ELECTRIC
DELIGHTS

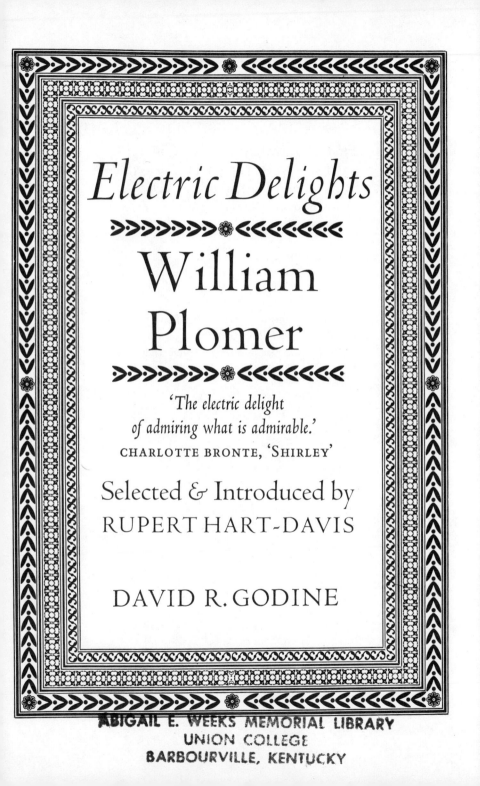

Electric Delights

William Plomer

'The electric delight
of admiring what is admirable.'
CHARLOTTE BRONTE, 'SHIRLEY'

Selected & Introduced by
RUPERT HART-DAVIS

DAVID R. GODINE

First U.S. edition published in 1978 by
D A V I D R. G O D I N E, *Publisher*
306 Dartmouth Street
Boston, Massachusetts 02116

L C 78-57682
I S B N 0-87923-248- X

PRINTED   IN   THE   UNITED   STATES   OF   AMERICA

Note: If I
ever make a book
of miscellaneous
pieces, dedicate it
to Rupert Hart-Davis

———————

Contents

Introduction

William Plomer often promised to collect his scattered pieces, and it must have been my urging him to do so that produced the note which I cannot resist printing on the dedication page. He had also written out the title and epigraph. If he had made the selection it would have been more homogeneous, but since this is likely to be his last published book (except for his letters) I feel that it should contain every uncollected article, story or poem that fully reflects his style, his admirations and his humour. All his books, manuscripts and papers are now in Durham University Library, but before they went there I picked out everything that seemed worthy of resurrection. Except for the marginalia and three poems, everything here has already appeared in print, as indicated in the note at the end of each item.

From his almost forty years of book-reviewing I have chosen those articles which deal with authors who meant a great deal to him, but I have not included anything about Virginia Woolf or E. M. Forster, because he wrote about them at some length in his *Autobiography*. Similarly I have omitted all his occasional writings on South Africa and Japan, since he has said his say on those countries in prose and verse. On the other hand I have included the Francis Kilvert essay: it was his last piece of sustained prose, and it sums up all his feeling for, and service to, the diarist. The varying lengths of his admirations – his electric delights – are not commensurate with his opinion of their subjects, but simply depend on the amount of space that the exigences of journalism required or allowed him to fill.

I sternly resisted the temptation to include otherwise unimportant reviews because they contained one of his telling phrases, as when he described the autobiography of John Cowper

Powys as 'a one-man eisteddfod' or wrote of a pretentious
American lady's memoirs: 'the drone of self-esteem is from time
to time broken by the shrill whine of the mosquito piercing the
dead horse'.

Having no telephone, William wrote more letters than most
people do today – witty, gay, enchanting letters, of which I hope
to publish a selection before long. He was a perfect friend and
companion, warmly affectionate and sympathetic, entirely loyal,
always full of jokes, and astonishingly observant. Once, staying
with Cecil Day-Lewis in Devonshire, he was taken for a short
motor-drive, during which he pointed out a dozen interesting things which Cecil, who knew the road well, had never
noticed before. I hope later to write some account of my forty
years' friendship with William, but in the meantime, remembering
him with love and sorrow, I will let his own self-epitaph speak
for him:

> Sometimes thinking aloud
> He went his own way.
> He was joky by nature,
> Sad, sceptical, proud.
> What he never would follow,
> Or lead, was a crowd.

Marske-in-Swaledale   RUPERT HART-DAVIS
November 1977

Personal

An Alphabet of Literary Prejudice

ARMIGEROUS people, said Gertrude Jekyll to Logan Pearsall Smith (as he tells us in his pleasing account of that lady in *Reperusals and Recollections*), never say *overcoat*, they say *great-coat*; in a recent novel by Nancy Mitford there is an upper-class character who condemns persons given to using the words *mantelpiece, mirror* and *notepaper* as beneath respectful attention; and a woman friend of mine lately told me that whenever she enters *table napkins* on a washing-list, the laundry returns the list with these words struck out and *serviettes* put in their place.

Prejudices of this kind are often so strongly, so fanatically cherished that one is reminded of the verbal taboos in primitive, highly formalized and ceremonious societies. Sometimes they are nothing more than signs of class consciousness and class solidarity, sometimes they are matters of individual taste and caprice and habit. They are tending, no doubt, to disappear, and in a classless society (which is obviously an impossibility) everybody would wrap their talents in a *serviette*, and few would bother to read *Alice through the Mirror*. Since these prejudices make for variety, why should they be condemned?

These little vanities, under the so distant and silent stars, are of the very stuff of human life. 'Without etiquette,' said a Frenchman of my acquaintance, when twitted on account of his ceremonious ways, 'where should we be? *There would be nothing left!*'

'BLIND SPOTS!' exclaimed Mrs Bovey-Tracey. 'But I'm all blind spots, I have them like a rash! What don't I like? I don't like allegories as a rule – they seem to turn so easily into nightmares or sermons, and I don't want to be frightened or preached at. Kafka and his English imitators are not for me. Historical novels, detective novels, novels about the future – no, thank you. Mysticism – oh no! Wasn't it Goethe who called it "unripe poetry, unripe philosophy"? Social realism? Oh dear no! Somebody once gave me Gladkov's *Cement*: it sent me scurrying to Turgeniev. Existentialism? More nightmares …

'Of course I'm immensely narrow and limited, because I only like ripe classics: I doubt if one can like Montaigne and Barrie – I like Montaigne. My narrowness is my nature, but other people narrow me down continually. I suppose it's because I'm a woman, but I can't help associating a writer with his admirers: that's why it's difficult for me to enjoy good contemporary writers.

'It all began at school, with a really awful "book-loving" schoolmarm. She was so insufferable – I mean *I* found her so insufferable – that she poisoned every well by merely pointing to it, and for me her enthusiasm tabooed its objects. So it took me years to approach Dickens and for years I had a horror of Daudet; she cut me off for ever from whatever enjoyment is to be had from Stevenson and Kipling. If only she hadn't referred to Stevenson by his initials! Thank goodness Mr Eliot isn't called "T.S.E."!

'I'm much too easily put off a writer by the antics of his admirers. I love Jane Austen, but when her admirers call themselves "Janeites" and begin smirking and making masonic grimaces at one another, whether in speech or in print, a blind spot rushes to my head, and I rush for consolation to some splendid but cultless old girl. In a case like that, Maria Edgeworth would do nicely. What a lot of little cults go on, don't they? When I hear some ninny talking knowingly about Henry James, let's say, or Max Beerbohm, I feel so *sorry* for James or Beerbohm, I almost begin to wonder if they're as good, in their different ways, as I know them to be – I wonder if I haven't been wrong to enjoy them. But perhaps I haven't really got any blind spots at all, for I know that even the best writers give footholds to all manner of pestiferous apes, and that one must allow for that. Nothing would induce me to read – no, I shan't tell you, he may be a friend of yours.'

CONTROVERSIAL writings are apt to be a great bore. 'My Leontion!' Landor makes Epicurus say in the *Imaginary Conversations*, 'you have inadvertently given me the reason and origin of all controversial writings. They flow not from a love of truth or a regard for science, but from envy and ill-will.' And not, one might add, from a love of literature. That love, according to Flaubert, is felt by no one, the morality of art being contained for everyone in that which flatters his interests. If only we could cherish our own interests without pecking and snapping at other people's! As one gets older and perceives more clearly that life is short and art long, one can indulge more easily in the pleasure of living and letting live – which means ignoring the activities of those contemporaries whose minds and works one finds distasteful. But some of our writers have grievances, and a Message, and a Missionary Spirit, and a sectarian outlook, and can only write in a pulpit, where they busy themselves with dividing the sheep from the goats, and the elect from the damned. But:

"Lor!" cried Mrs Boffin. "What I say is, the world's wide enough for all of us!"

"So it is, my dear," said Mr Boffin, "when not literary. But when so, not so."

DEATH is a great evoker of cant and cliché. Memorial notices written by a dead man's friends have often revealed the poverty of their minds and emotions. Real emotion is likely to be eloquent or silent; if it finds expression in flat or trite phrases it seems, though it may not be, unreal. Some years ago I made a study of such notices and was much struck by the seeming poverty of head and heart that had made them possible and public. Nothing could be feebler than the choice of adjectives. Again and again I read of *unremitting* labour or toil, of *consummate* tact, of *indefatigable* industry, of *unabated* zest, of *selfless* devotion, of *utter* unselfishness, of *inflexible* determination, of *deep* loyalties, of *long* experience, of *varied* responsibilities, of *indomitable* courage, of a *keen* sense of humour, of *infectious* laughter or cheerfulness, of *sterling* integrity, of *conspicuous* success, of *untiring* energy, of *unfailing* generosity.

There is admittedly something pathetic in the effort to believe, or to make others believe, that the virtues of a deceased person were absolute, constant or extraordinary, but this effort implies

obedience to the maxim, *De mortuis nil nisi bunkum.* To overpraise
the dead is to transfer the phrase 'Here lies' to the memorialist.

Can it be believed of any human being (I quote) that 'all children
and animals worshipped him', that 'he achieved instant popularity
with everyone', that 'he was loved by all', that 'he was quite
incapable of a mean thought', that 'no one who met him could fail
to be influenced by him', or that 'he had an immense affection for all
animals'? Did he cherish wart-hogs and dote on hyenas, did he take
the skunk to his bosom?

The effort to prove that the deceased was a superman often took
the form of saying that 'if ever there was a born soldier', or 'saint
on earth', or 'leader of men', 'it was he'. Or, 'One felt instinctively
that here was an individual of no ordinary mould.' There were
many variations on the theme that the world would be 'the poorer
for his passing', that his death had 'cast gloom over a wide circle',
or that he had 'left a gap which could never be filled'. In one
instance his claim to that distinction which must apparently be
proclaimed, even about the most commonplace man, was that
'he was a zealous beagler'; in another that 'of boomerangs he had a
large collection'. This was however welcome, for it did distinguish
the man from others.

'Is it not strange,' asks Mr Forester in *Melincourt*, 'that even the
fertility of fiction should be so circumscribed in the variety of
monumental panegyric?' 'I have often thought,' replies Mr Fax,
'that these words of Rabelais would furnish an appropriate inscription for ninety-nine gravestones out of every hundred:—*Sa
mémoire expira avecque le son des cloches qui carillonèrent à son enterre-
ment.*'

'EVERYBODY can write one good book' is one of the most idiotic
sayings imaginable. It is not even true that everybody has the
material for one good book or even for one good article, for
'material' is not what has happened to you but the effect upon you
of what has happened. Years of experience as a professional reader
teach one that a good many people can write a book which is
neither good nor bad, and even a brief experience as an ordinary
reader shows that a good many publishers publish books which are

neither wise, useful nor necessary, which are not without merit but are not good, and which have faults but are not really bad. Illiteracy is far less to be condemned than pretentious – yes, and industrious – mediocrity. 'I do want you to meet Miss Leighton-Buzzard,' said Mrs Bovey-Tracey (to whom I have already alluded), asking me to dinner the other day; 'she's such an interesting woman, and most unusual. She *doesn't write*, you know.'

'FOLLOWING the visit of General Bazooka to Aldershot, an official enquiry is to be held into the recent disturbances.' Obviously if the enquiry is still to be held, it must follow the general's visit. The word *following* is intended here to mean *as a result of*. Its now indiscriminate use may be ascribed to journalists who find it easier or cheaper to telegraph one word instead of four, but I find it irritating, especially when it is used to mean *after*, which is a shorter word. Thus: 'General Bazooka is expected to return to London, following his visit to Aldershot.'

GAY, in *The What D'Ye Call It*, introduced among his characters the ghost of a miscarriage. In the same 'tragi-comi-pastoral farce' there is a speech by Peascod which reminds me of the more effusive kind of reviewer:

> Lend me thy handkercher – *The Pilgrim's Pro*——
> [*Reads and weeps.*]
> (I cannot see for tears) *Pro-Progress* – Oh!
> *The Pilgrim's Progress* – *eighth* – *edi-ti-on*
> *Lon-don* – *printed* – *for* – *Ni-cho-las Bod-ding-ton:*
> *With new ad-di-tions never made before.*
> Oh! 'tis so moving, I can read no more.
> [*Drops the Book.*]

'HAWORTH I must see tomorrow,' I told the old Yorkshireman, 'whatever the weather's like.' He was evidently amused and a little puzzled that anybody should want to see Haworth. It was only a few miles away from the place where he had lived all his life. He was a shrewd man, a kind man, a skilful farmer, but I don't think he had ever heard of the Brontës. His comment on my resolution was certainly free from literary prejudice. 'Ah, Haworth,' he said. 'That was where they raked the moon out of the pond, so they used to say when I was a lad.'

IMAGINARY lines by great poets sometimes form themselves in minds with a satirical bent. A friend of mine used to recite with glee a line which he said could be found in the *Idylls of the King*:

> Adown the glade a-jumpt the harlot.

It was a little difficult to swallow 'a-jumpt', though I thought it *ben trovato*. In fact the last four lines of *Merlin and Vivien*, which might well be part of a parody, run as follows:

> Then crying, 'I have made his glory mine,'
> And shrieking out 'O fool!' the harlot leapt
> Adown the forest, and the thicket closed
> Behind her, and the forest echo'd 'fool'.

JAPANESE poetry has taken various forms. I have a prejudice in favour of the seventeen-syllable poems variously known as *haikai*, *haiku* and *hokku*. The late Professor Basil Hall Chamberlain, that eminent japanologue, suggested that they correspond to lines like

> The linnet born within the cage,
> That never knew the summer woods,

or

> And Autumn laying here and there
> A fiery finger on the leaves,

which in English cannot stand alone. He might have found better examples. Broadcasting not long ago about Charles Turner, the brother of Tennyson, I quoted two almost perfect *haikai*, extracted from his sonnets and well able to stand alone. Here they are:

> Still falls the summer night – the browsing horse
> Fills the low portal with a grassy sound.

and

The low of oxen on the rainy wind,
Death and the Past, came up the well-known road.

Haikai have been imitated in Europe, without much effect: in
Europe we are seldom content with small mercies.

KELLY, I mean Hugh Kelly, the Irishman who in 1768 produced a
play called *False Delicacy*, made more money out of it than he had
ever seen before. This had a happy result, for it is said to have
transformed him from 'a low, petulant, absurd and ill-bred
censurer' into 'the humane, affable, good-natured, well-bred man'.
Perhaps it did, but the man I admire is the man who stays humane,
affable, good-natured and well-bred in spite of poverty. 'A society
of *poor* gentlemen upon whose hands time lies heavy', said the
admirable J. B. Yeats in one of his letters, 'is absolutely necessary to
art and literature.' If this is true, art and literature must be growing
needy.

LOG-ROLLING is regarded as a reprehensible exercise by persons
who have no logs of their own to roll, or not enough strength to
roll other people's logs. The term is applied, says the dictionary, to
mutual help – (what can be more desirable, more virtuous?) – but
'esp. to unprincipled political combinations and puffing of each
other's works by author-reviewers.' If log-rolling is unprincipled,
then it is bad, but let us at least admit that there are good logs and
bad, and good and bad ways of rolling them. To puff means 'to
advertise (goods) with exaggerated or false praise'. Well, we have
all seen author-reviewers puffing each other's works and unprincipled combinations with exaggerated or false praise. In doing
so, they make fools of themselves and each other. Can we not
perceive that the logs are hollow or rotten and trundle along with
too light and bounding a motion? Need we be taken in by exaggerated or false praise? If we are taken in, we have only ourselves
to blame.
    Do not the virtuous roll each other's logs? They do, and rightly:
it is part of their striving after virtue. In all walks of life do we not
see and commend and gain by mutual aid? If your friends don't

help you to roll your log, nobody else will; and it is part of your duty to your friends to help them to roll theirs. I knew a woman who was accused of being unable to see, or at least unwilling to admit, any faults in her children. 'It is not my business to do so,' she said. 'There are plenty of people in the world who are ready to find fault with them and to put obstacles in their way. I am their mother.' Such partiality is sublime, though it may not always be wise. The term log-rolling seems to be used almost invariably in a pejorative sense. Why should it be? Properly performed, it is a noble exercise, so frequent, necessary and universal that one cannot imagine life without it.

MIXED METAPHORS, like abortions and contortions, can be strangely impressive. During the recent war, a certain European newspaper remarked that

> the tortuous whispering-propaganda, like a thousand-headed hydra, has once again acquired a well-trained accomplice in the sphere of mixing mental poison. The hand which keeps order in the country should strike not only at those who make a habit of passing on the poisonous mushrooms of the enemy radio and other rumour-mongers, but should also quickly find an appropriate cage for these birds of ill-omen.

On 7 June 1940, *The Times* printed a letter, over the signature G.M.Y[oung], drawing attention to the record in Hansard of a Member of Parliament's protest against what he considered the superabundance and parasitic nature of the staff of a new Ministry:

> I can assure the Minister (the Member had said) that anyone in his position will require to have courage and a double-edged scythe to cut down and winnow away the army of barnacles that have got into that establishment.

Let us examine this slapstick utterance. 'Army' as a collective noun for barnacles is perfectly wrong, because the main thing about an army is its mobility, and the main thing about a barnacle is its adhesiveness. It is true that this particular army was said to have 'got into' an establishment, and it has also been said that an army

marches on its stomach, but barnacles on the march into an establishment can hardly be looked for. Having got in, they were to be 'cut
down'. Now armies have been cut up or mown down, and perhaps
cut down, but when composed of barnacles they had better be
scraped or chipped off the surface to which they have stuck. If
barnacles are susceptible of being 'winnowed away', they must be
like chaff; but it would not be easy to say what residue, let alone
what useful residue – particularly in a Ministry – would be left after
their dispersal by some stronger wind than could be produced by
the agitation of a scythe. To winnow with a scythe would be a
strange feat, not without risk, especially if the scythe were double-
edged and even though both edges had previously been blunted
by the cutting down of regiment after regiment of barnacles.

A purist in prose could hardly help harbouring a prejudice in
favour of the mixing of metaphors – by other people – since the
detection of it would make him feel superior, and might also make
him laugh, for mixed metaphors come tumbling out of muddled
minds, spinning head over heels like clowns. Yet the minds that
evolve them are sometimes clear, and they are not necessarily
absurd, especially in poetry.

NICE clean books are sought after by orthodox book-collectors,
who keep them in glass-fronted bookcases, and read them – if they
read them – with gloves on their hands. This was the habit of K.,
and it was an irritation to his sister, who was denied access to his
collection. Miss K. was a literary lady who smoked in bed, trod her
slippers down at the heels, wore woollen stockings and never
mended her underclothes. To annoy her brother she used to leave
her own books about, with her place in them marked by a bacon
rind. Once he wished to refer to one of her books, but the page he
wanted had been permanently united to its opposite by what looked
like a spoonful of mulligatawny soup, so a reference remained
unverified.

There is a good deal to be said for a middle course. Not a collector,
I like books in their original editions, humanized by use, but not
torn or defaced. An occasional squashed gnat between the pages,
with its suggestion of fine summer evenings, gives me no pain; I

do not shrink from a faded spine, a foxed fly-leaf, or an ex-library copy. I like for instance these two volumes of *The Professor*, by Currer Bell, with the bookplate of a country gentleman and the later one of the Stafford Working Men's Club Free Library ('Open on Saturday Evenings, from Eight to Nine o'clock'). I like too this copy of *In the Year of Jubilee*, with the roneo'd bookplate, ornamented with a scroll and bulrushes, of the Bunhill Row Book Club, Founded 1887, and recording that it was bought for half-a-crown on 14 September 1896, and was read by Wm. C. (the Hon. Secy.), E.B., A.W.C., J.H., K.C., G.R., and Mrs Sutton. Ah, Mrs Sutton, what did you make of it, and where are you now?

OVERALL as an adjective is now in frequent use. I can't say I like it. Of Winston Churchill's speech at Fulton, Missouri, I read in an English Sunday paper: 'To an elemental power of style and phrase … he added an overall polish of expression.' The process of adding a polish to an elemental power is not specially clear, and the word *add*, by the way, is also too much used by journalists.

> Speaking at Bootle about the new communal toothbrushes, the Minister of Dental Affairs said they would soon be in full production. 'That is,' Mr Caries *added*, 'if no bottlenecks supervene.'

Here *added* only means *said*: if the Minister had uttered a brilliant epigram, there might have been some point in writing *added*.

PERRAULT's writings seem to me like small diamonds of the first water. He says, in the dedication to *Les Souhaits Ridicules*, that

> c'est la manière
> Dont quelque chose est inventé,
> Qui, beaucoup plus que la matière,
> De tout récit fait la beauté,

but this does not explain the secret of his own *manière*, the graceful directness and euphony of his verse as well as his prose, or his gaiety:

> A peine acheva-t-il de prononcer ces mots

> Que sa femme aperçut, grandement étonnée,
> Un boudin fort long, qui, partant
> D'un des coins de la cheminée,
> S'approchait d'elle en serpentant.

I would rather have those five lines than the complete poems of Swinburne.

QUEENIE'S WHIM is a title I cannot forget. It is the title of a novel I do not expect or want to read. The novel was by Rosa Nouchette Carey, whose readers must now be fewer than they were.

REST, a good long rest, ought to be given to a number of over-worked words. *Sensitive* is one of them. It is much used by reviewers to denote merit. 'Another of Miss Corona Portable's *sensitive* studies of life in Baron's Court.' 'In her new film, Heather Honey gives a *sensitive* interpretation of a nymphomaniac mannequin.' Probably all that is meant is that Miss P. appears to have some idea of what she is talking about, and Miss H. some idea of how to act her part. *Sensitive* has become a canting epithet of the present day, like *hectic* and *intriguing* fifteen or twenty years ago.

Another down-at-heel bit of smartness is *cross-section*. 'Miss Portable gives us another of her sensitive *cross-sections* of life in Baron's Court.' People used to talk about 'a slice of life', but life is not a piece of cake: what is meant is that Miss P. had produced what is, or is meant to be, a true or plausible or typical account of life as it is presumed or known to be usually lived in Baron's Court.

Equally tiresome is the word *scene*, which is used indiscriminately by writers who ought to know better. 'Miss Portable gives us another of her sensitive cross-sections of the Baron's Court *scene*.' We get 'the London *scene*', meaning life in London, or simply London; and even 'Major Mashie has long been prominent in the golfing *scene*'. When Tennyson's brother, Charles Turner, in one of his sonnets apostrophized a country landscape as follows:

> Sink deeply in my heart, surpassing scene!

Coleridge was provoked to write, 'Suffer me, my dear young Poet, to conjure you never to use this Covent Garden and Drury Lane word unless some distinct allusion or reference be made to a Theatre. This "scene and scenery" (are) villainous slang fineries of the day.' What a long day it has been!

And a long taboo might well be imposed on *aware* and *awareness*, words much used at present by half-baked writers and bluestockings not fully fashioned.

SCOTS AND SCOTTISH are Scotch to me. I regard them as localisms proper no doubt in the mouth of a Scotchman but affected in that of an Englishman, who might as well talk of *Paree* and *München* as call a Scotchman a Scotsman. I have never walked in a *Scots mist*, or revived myself with *a drop of Scottish*, or supped off *Scottish broth*, followed by a piece of *butter scots*. If the word *Scotch* was good enough for Burns and Scott (and it was), it ought to be good enough for anybody else derived from the same part of the world. *Scotch* is good English, and only derogatory when applied to shortcomings.

Some Scotchmen, fearful lest their oddly-shaped northern promontory (which so many have left for more lucrative regions) should be less of an obsession with others than it is with themselves, would have us say *Britain* when we mean *England*. I wish them all a Merrie Britain.

TRAMPLEASURE, a surname which used to appear and perhaps still appears in the London Telephone Directory, by its unexpectedness became famous. If one were immortal, one might find time to read that book: it contains more characters than all the novels chosen by all the book clubs. Glancing through a few pages of it (not, I believe, the latest edition), I once found time to salute Mr Bang and Mr Bluglass, Mrs Bitchell and Miss Bluff, the firm of W. C. Beetles & Co., Leslie Fly & Geoffrey Gush, Leon P. Flageolet & Dr Fredoon Famrose, Mr Haddock, Mr Halfhead, and the heraldic-sounding Mr Griffinhoofe. Such names are eloquent of the diversity of life in London, and of the ancient mysteries of etymology.

UNNECESSARY is the too common use of certain adverbs in spoken and even in written English. An undergraduate at Oxford was lately

asked by his tutor why he used the word *actually* so often: they had
just exchanged the following questions and answers:

TUTOR: Where are you going now?

UNDERGRADUATE: Well, *actually* I am on my way to lunch.

TUTOR: Have you seen your brother?

UNDERGRADUATE: *Actually*, I haven't.

TUTOR: Has he been doing any work lately?

UNDERGRADUATE: I don't know whether he has, *actually*.

It is all too easy to fall into the habit of using this word too often:
it generally means nothing. I remember once hearing a man,
accused of an attempt on the chastity of a member of the opposite
sex, say, 'Well, I mean, I did sort of, don't you know.' All he meant
was, 'I did.' I think *actually* was not then so commonly used as it is
now, or he might have worked that word in too.

Actually seems to be a weakness of persons more prosperous and
ostensibly better educated than those who keep trotting out
definitely, which is sometimes used by itself to mean *Yes*. Liars
perhaps think it a more convincing affirmative. Actually, I find
Yes definitely more emphatic.

VAINGLORY was one of my three favourite bedtime stories during
the blitz. (The others were Osbert Sitwell's *Triple Fugue* and Gib-
bon's autobiography.) As the bombs were falling and the guns
banging, I went through *Vainglory* several times, then marked with
a pencil all the jokes I liked best, then took the book up from time
to time in order to enjoy these jokes again.

In one sense, Firbank is a realistic novelist: he noticed that people
don't listen much to one another, that in conversation they pursue
their own thoughts rather than other people's, and that much of
what they say is calculated to advertise their own importance,
beauty, cleverness, knowledge or taste. He had a sharp ear, especially
for the talk of women, especially middle-aged, idle, rich Edwardian
women with pretensions to culture. He loved their talk for its
graceful absurdity and for its constant betrayal of their vanity.
Sometimes the talk in his books reminds one of Swift's *Polite
Conversation*, but that is recorded rather than invented, and Firbank
invents rather than records.

As Lady Anne Pantry said of the writer Claud Harvester:

His work calls to mind a frieze with figures of varying heights trotting all the same way. If one should by chance turn about it's usually merely to stare or to sneer or to make a grimace. Only occasionally his figures care to beckon. And they seldom really touch.

Life is very like that. 'You may kiss me,' says Mrs Shamefoot, 'but kiss me carefully.' In other words, what is essential is that she should maintain her own image of herself, her *persona*: a relationship, a contact, with somebody else is only of interest if it serves that end. And it was Mrs Shamefoot who observed that glass over an oil painting

makes always such a good reflection, particularly when the picture's *dark*. Many's the time I've run into the National Gallery on my way to the Savoy and tidied myself before the Virgin of the Rocks ...

Yes, on the whole *Vainglory* is the best Firbank. The cathedral town of Ashringford is a long way from Barchester; it will never have so many visitors; but a faithful few will return again and again – they like the atmosphere.

'Thérèse will sometimes say to me that that melancholy Miss Wintermoon must have gone away *at last* when suddenly up flies her window and a hand shakes a duster into the street.'
'In Ashringford there's chatter enough indoors. You'd be surprised.'
'Well, I never know what goes on, except when the sow gets into the Dean's garden. And then I hear the screams.'

WALT WHITMAN, that great poet, had something sly and roguish in his nature. It can be discerned especially in the accounts of him as an old man. What he lacked was irony, wit and humour. Blowing an enormous trumpet, unique in shape and tone, he rode into a New Jerusalem (populated entirely by creatures of his own fancy) with his face to the tail of the ass, Democracy. How different was Whitman's contemporary, Herman Melville (these two were born in the same year) – Melville, who forecast 'the Dark Ages of Democracy'. Each was right, since each was himself, and one would not wish and could not imagine either in the least otherwise than he was. A reader capable of appreciating both these writers in their mid-career might justifiably have claimed freedom from critical prejudice, a perceptiveness and mellowness. It is easier to be wide and bland and eclectic about the long dead than about the living, especially about the young, especially about the new and unfamiliar and difficult, especially about the successful.

Swift ridiculed the music of Handel and the generalship of Marlborough; Pope the perspicacity and the scholarship of Bentley; Gray the abilities of Shaftesbury and the eloquence of Rousseau. Shakespeare hardly found those who would collect his tragedies; Milton was read from godliness; Virgil was antiquated and rustic; Cicero Asiatic.

You have been listening to Walter Savage Landor in his imaginary conversation between Southey and Porson. Now go away and beware of running down your contemporaries.

XENOMANIA in the form of charity is endemic among the English. It is in a sense a literary prejudice, for it has largely been engendered by the Bible.

> Their Bibles for the heathen load our fleets;
> Lo! gloating eastward, they enquire 'What news?'
> 'We die,' we answer, 'foodless in the streets.'
> And what reply your men of Gospel-views?
> Oh, 'they are sending bacon to the Jews.'

(No prize is offered for guessing which poet of the last century wrote these lines.)

> Their lofty souls have telescopic eyes,
> Which see the smallest speck of distant pain,
> While, at their feet, a world of agonies,
> Unseen, unheard, unheeded, writhes in vain.

'We wish', wrote *The Times* in 1844, 'people could be brought to be chivalrous and warm about English poverty ... However laudable the anti-slavery feeling may be, a nation that feels for African negroes, and does not feel for its own poor, is convicted of cant.' We must walk warily. Charity begins at home, but ought it to stay there? Shall we, or shall we not, subscribe to Lady Fimble's Fund for Spavined Soviet Horses, to the Help Hungry Asia Fund? Shall we support the flag-day for Saving Ruritanian Babies? Or not? If we refrain, are we being selfish and uncharitable? If we subscribe, are we really promoting peace and international amity, or are we merely impoverishing ourselves and being regarded abroad as gullible and squeezable sentimentalists? By giving to remote aliens one may protect oneself from ingratitude nearer home, but may it not be better to be 'warm about English poverty' than to be 'convicted of cant'?

YESTERDAY, that is to say before the last war, I thought of making a glossary of the rhyming slang used in a circle in South London that I used to frequent, but there was something tiresomely facetious, something utterly pointless about it. It was part of the Cockney language, which must be dying out – the language in which a farthing is a *frobley*, a penny a *coal*, threepence a *tray*, sixpence a *sprarzey*, a shilling a *chip*, half-a-crown *half-a-tosh*, five shillings a *caser*, ten shillings a *calf*, and a pound a *oncer*. These words were used by men and boys, seldom by women and girls. This was not surprising, for in primitive societies it is usual for certain words to be used exclusively by men and certain other words by women.

ZULU is a written as well as a spoken language. It sounds much grander than the debased Dutch and unsonorous English spoken in the same part of the world. One can imagine *Macbeth* in Zulu – but not its translator, at least not yet. If Zulu does not become extinct, there may some day be a Zulu literature. The Zulus have not been without influence on English thought, for it was largely because of the intelligent questions, the awkward questions, asked by his Zulu converts that Bishop Colenso was led to undermine Victorian fundamentalism.

[*Windmill*, 1946]

A Writer's Faith

When I begin to think about what I believe I find that not all my beliefs are fixed and unalterable. I am not alone in this. Religious believers sometimes have doubts, and their faiths may weaken or be discarded. Political believers sometimes change sides. Private beliefs are not always unshakeable: the husband who believes absolutely in the chastity of his wife, the wife who believes absolutely in the faithfulness of her husband, are each liable to be confronted with evidence which makes nonsense of perhaps the most cherished belief.

A good deal of amusement can be had by noticing how firmly we human beings cling to irrational or trivial beliefs. We may encounter the man who believes he can foretell the end of the world by some fanciful calculation, or the woman who believes that some little form of speech or behaviour is the acme of refinement, until she finds that among people she looks up to it is considered a mark of vulgarity. I suppose we have all at some time or another felt our faces grow hot or grow pale on discovering some precious belief to have been an illusion. A thinking man, because he looks at more than one side of a question, is particularly likely to change his mind. Walt Whitman said, 'I contain multitudes,' and I think it was Renan who said that an intelligent man can hardly help contradicting himself at least once every day.

The most strengthening and comforting beliefs are those which we feel we have proved true by our own experience. This does not invariably make them true, but we can test their truth by finding out whether they resemble beliefs held by persons of sound mind among our acquaintances, or in other times and places. The purest, oldest, and most distinguished forms of religious belief in the world have certainly been held by a great variety of the most distinguished minds, and it is hard to suppose that they can all have been altogether wrong. I used just now the words 'strengthening' and 'comforting' as if belief was a sort of hot drink or a tonic. And why not? Why should not a belief warm and strengthen one? Life can often be chilling, exhausting, and disheartening: when it is one is sustained by belief, or one would hardly be able to go on living.

Like anybody else I believe a great many things. One of the things I most strongly believe is that art is important and valuable. I am, if you like the word, an aesthete. I do not say it either boastfully or apologetically; I state it as a fact. You may at once require me to state also what I mean by 'art', and what I mean by 'important and valuable'. Briefly, by 'art' I mean the most persistently admired and therefore the most durable creations of the best minds and sensibilities in the use of language, which is literature; in the use of sound, which is music; and in the use of materials, which means the fine and applied arts and crafts, particularly painting, sculpture, and architecture.

By 'important and valuable' I mean that not to have enjoyed any of these things in one's life is to have missed some of what are generally held by educated people to be some of the greatest achievements of the greatest men, the most passionate, the most disinterested and truthful, the richest, the most beautiful efforts of the human head, heart, and hand. I believe in art because I believe in imagination, skill, and pleasure – three of the many things involved in the making of a work of art.

I believe in art because of its ability not only to console one when life is disheartening but for its power at any time to make life less disheartening and more exciting, to make life fuller and happier, when it already seems full and happy – when one is young, for instance, and in love, and beginning to succeed in one's chosen work. I believe in art because I believe in the artist. I believe it is the function of the artist always to make us see or hear or understand in a new way. It is because the artist's vision or technique is always new that it is not always immediately acceptable; it has very often happened that works of art have not been appreciated in the lifetime of those who made them.

Now two questions seem to me to arise. Why am I proclaiming a belief in art rather than in science, let us say, or in some political or economic doctrine? And what has this belief meant to me in my own life? I am certainly not proclaiming an exclusive belief in art. I am not denying that science may be useful, that political doctrines may be enlightened, or that trade may be necessary. I am simply saying that I believe art to be more significant than these things, more rewarding, more revealing, more durable, and on a higher level of human activity.

When we come to the question of what my belief in art has meant to me in my own life, I would say that it has meant first and foremost a battle. I do not mean a battle against any wavering or weakening of that belief held by me, but a battle against the pressure of the everyday world. It is all very well to find oneself a little aesthete – and I think I may say an artist as well, because I have done something to create as well as to enjoy; but I did not find my inclinations altogether protected, fostered, or indulged. I did not grow up in a family or in a society of leisured and cultivated aesthetes. My education and the social milieu in which I mostly found myself when young were conventional, practical, and philistine.

At the age of seventeen, for instance, I was living in a remote place in Africa, not by my own choice, and the only books I had were a handful I had brought with me. They included the poems of Blake and of Rimbaud, and the letters of Vincent Van Gogh. It occurs to me now that one could hardly choose from the nineteenth century or from any other time three men, three artists, more single-mindedly devoted to their art or more isolated from their contemporaries.

With such great examples before me, how could I fail in my obscure and small and immature way to see that the world of imagination and of art was worth all one's loyalty? Its shapes were more defined, its colours were clearer, it was nearer to the truth than the everyday world. Through later life, the dangers of war, the drudgery of duty and responsibility, the waste and folly of ordinary existence, the strain and anxiety of public and private life, my belief in the values of art has remained constant because they themselves have remained constant.

[*London Calling*, 30 May 1957]

On Not Answering the Telephone

If, at the end of a conversation, somebody says to me, 'As soon as I know, I'll ring you up,' he is taking too much for granted. He is proposing to attempt the impossible. So I have to say, 'I'm afraid you can't. You see, I'm not on the telephone. I just haven't got a telephone.'

Reactions to this are various. Some people say: 'Oh, but you must have a telephone!' as if they thought I had mislaid it somewhere, or forgotten about it. Some people say: 'How terribly inconvenient! How can you do without a telephone?' And some say: 'Oh, you wise man, how I envy you!' But the usual reaction is astonishment, and although I regard myself as a quiet, conventional sort of character, I find myself being stared at as a wild or wilful eccentric, especially when somebody says: 'Well, if I can't ring you up, perhaps you'll ring me up,' and I reply, 'Perhaps; but I'm more likely to write to you.'

Why don't I have a telephone? Not because I pretend to be wise or pose as unusual. There are two chief reasons: because I don't really like the telephone, and because I find I can still work and play, eat, breathe and sleep without it. Why don't I like the telephone? Because I think it is a pest and a time-waster. It may create unnecessary suspense and anxiety, as when you wait for an expected call that doesn't come; or irritating delay, as when you keep ringing a number that is always engaged. As for speaking in a public telephone box, that seems to me really horrible. You would not use it unless you were in a hurry, and because you are in a hurry you will find other people waiting before you. When you do get into the box, you are half asphyxiated by stale, unventilated air, flavoured with cheap face-powder and chain-smoking; and by the time you have begun your conversation your back is chilled by the cold looks of somebody who is fidgeting to take your place.

If you have a telephone in your own house, you will admit that it tends to ring when you least want it to ring – when you are alseep, or in the middle of a meal or a conversation, or when you are just going out, or when you are in your bath. Are you strong-minded enough to ignore it, to say to yourself, 'Ah, well, it will all be the same in a hundred years' time'? You are not. You think there may be some important news or message for you. Have you never rushed dripping from the bath, or chewing from the table, or dazed from the bed, only to be told that you are a wrong number? You were told the truth. In my opinion all telephone numbers are wrong numbers. If, of course, your telephone rings and you decide not to answer it, then you will have to listen to an idiotic bell ringing and ringing in what is supposed to be the privacy of your own home. You might as well buy a bicycle bell and ring it yourself.

Suppose you ignore the telephone when it rings, and suppose that, for once, somebody has an important message for you. I can assure you that if a message is really important it will reach you sooner or later. Think of the proverb: 'Ill news travels apace.' I must say good news seems to travel just as fast. And think of the saying: 'The truth will out.' It will. But suppose you answer the telephone when it rings. If, when you take off the receiver, you say 'Hullo!' just think how absurd that is. Why, you might be saying 'Hullo!' to a total stranger, a thing you would certainly think twice about before doing in public, if you were English.

But perhaps, when you take off the receiver, you give your number or your name. But you don't even know whom you are giving it to! Perhaps you have been indiscreet enough to have your name and number printed in the telephone directory, a book with a large circulation, a successful book so often reprinted as to make any author envious, a book more in evidence than Shakespeare or the Bible, and found in all sorts of private and public places. By your self-advertisement you have enabled any stranger, bore, intruder, or criminal to engage you in conversation at a moment's notice in what ought to be the privacy of your own home. It serves you right if you find it impossible to escape from some idle or inquisitive chatterbox, or from somebody who wants something for nothing, or from some reporter bent on questioning you about your own affairs or about the private life of some friend who has just eloped or met with a fatal accident.

But, you will say, you need not have your name printed in the telephone directory, and you can have a telephone which is only usable for outgoing calls. Besides, you will say, isn't it important to have a telephone in case of sudden emergency – illness, accident, or fire? Of course you are right, but here in a thickly populated country like England one is seldom far from a telephone in case of dreadful necessity. All the same, I felt in instant sympathy with a well-known actor whom I heard on the radio the other day. He was asked: 'Suppose you were left alone to live on a desert island, and you were allowed to take just one luxury with you, what would you choose?' 'I would take a telephone', he said, 'and I would push the wire into the sand, and my greatest pleasure would be to sit and look at it, and to think "It will never ring, and I shall never have to answer it." '

If, like me, one is without a telephone, somebody is sure to say, 'Oh, but don't you find you have to write an awful lot of letters?' The answer to that is, 'Yes, but I should have to write an awful lot of letters anyway.' This may bring the remark, 'Ah well, if you don't have a telephone, at least you must have a typewriter.' And the answer to that is 'No.'

'What, no telephone and no typewriter! Do please explain why.' Well, I am a professional man of letters, and when I was younger I thought a typewriter would be convenient. I even thought it was necessary, and that editors and publishers would expect anything sent to them to be typewritten. So I bought a typewriter and taught myself to type, and for some years I typed away busily. But I did not enjoy typing. I happen to enjoy the act of writing. I enjoy forming letters or words with a pen, and I never could enjoy tapping the keys of a typewriter. There again, there was a bell – only a little bell that rang at the end of each line – but still, a bell. And the fact is, I am not mechanically minded, and the typewriter is a machine. I have never been really drawn to machines. I don't like oiling, cleaning, or mending them. I do not enjoy making them work. To control them gives me no sense of power – or not of the kind of power that I find interesting. And machines do not like me. When I touch them they tend to break down, get jammed, catch fire, or blow up.

As with telephones and typewriters, so with cars. I obtained my first driving licence in South Africa at the age of seventeen, having been taught to drive in the rush hours in the middle of the busy city of Johannesburg. I needed the car for use in another part of Africa where in those days there was hardly any motor traffic. The actual process of driving soon became automatic, and my sole idea was to get from one place to another as soon as possible. I therefore drove fast, and within a week or two the speedometer was broken. I never had it mended. I was not a reckless driver. I did not lose control of the car, even on rocky or sandy tracks or driving with chains through deep mud. I never killed or injured anybody. But I was bored, and if circumstances had allowed I should have preferred to walk. Nowadays, living in an overcrowded country where traffic is continually on the increase and often congested, and where driving is controlled by a great many rules and regulations, I feel no temptation whatever to drive a car.

But, you may say, am I not aware that we are living in a machine age? Am I trying to put the clock back? Am I an escapist, a crank, or a simple-lifer? Not at all. It is as a matter of preference, not principle, that I choose, as far as possible, to do without these things – a telephone, a typewriter, and a car. If other people are willing – and they seem entirely willing and even eager – to make and use machines for my benefit, I am not less willing to let them do so. I am perfectly ready to pay to be driven about in trains, cars, or aircraft, to take lifts instead of walking upstairs, and to use moving staircases instead of unmoving ones. But I do not wish to be domi-nated by machines. I do not want to oil them, mend them, or clean them. I do not want to feed a typewriter with sheets of paper, to lose the use of my legs by travelling always by car, or to be sum-moned, with or without warning, by the telephone.

Is there any conclusion to be drawn from my obstinacy and wilfulness, my escapism, if you like to call it that? I think perhaps I had better try to justify myself by trying to prove that what I like is good. At least I have proved to myself that what many people think necessary is not necessary at all. I admit that in different circumstances – if I were a tycoon, for instance, or bedridden – I might find a telephone essential. But then if I were a secretary or a taxi-man I should find a typewriter or a car essential. Let me put it another way: there are two things for which the English seem to show particular aptitude: one is mechanical invention, the other is literature. My own business happens to be with the use of words – but I see I must now stop using them. I have just been handed a slip of paper to say that somebody is waiting to speak to me on the telephone. I think I had better answer it. After all, one never knows, it may be something important.

[*Listener,* 13 August 1959]

Conversation with my Younger Self

WILLIAM PLOMER: If I am to have a talk with you, my younger self, I must find out who and what you were. I can only imagine you from the time when you were beginning to be conscious – or rather when I remember you as having been conscious. There is plenty of evidence of your earlier existence. Here, for example, is a photograph of a child of two, in a white frock and with fair, almost white, hair. The child is sitting in the sun on a lawn thickly covered with daisies and is looking attentively at an open book. I know who the child is, and that this is the lawn of a country house in Nottinghamshire, and I know why you are there, and that the house belonged to our grandmother; and I think, but I am not sure, that you were conscious of the many brilliant daisy-faces around you, and of their crimson buds and fringes of white petals, and of the pungent, characteristic smell of the round yellow cushions in their centres. I also know that you were already a kind of displaced person, and that this fact is important if I am to try and understand you.

Not much more than a year later, consciousness has taken over, and the senses are awake – but in what a different world! The child is now back in tropical Africa, where it was born; it has been displaced again. As you are small and near the ground, naturally attracted by all things bright and beautiful, and already taught to notice things, you notice wild flowers and pick them. You are strongly responsive to their colours, forms and scents. Would it be fanciful to say that the smell of the daisies in Nottinghamshire touched some atavistic nerve, since, for a thousand years and more, daisies were known to the generations of men and women from whom you are derived; while the strong, exotic odours of veld-flowers in the Northern Transvaal excited you by their absolute newness and strangeness? At least the contrast indicates that in trying to carry on a conversation with you, I shall find a divided self, or two selves, and must remember which one I am addressing.

If a child is to grow up with a reasonable degree of stability and self-confidence, a good many conditions have to be fulfilled. It must be adequately nourished and cared for, it must enjoy the security that comes from knowing that its parents love and protect and understand it, and it ought to have children of its own age to play with. And it seems desirable that as it grows older it should have a settled home, so that it can grow up in a society in which its own place is as unambiguous as that of an actor playing even the smallest part in a play with a large cast. But not all these conditions were yours; you were not merely a displaced, but an often displaced, child. Sometimes both parents were present, sometimes only one; sometimes both were 6000 miles away, for months or years. Generally there were no other children to play with; you had no sister; a brother died young, and there was no other brother until you were nearly eight years old. So you were in effect an only child.

As we were born very soon after the death of Queen Victoria, you were an Edwardian child, and our parents were Victorians, with something of the magisterial confidence of property-owning Victorians: if they had any religious, political, or social doubts, there was no sign of them. Why did they not succeed in instilling their confidence, their unquestioning acceptance of conventional standards of belief and behaviour, in their small, smiling offspring? Yes, as a child you were often smiling, partly because you were pleased and amused, but it was often merely a shy smile, a nervous, uncertain, propitiatory smile. Of what were you uncertain and apprehensive? Of the behaviour of adults. I see now how right you were not to trust them. At an early age you saw manifestations in a certain adult of what I now know to have been neurosis, which tended to show itself in brain-storms and terrifying aggressiveness, sometimes directed against your small self. At the age of five you were in England, separated from your parents, and in a situation where several adults of both sexes amused themselves by teasing you. They pretended that an object you were fond of was in fact conspiring against you and unfaithful to you, and seeing that you

took this seriously, they continued, with guffaws. They were not
ill-disposed towards you, not at all; they were protective. I think
they thought they were preventing you from growing up soft.
At best, their behaviour can be called unimaginative. To you it was
painful and distressing, to me it seems cruel. I think we are in agreement about it. I can recognize now that odious trick of worming out
the most private and cherished feelings of a docile person in order to
gain power over him or her. It is liable to be used by parents,
schoolmasters and priests. Even with good intentions, it is the taking
of an innocent hostage, it is cold blackmail. God preserve me, in
what is left of my life, from being either the victim or the doer of
such a thing.

But nothing of that sort happened in Africa: oh, no! And if I
ask you, my articulate younger self, why, you can answer for that
far-off small self to whom you are nearer in time.

YOUNGER SELF: I am a white child in a remote part of Africa. I am
cared for by my parents. I am also cared for by a black nursemaid,
and, when she is absent, sometimes by a black house-man or house-
boy. They move about the house quietly, on bare feet. It is they
who cook, who clean, who wait at table, who wash our clothes and
dig our garden. When the huge flames of a grass fire threaten our
house, it is they who make it possible to attack and defeat the fire.
When lions roar at night, I feel wonder, not fear; our kind black
servants have given me confidence. Dignified and gentle in their
manners, they seem to be always patient and good-humoured.
They seem to me beautiful too – their backs are so straight, their
teeth are so white, their skins are so smooth, their hair is as nice to
touch as a lamb's back, they seem warm and calm and gay. And
above all, when I am naughty, they don't scold or fly into a rage –
they laugh.

WILLIAM PLOMER: Well, yes. I suppose it would be no good telling
you about the crudities of tribal life, the inhumanities of African
history (almost as bad as those of European history), the horrors of
witchcraft. Ah, you small person, you small privileged person, you
are seeing these good black souls on their best behaviour, so you

take an extremely favourable view of them. They are dependent upon our father and mother, and are anxious to please them.

I cannot expect you to discuss with me the rights and wrongs of such a situation. I certainly do not hold it against our parents that they were engaged in colonization – a word that one never hears nowadays; it has been ousted by skilful anti-Western propagandists, who have succeeded in making the world call it 'colonialism' and condemn it outright. Our father was a civil servant. He was not oppressing anybody or trying to get rich quickly. For a small salary, in a lonely place and a trying climate, in conditions that were often difficult and sometimes dangerous, he was doing his conscientious best to help a primitive society to enjoy some of the advantages he had himself enjoyed. If one asks *why*, well, he was in some ways rather vague, and had drifted into this line of duty; and our mother, for whom it was in every way more of a trial, had undertaken, in her marriage vows, to be a help to him. (Like many another woman, she had little foreseen what she had let herself in for, but she was a woman who kept her promises.) If their proceedings were colonialism, it is a pity, in some ways, there hasn't been more of it. But long before the word 'colonialism' was ever heard, you had grown up unable to accept what was taken for granted about the relation of white people to black people. To you they were all people, and so they are to me, and of all gradations, like other varieties of human beings, between the insufferable and the adorable.

Just at the beginning of the First World War, you find yourself placed in a large Victorian country house on a hilltop in Kent. My poor child, it seems hard to believe today, but whenever you arrive or leave there you are wearing a bowler hat and *carrying* a pair of gloves. I stress the word *carrying*, because it is not thought *comme il faut* to put them on, and yet it is thought unseemly to be seen without them. What awful nonsense! I suppose it was some sort of status-symbol. Let me congratulate you on having asked if there was really any point in it. That great house was a preparatory school, and it is no good our pretending that it was a delightful example of its kind. In case anybody is listening to us, we must not give them the idea that you are sorry for yourself, or that we are

rehearsing a hard-luck story together. That would not be true,
and in any case might put them right off. In fact at your prep school
you are immensely privileged. You have got a good constitution,
you are not actually starving, you are learning to read Virgil, you
keep having interesting holidays with affectionate relations and
friends. Why do you hate your headmaster so much? After all, you
are a playful boy, used to giving and receiving affection.

YOUNGER SELF: I know one is supposed to try and love one's
enemies, but there isn't a single thing I like about him. You've just
used the words 'affectionate' and 'playful'. But here playfulness
means organized games, and if one were to show or be shown
affection, I'm sure one would be punished. I wouldn't mind the
headmaster not being a young man, if only he were a bit fatherly.
He seems to me very, *very* old – over sixty, at least. Well, as this is
1915, he must have been born soon after 1850. You feel that he has
never changed his ideas since he grew up, and that he must have
been brought up in a horrid Victorian way that he has never
questioned. I used to enjoy church, but he seems to make religion
dull and joyless. Not love and praise but sin and duty are what he
harps on.

WILLIAM PLOMER: You're right. He was a muscular Evangelical of
the grimmest 1850 sort, a left-over, a time-lag.

YOUNGER SELF: We are never to be idle, or to enjoy ourselves in
our own ways, or to be interested in the arts or in nature. We are
surrounded by marvellous woods and what is still real country: it
is all strictly out of bounds. Cricket is thought a thousand times
more important than music or painting. In fact they are not thought
of at all. Physical discomfort is supposed to harden us, but why
should we be hardened? Who wants to be a fossil? We sleep in cold
dormitories and on winter mornings sometimes have to break the
ice on our miserable shallow tin baths. What *is* the sense of that?
It keeps the headmaster's coal bill down, and although he lives in
comfort himself, his principle of forcing us, the boys, to lead a
cheerless and ascetic existence helps to fatten his own pocket. He

has poisoned my joyful religious feelings, he has almost destroyed my pleasure in athletics, he has tried to make me believe that anything to do with sex is wrong and guilty. He thinks he is making a man of me, but he has made a rebel of me. I hate almost everything he believes in, and perhaps most of all his unquestioning smugness about the war. I not only despise him but I feel there must be something seriously wrong with the civilization that has produced him.

WILLIAM PLOMER: All bad things come to an end. Now you have got away from your prep school, isn't it rather a relief to be at a public school?

YOUNGER SELF: Oh yes, immense! You suddenly feel that you are somebody, that you can expand, that you aren't just the helpless victim of an odious and petty tyrant with neither heart nor imagination.

WILLIAM PLOMER: You have now been a year at Rugby and you are having bother with your eyes and are told that until you are grown up you must stop reading and lead an open-air life. The question arises whether you are to do this in England or in Africa. You are barely fifteen. That enlightened woman, our mother, gives you the choice.

YOUNGER SELF: Naturally I choose Africa. I should think almost any boy would. Do you regret my choice?

WILLIAM PLOMER: Regret? Life is so short that one can't sit about saying 'Supposing I had done this or that.' For me the result of your choice has been that the life I look back on in youth and early manhood was utterly unlike that of anybody else I know. But here you are back in Africa yet again, and intensely English, and you must, once again, be feeling very much a displaced person?

YOUNGER SELF: I am.

WILLIAM PLOMER: Very isolated, even lonely.

YOUNGER SELF: Yes. And I shall go on feeling like that. I don't think I shall ever be what is called a good mixer – nor, I dare say, will you.

WILLIAM PLOMER: I think not.

YOUNGER SELF: I find myself cut off from persons of my own age with the same sort of experience, tastes, and hopes. There don't seem to be any of them here.

WILLIAM PLOMER: Are you unhappy?

YOUNGER SELF: I am not unhappy by nature, but now, when I am growing up, I sometimes burst into storms of tears which I cannot explain. It is not from self-pity, but from a sort of bewilderment and frustration.

WILLIAM PLOMER: But when you were smaller you were so fond of the Africans. Aren't you able now to develop new friendships with any of them?

YOUNGER SELF: No. How can I? The freedom of a child has come to an end. As an adolescent I am hedged in by racial taboos which I am not in a position to break, however much I want to.

WILLIAM PLOMER: I can imagine that your isolation and bewilderment may be making you melancholy. What sustains you?

YOUNGER SELF: Three things, I think. The affection of my parents; anger with the injustices and stupidities of my environment (and anger is a good antidote for melancholy); and a kind of confident hope, or hopeful confidence.

WILLIAM PLOMER: What have you got to be so confident about?

YOUNGER SELF: Surely it is not unusual or inexcusable to be a bit cocky when young? I am full of physical and nervous energy, I want to find out about life. At the same time I am conscious of a

creative talent. I have already begun to write. I feel I have things to
say which nobody else has said, that I shall say them in my own way,
and that they may be worth saying.

WILLIAM PLOMER: But you are only half educated. Your responses
to life and your surroundings are hardly reasoned: they are
emotional, intuitive, and disordered. I see you regard yourself as
an artist, and are driven on by some kind of creative urge. But I
doubt if this motive is quite unadulterated. Are you ambitious?
Perhaps you simply want to make money, and are longing for
fame, or popularity, and power?

YOUNGER SELF: I will try to give you an absolutely honest answer.
I think it is true that my ambitions, as a writer, are strictly functional.
I wish to control the medium in which I am working. I wish, in my
writing, to be exact and free. In aiming at precision I have something in common with a craftsman, a scholar, an engineer, or a
scientist. But what do I mean by freedom? I mean freedom to
choose and define my subject matter, and the attainment of flexibility in the treatment of it. I suppose I also want such freedom to
write as can be afforded by a reasonable allowance of health, leisure,
stimulating or fertilizing experience, and helpful influence or conditions outside myself.

WILLIAM PLOMER: But what about money?

YOUNGER SELF: I have no idea of making money or, I think,
expectation of making a living by writing: naturally I shall be
pleased if any of my writings bring me useful amounts of money.
And as for fame, I have no expectation of popular success, or desire
for such a thing. The fame I should like would be for whatever gifts
I have and exercise to be recognized. I should like my writing to be
found vigorous and fresh and pleasing by persons whom I respect
or like, by my approximate coevals and equals, and also by persons
unknown to me, older or younger than myself, or perhaps even not
yet born. You also said something about power. I hope for the
power to cultivate my understanding and my art of writing. I

suppose that that implies some wish to influence other people, even if only by interesting or entertaining them.

WILLIAM PLOMER: And now you are nearly grown up.

YOUNGER SELF: Yes, I am nineteen, and I am writing a novel.

WILLIAM PLOMER: That's not a very unusual coincidence.

YOUNGER SELF: But it is an unusual novel. You may not have read it lately, but you can look back, whereas I can only look forward. Would you say, on the strength of this rather intense novel and of the work which is going to follow it that they go some way towards justifying my belief in myself?

WILLIAM PLOMER: I think we had better leave it to other people to judge that, don't you ? I do not myself think that your first novel is any great shakes as a novel, but I do think it rang a bell – an alarm bell, if you like. It at least did something to shock a few people into facing the explosiveness of a way of life in Africa that had up to then been taken for granted. It has been said more than once that in your early work are to be found the archetypes of the two human situations from which all subsequent South African fiction has sprung – the story of mutual sexual attraction between persons of the two different races, and the story of the innocent, indigenous African who is corrupted by the white man's big city – which is almost invariably Johannesburg. By accident or design, you did go straight to the two main points about South Africa – that racial relationships were not merely political or economic, but emotional; and that the effect of industrialization upon the African was profoundly disturbing and was bound to have political consequences.

YOUNGER SELF: So I did make something new?

WILLIAM PLOMER: At least you saw what was important. But that is quite enough about Africa. Your novel and your short stories were published, they were noticed, the seed you sowed is still growing; and Americans, and Africans nowadays too, write theses about it. But here you are, in your early twenties, no longer in Africa, but quite settled down in, of all places, Japan. What on earth are you really doing there?

YOUNGER SELF: I am doing what I could not do in Africa – living among people of a race remote from ours without exposing myself to guilt or persecution. Not only do they treat me with hospitality, kindness and courtesy, but I think they approve of my efforts to fall in with their habits and customs and to look at things from their points of view.

WILLIAM PLOMER: Why do you say 'points of view' in the plural?

YOUNGER SELF: A split personality must surely have at least two points of view. The Japanese live in a state of strain and crisis, and are torn between the past and the future. Under the violent pressure and threat of change, they half cling for safety to tradition and habit, but safety compels them to adapt themselves to what is strange and new. Living among them while they are in such a state of turmoil, I have a special sympathy with the young in their hopes and despairs and bewilderment, and especially in their awful lack of freedom of speech and even of movement. They cannot travel, and are weighed down with family and patriotic responsibilities and conventions. I think they envy me my freedom: I wish I could share it with them.

WILLIAM PLOMER: You are writing fiction about Japanese men and women. Recalling what you said, I feel sure you won't expect a popular success or a large sale in England for it, or even that much notice will be taken of it.

YOUNGER SELF: How could I? The English as a rule have little curiosity about people of distant races and places. And I fear that people only read books that flatter their own interests, prejudices, or fantasies. But why do you ask me so many questions? I thought we were supposed to be having a conversation, not an interview.

Now let me ask *you* a question. What do you think of my writings about Japan?

WILLIAM PLOMER: It would be rather unseemly for me to blow your own trumpet (or is it mine?), but I think you do write about the Japanese without patronizing or sentimentalizing them. I would go a little further: I think you foreshadow the danger and folly of Japanese militarism.

YOUNGER SELF: What, another alarm bell? Do you think it is the function of your younger self merely to go about the world ringing the tocsin? You talk to me as if I am some sort of journalist or political commentator.

WILLIAM PLOMER: Not at all. As I told you, I think you have more imagination and intuition than intellectual power or training, and I think this sometimes enables you to see what is going to happen more clearly than is possible for more conventional minds. But now we are in the late 1920s, and you have decided to return to England and settle there. What are your motives?

YOUNGER SELF: I have accustomed myself to Japanese life and have formed emotional attachments here in Japan, and the Japanese have honoured me by asking me to stay. But what would become of me? Should I 'go native', as they say? If so, how could I help becoming an oddity? I should always be an alien here, and to settle in Japan permanently would turn me into a permanently displaced person. After all, I have no roots here.

WILLIAM PLOMER: Is that chiefly why you are going back to England, to draw nourishment from your roots?

YOUNGER SELF: Can't you imagine how isolated I feel, and how very far east I am, not merely in the geographical sense? I am completely cut off here, *completely*, from Europeans, from Englishmen, of my own age, kind, and inclinations. Surely you can understand that a young man might need badly to associate with others of his own generation, and that a writer might want to meet other writers in his own language, and might want to soak himself and disport himself in the particular stream of civilization he can call his own.

WILLIAM PLOMER: I understand all that. But surely there is also the question of love and sex. You aren't young for nothing. I don't want to pry unduly into your private life, particularly as we are liable to be overheard – one never knows. You talk so solemnly about exchanging ideas and so on, but unless your inclinations are purely exotic, I imagine you might want to exchange kisses as well as ideas in your own country.

YOUNGER SELF: You have reached a point where I think you ought to mind your own business.

WILLIAM PLOMER: All right. I have another question to ask about your intended return to the land of our ancestors. You speak of your feelings of isolation here in Japan. Has it not occurred to you that a new kind of isolation may await you in England?

YOUNGER SELF: How do you mean?

WILLIAM PLOMER: Well, you know, England is not a country that welcomes everybody with open arms. Nor has it any particular reason to welcome you. You are not famous or notorious. You are not rich enough to enjoy the kind of freedom that money gives. You have no circle to re-enter or close friends waiting to be reunited with you. You have drifted away from the persons, and indeed from many of the values and accepted ideas prevailing in England when you were a boy. You have admitted that you are not a good mixer. I think you are deficient in worldly ambition, and I don't think you are likely to push or advertise yourself or to marry the kind of woman who would push you along. I don't even see you joining some decent club. In fact I think you are an un-clubbable young man. Your only assets, so far as I can see, are your youth, such talent and intelligence as you seem to possess, and a certain independence of nature. My guess is that, partly by choice and partly from necessity, you may find yourself living, for some years at least, a rather solitary, marginal life.

YOUNGER SELF: Such a prospect wouldn't really daunt me.

WILLIAM PLOMER: I doubt if you realize how different you have become, how tremendously *dépaysé*. From living with the Japanese you have become uncommonly formal in your manners and speech. This won't go down well in England now, in 1929, just when manners have so greatly loosened up. When you land in England again you will not merely be conscious of broken links with people and places: you will find that in the ten years since 1919, when you were last there, great changes have taken place. And I doubt if you have yet overcome that shyness you had when you were much younger. My guess is that you will not merely feel once more like a newly displaced person, but almost like an alien.

YOUNGER SELF: Very well, then perhaps I shall be able to look at England and the English with something of the detachment of an alien, and see them as they really are. I hope that in time I shall find myself reassimilated. I am not a specially envious person, but I do rather envy you your obvious feeling of being at home. And I like to think that I may look forward to enjoying it myself.

[Broadcast on 12 December 1962. The older self was spoken by the author, the younger self by Denis McCarthy. Printed in an edition of 25 copies, 1963]

Admirations

I

Prose Writers

Ivan Bunin

M. Ivan Bunin is perhaps the most distinguished of the Russian writers who are living in exile. He is best known in this country by a story called *The Gentleman from San Francisco*, which, with three others, was translated by D. H. Lawrence, S. S. Koteliansky and Leonard Woolf. A novel called *The Village* has also appeared in English, and about ten years ago Martin Secker produced a volume of *Fifteen Tales* in a translation which was often clumsy and irritating but could not mar the clear outlines of the original. M. Bunin is a sound and brilliant writer, highly individual and highly skilled. His honesty lies partly in his always remaining true to his nature, which, like everybody else's, is the product of a particular set of circumstances, and partly in the clear gaze he has always directed at his surroundings. His writing is always concise and graphic, with profundity beneath its lightest effects, and his view of the world is his own. He is, in fact, an artist.

There is a fashion for dragging political prejudice into the appraisal of literature, and there are many no doubt ready to speak scornfully of M. Bunin because he is not at this moment in Moscow expressing an exuberant faith in the dictatorship of the proletariat and describing the daily lives of those who labour to bring it about. But a careful study of his work will show that he is not a Utopian, nor a man likely to devote himself to any political formula. There are quite enough people in the world ready to tell the world what it *ought* to be like; M. Bunin is one of those who spend their lives trying to find out what it *is* like. In so far as a bias may be detected in him, it is not unnaturally the bias of the race and class from which he sprang and which gave him the advantages he has enjoyed – his zest for life, his culture, his mysticism – but his sympathies are not confined to the aristocrat and the bourgeois.

The Well of Days is described as 'an autobiographical novel of

Russian country life fifty years ago, seen through the eyes of a sensitive child with a passion for poetry'. With all its vividness, it has an atmosphere of sad and dreamlike remoteness which cannot only be accounted for by the fact that it is made up of memories. The prevailing note is one of nostalgia. Nostalgia for what? Not simply for the past. For the unknowable, perhaps. A 'yearning for a future where all the loveliness and joy of this world seemed to lie in store' or an 'anticipation not merely of happiness, of its peculiar fullness, but also of something else in which, once it came, that essence, that meaning, would at last suddenly reveal itself and be grasped' – all this could no doubt be explained away glibly enough as the decayed sentimentality of a bourgeois *déraciné*: but the explanation would not be a true one. Nostalgia is a real emotion – for some people one of the most profound emotions – and long before the War or the Revolution it was present in M. Bunin's work. With him it seems almost a religious emotion; it seems to suggest the soul bewildered and seeking for home.

There is no special point in comparing the reminiscent Bunin with Aksakov. The perspective is different, the style is different, but the strange old Russian countryside and its feckless, temperamental inhabitants are easily recognizable. The book is never anything but Russian. At times it gives one the feeling of being in the presence of an Orthodox priest who mutters, in an air either loud with bells and heavy with incense or hushed on account of death, incantations which express a yearning for heaven and yet stir the heart with earthly emotions. And all the time it makes the reader feel like an eye-witness of the scenes it describes. Few writers can ever have ventured to employ a style so heavily harnessed with adjectives. Just as a worshipped ikon is loaded with jewels, just as a painter with a 'feeling for paint' lovingly enriches his canvas, so M. Bunin, striving to reanimate a world passionately apprehended in youth, tends at times to be over-lavish in style. But from the well of days he has drawn a lovely picture of a temperament, and of a vanished society and time, and his translators (Gleb Struve and Hamish Miles) seem to have done their job to perfection.

[Review of *The Well of Days, Spectator,* 14 July 1933]

Lenin's Favourite Novel

A friend of mine who knew Lenin's widow once asked her whether he ever read novels, and if so, what novel he liked best. She answered that he sometimes did read novels, and that there was one in particular which could be called his favourite. One might spend a long time guessing what this book was, but directly the answer is known it seems, like the answers to so many puzzling questions, almost obvious. The book in question was Balzac's *Country Doctor*, which deals with matters that meant much to Lenin. It is possible that it put ideas into his head, and likely that it clarified ideas already there, for it is among the functions of classic writings, including novels, to confirm our suspicions, to show us that what we think new is not new at all, to remind us that the conclusions we have drawn, perhaps painfully, from our own experience (congratulating ourselves, no doubt, on our intelligence) have been drawn more neatly and more profoundly by others long before, and, in dealing with the particular, to hint at or lay down certain general principles which hold true to human experience in vastly different times and places.

One might say that among novelists – even among French novelists, Stendhal, Proust, whom you will – Balzac is most of all a man of the world. That is to say that he is the most aware of what goes on in the world and the best able to convey images of human behaviour with a proper sense of proportion. It is therefore fitting that he, like Shakespeare, should be read by men whose business is with government, in order that they may understand better what they are about. In *The Country Doctor* he is dealing directly with the subject of government, both in practice and in principle. Simply as a novel, the book makes a powerful, lively and enduring impression, but one does not remember it least as a vehicle for ideas, and for one idea in particular – that there can be no form of government more admirable than a benevolent dictatorship.

The dictatorship held up to us as an example is that of the country doctor himself, Benassis, who has settled in a region not far from Grenoble, but backward, and 'completely outside the social movement'. As a distraction from private sorrow he has 'resolved to educate this country as a tutor educates a child'. From the beginning he has had uphill work. He was up against ignorance and apathy. Like the begging friar, he says, he has had to make *soup of pebbles*. How did he do it? In the first place by creating needs, by raising the standards of living, for 'people without wants are poor'. His economic theory was not founded on anything so narrow as self-sufficiency: he understood the need for trade with the outside world. Energetic, firm, and endlessly resourceful, he has won the confidence and affection of the locals, completely reorganized their lives, and brought them prosperity. He has become 'the oracle of the canton'.

To him comes a military man, Genestas, who for reasons of his own wishes to find out if Benassis is all that he is said to be. Both admirable men, they take to each other. The doctor receives the soldier as his guest, shows him round, and explains at length what he has done for the neighbourhood and how and why he has done it. At one point there is a symposium in the doctor's house attended by such symbolical figures as a priest and a lawyer, where the general principles behind the doctor's activities are expounded. At the end of the story he dies, and somebody says, 'He was the Napoleon of our valley.'

The reader sees Benassis as a man of strong individuality, a practical idealist, one who seems moved to action by intellectual passion, a reasonable fanatic. Was not Lenin something of the same sort? Did he not see in Benassis a reflection of himself, and did he not find the likeness in some points startling? For instance, when the doctor permits himself such observations as that 'perhaps it is even a social theft to consume without producing anything,' or that 'with the people, it is necessary to be always infallible,' or that 'constancy is the highest expression of strength,' or that 'a man who conceives a political system should, if he feels in himself the strength to apply it, be silent, seize the power and act.'

The beauty of the book, from a Marxist point of view, is no doubt that it is so largely about the material interests of a community. Having made his resolution to devote himself to the betterment of this community, Benassis had hesitated whether to be a curé, a doctor, or a justice of the peace. Comparing the functions of doctor and priest, he remarks that the peasant listens more willingly to a man who cures his body than to one who talks about saving his soul: so he became a doctor. He had to deal with peasants, who in the first place had bellies to fill:

> I haven't made any idylls about my people, I have accepted them for what they are – poor peasants – neither entirely good nor entirely wicked ... I understood, above all, that I could act upon them only through calculations of self-interest and immediate benefit. All peasants are children of St Thomas, the doubting apostle: they always want words to be supported by facts.

But self-interest is not peculiar to peasants. Society as a whole has no other support than egotism. The great man who will appear in the rôle of saviour will 'doubtless avail himself of the spirit of individualism to remake the nation; but, while waiting for this regeneration, we are still in the age of material interests.'

So far, Lenin may have felt, so good. But presently the question of religion has to be faced. Benassis–Balzac is pretty definite. Formerly, he says, he had regarded Catholicism as 'a mass of bigotry and superstition, skilfully manipulated', which under any intelligent system should be reformed, but as a result of his labours among the peasants he has come to recognize it as 'the only force which can bind together the social elements and give them a durable form'. Furthermore, it has 'political utility'. The dogma of the life to come is 'not only a consolation, but still more an instrument adapted to govern with'. Has not Russia since the Revolution been entirely governed by the dogma of the life to come, and has not Lenin himself become that 'visibly-honoured god' without which human laws have no strength? Substitute Communism for Catholicism, Lenin may have felt, and the difficulty is solved: you have got your religion ready-made, and there will be plenty of time later on to build the temples and hunt the heretics.

Government in Russia, as in Germany and Italy, seems to have proceeded precisely according to the maxims laid down by Benassis. 'Who votes', he says, 'discusses. Powers discussed do not exist ... The proletarians seem to me the minors of a nation, and should always remain in a state of tutelage ... The tutelage of the masses seems to me, then, to be a thing just and necessary to the sustaining of a society.' If a strong man appears amongst the proletariat, he should be assimilated by the government lest he encourage the masses to revolt. Discussions, parliaments, democracies, are just a waste of time, for 'at the end of all deliberations will be found Mirabeau, Danton, Robespierre or Napoleon – pro-consuls or an emperor.' 'A deliberating assembly which discusses the dangers of a nation, when it is necessary to make it act, does that not seem to you ridiculous? ... Power, the law, should be the work of one man only ...' Finally, we are given a somewhat idealized portrait of the desired dictator:

> To be able to see always beyond the present moment and in advance of destiny, to be above power and to remain in it only through a consciousness of his utility without any self-deception as to his own strength; to discard his passions and even all commonplace ambition in order to remain master of his faculties, to foresee, to will and to act incessantly; to make himself just and absolute to maintain order on a large scale, to impose silence upon his heart and to listen only to his intelligence; to be neither suspicious nor confident, neither doubting nor credulous, neither grateful nor ungrateful, neither unprepared for an event nor surprised by an idea; to live, in short, through the sentiment of the masses, and to dominate them always by extending the wings of his intelligence, the volume of his voice, and the penetration of his eye; in seeing, not the details, but the consequences of everything – is not this to be a little greater than a man?

Does Hitler come up to this standard? Does Mussolini? Does Stalin? Did Lenin? I think Benassis comes nearer to it than any of them.

Why, then, did he not employ his talents where they would have had more scope? Perhaps because he remained too human and too imaginative and too modest. In fact one is left wondering whether perhaps he is not a little too good to be true. Balzac seems to have had the idea of creating a minor Napoleon – but he has made him virtuous. At least Benassis knew something which the revolutionary autocrats of our time do not seem able to get into their heads, that 'ideas which suit one country are fatal in another.'

[*Spectator*, 6 August 1937]

Herman Melville

Herman Melville died in New York in the autumn of 1891. Once famous, he had been almost forgotten. That neglect is not to be wondered at, for he had gone where the world never follows, into the dark places of thought where questions are asked that never get an answer by reasoning. They may get an answer through religious faith, but Melville had no religious faith. He saw what the world was and he saw what it might be, and the difference between these two visions sent him into a kind of trance. In the bustling, money-making New York of the later nineteenth century he lived as withdrawn as a hermit in a cave, and if the world had asked him what conclusions he had come to, it would not have liked his answer. He might have answered that he had found out that there was more evil than good in the world, and no remedy for it. Or that Fate rules everything, and there is no such thing as free-will. These are answers which the world never likes to hear, for it is largely kept going by ignorant optimism and the strange belief that a man is the master of his soul and body. 'By heaven, man,' wrote Melville, 'we're turned round and round in this world like yonder windlass, and Fate is the handspike.' That may have been the voice of a hermit, but it was a seafaring hermit. There were three Melvilles in one – the sailor, the writer, and the hermit. They were all in him at the beginning, and they were all part of him to the end. First the sailor was most active; then the writer, who remembered the sailor; then the hermit who dwelt on the memories of the old days at sea and on all the questions that had arisen in the mind of the writer. And it was the hermit who got into the deepest waters of all.

Melville's father was a well-to-do merchant with a large family. He lived on a fine scale, but when Melville was only thirteen, his father died bankrupt and the boy was thrown on the world. He worked in a bank, in a store, on a farm. 'Talk not of the bitterness of middle age and after-life,' he wrote. 'A boy can feel all that, and much more.' At eighteen, he ran away to sea. His first voyage was a rough one. He had grown up in a genteel home and is thought to have been a member of a Juvenile Total Abstinence Association and Anti-Smoking Society, which had not exactly fitted him for the forecastle. The voyage took him to Liverpool and back. His father had told him what a fine city it was, but when he got there he did not find it all he had hoped: he found that people in England had their troubles, just like the Americans. When he returned to the United States he spent three restless years teaching and trying to write. Then he joined the crew of a whaler bound for the South Seas.

In the last century the South Sea Islands became a place of romantic escape for Europeans who were tired of Europe or Americans who were tired of America. But they were already too late, most of them. A writer like Stevenson, a painter like Gauguin, and all the swarm of adventurers and outcasts, they were really too late. These regions had already been corrupted by Europe and America: the trader and the missionary, alcohol and venereal disease, had already done their work. Melville was the first imaginative writer to reveal the islands to the Western mind. When he arrived in the Marquesas Islands, exactly a hundred years ago, it was still possible to find what he called 'authentic Edens in a pagan sea'. He had had a bad voyage out – there was much trouble on board – and together with a shipmate, Toby Greene, he deserted his ship. These two made their way to a remote valley, where they were welcomed and held in a kind of playful captivity by the natives. Today nobody lives in that once happy valley, and it is all overgrown. Its once happy life would have vanished from human memory if it had not been recorded by Melville in *Typee*.

> There seemed to be no cares, griefs, troubles or vexations in Typee ... The natives appeared to form one household, whose members were bound together by the ties of strong affection ... Above all, there was no money. All was mirth, fun and high good humour.

Years later he wrote:

> But tell, shall he, the tourist, find
>   Our isles the same in violet-glow
> Enamouring us what years and years –
>   Ah, Ned, what years and years ago!
> Well, Adam advances, smart in pace,
> But scarce by violets that advance we trace.

Very well: but why did he leave his earthly paradise? Didn't he know when he was well off? The answer is that a civilized man cannot settle down for good among primitive people if he is also young and restless. 'Once more the sailor's cradle rocked under me, and I found myself rolling in my gait. By noon, the island had gone down in the horizon, and all before us was the wide Pacific.'

After various adventures, Melville joined the United States navy as an ordinary seaman, and in his book *Whitejacket* he has left us a detailed and wonderful account of life in the American navy of his day, the good with the bad. He was greatly shaken by having to witness the then customary punishment of flogging. He could not understand how any man could order or inflict such a cruel indignity on another, or how any man could survive it without being broken in spirit if not in body. So vividly did he describe this horror in *Whitejacket* that the book is said to have had more influence than anything else in abolishing corporal punishment in the American navy. A copy of the book was placed on the desk of every member of Congress, and a law was passed soon after, abolishing flogging in the navy without substituting any other mode of punishment.

All his life Melville was something of a hero-worshipper, and while he was serving on an American warship he met a man whom he idealized and idolized, an Englishman whom he writes of as Jack Chase and describes as handsome, frank, charming, bold, good company, an excellent seaman, better than a hundred common mortals, and full of good sense and good feeling. To this man, a little too perfect to seem true, Melville offered his 'best love'.

After all this, Melville was still only twenty-five. It was then that he came home and began to write his books, and until then, he afterwards said, he had had no development at all, by which he seems to have meant that until then he had not begun to think, because he had been too busy living. He certainly had plenty to write about. Soon after he had written his first book, which attracted a great deal of attention, he got married. He hoped to support his family by his pen, and if he did not succeed it was not for want of trying. He wrote four books in four years and quickly became famous, for the public loves a novelty and he had something to say they had never heard before. Some offence was caused, however, by what he wrote about missionaries in the South Seas. 'If some books are deemed most baneful,' he wrote, 'and their sale forbidden, how then with deadlier facts? Those whom books will hurt will not be proof against events. Events, not books, should be forbidden ... Ill or good men cannot know. Often ill comes from good, as good from ill.'

After a visit to London (where he saw the public hanging of a man and wife convicted of murder, and the crowd roaring like wild beasts), Melville settled down with his wife and children in an old farm-house in Massachusetts. But he seems to have felt very much alone. His wife was in no sense his intellectual equal, and she was not even a particularly good housekeeper. As for the people who lived round about, they were staid, hard-working and narrowly religious. They were anything but genial. Once when Melville tried to entertain a gathering of them with stories of the sea and of his wanderings, they listened in silence, and at last one farmer said, 'Friend, we know nothing of that here.' Young as he was, Melville already thought much about his past, and his mind was already turning to deeper things – not only to experience, but to a search for any possible meaning in experience. Driven in upon himself, he yet needed to give himself more than he could give himself to his wife and children, or to the farm, or to his neighbours. He gave himself up to the writing of his greatest book, *Moby Dick*, and while he was writing it he met Nathaniel Hawthorne, fifteen years his senior, to whom he gave, or tried to give, himself in an unsought outpouring of hero-worship and intense emotional friendship. Unfortunately he could not give himself freely to the book, because, as he said, 'What I feel most moved to write, that is banned – it won't pay. Yet write altogether the other way I cannot. So the product is a final hash; and all my books are botches.' He also knew that he was writing too grandly for a public chiefly interested in money-grubbing. 'Though I wrote the Gospels in this century, I should die in the gutter.' And he could not, like Whitman, make comforting visions out of the everyday life and simple men in the street. He was also highly suspicious of democracy.

Moby Dick is a story of the sea, of whaling, and of the strangely assorted crew of a whaler, whose captain, Captain Ahab, is bent on the pursuit of one particular whale, a white whale, nicknamed Moby Dick. In the end Ahab finds the white whale, but it is not a happy ending, it is a fatal one. The story is full of wild visions and adventures, full of quaint learning and practical knowledge of old-time methods of whaling, full of splendid rhapsodies, but while you read you realize that it is full of hidden meanings. Just as the sea is out of your depth, so this story of the sea takes you out of your depth. Melville was always fascinated by the sea. It was for him the supreme mystery of the visible world. He thought that men were more mysterious than women, and he once compared them to the sea and the sky. While most people look up sometimes into the sky and wonder about space and eternity, Melville looked down into the sea and wondered about good and evil:

> It was a clear, steel-blue day. Air and sea were hardly separable – only the air was transparently pure and soft, with a woman's look, and the robust and man-like sea heaved with long, strong, lingering swells, like Samson's chest in his sleep. Hither and thither on high glided the snow-white wings of small, unspeckled birds – these were the gentler thoughts of the feminine air. But to and fro in the deeps, far down in the bottomless blue, rushed mighty leviathans, swordfish and sharks – and these were the strong, troubled, murderous thinkings of the masculine sea.

Strong, troubled, murderous thinkings went to the making of *Moby Dick*. Captain Ahab thought of the white whale as evil, an embodiment of all the evil in the world, but Melville did not believe that good and evil could be so easily distinguished that goodness

could be simply represented by a brave seaman who tries to stick a
harpoon into a whale representing evil, like St George and the
dragon. What he leads us to believe is that Ahab is a kind of mad-
man, a man perhaps who had suffered so much that he wished to
avenge himself for his sufferings upon some formidable being – like
the Devil or Hitler – whatever effort it might cost him. Ahab can
perhaps be seen as every man who struggles against fate – against
disappointme.\t, frustration, sickness, poverty, loneliness, un-
faithfulness, oppression or a ruthless enemy – like a hero; and
Ahab's, like all heroism, had to be its own reward.

Although Melville, while he was writing *Moby Dick*, was like a
man possessed, we have his own word for it that he could not give
himself to it wholly. This great book did not bring him sufficient
reward, either in fame or money, for the effort it cost him or the
result he achieved. 'Though the world worship mediocrity and
commonplace,' he said, 'yet hath its fire and sword for contemporary
grandeur.' Nor did his friendship with Hawthorne bring him what
he had evidently expected, for Hawthorne could not respond to the
offer of Melville's heart, and withdrew. Melville shut himself up
more and more in his own thoughts. He wrote other books, but
they were not to the popular taste. His health suffered, he grew
moody and low in spirits, so at last he went for a long tour in
Europe. When he returned, he gave lectures upon it, but people
did not go to listen to him, they went to listen to 'the man who had
lived among cannibals' – for that was how they still thought of him.
Having a family to support, he became an Inspector of Customs in
New York City, and continued in that employment for a quarter
of a century, only retiring three years before his death.

In those long years in the customs-house, which was commonly
regarded as 'a refuge for nonentities, failures and nondescripts',
Melville was very much alone. He had a home, it is true, and his
wife stood by him for more than forty years, but although one
daughter lived at home and another was happily married, one of
his sons had run away from home and the other had been found
shot dead – whether it was accident or suicide remained in some
doubt. Melville was not always melancholy, for a man who saw
him five years before his death said that he bore nothing of the

appearance of a man disappointed in life, but rather had an air of
perfect contentment, and his conversation had much of his jovial,
let-the-world-go-as-it-will manner. Let the world go as it will!
Melville might well have said that, for he did not belong to his
world, the busy, pushing, go-getting New York of the later
nineteenth century. He saw around him what he called 'the triumph
of the insincere, unanimous mediocrity', and he did not like it. He
did not trust the machine age. Technical advances, he thought,
meant spiritual retreats. What a true prophet he was!

> Your arts advance in faith's decay:
> You are but drilling the new Hun
> Whose growl even now can some dismay;
> Vindictive in his heart of hearts,
> He schools him in your mines and marts –
> A skilled destroyer.

Melville did not live to see the new Hun let loose, but he lived
long enough to write another masterpiece, *Billy Budd*. This was
spared by his widow's hand after his death: what she destroyed we
shall never know. In it he wrote that will-power was a term not
yet included in the lexicon of science. He was a determinist to the
last: great forces behind everyday life, not mere human impulses,
seemed to him to govern human existence. It is true that he once
wrote that it was better to live in a fool's paradise than in wise
Solomon's hell, but it was not possible for him. He nursed to the
last his own secrets, his own hidden fire. 'In fervid hearts, self-
contained,' he wrote, 'some brief experiences devour our human
tissue as secret fire in a ship's hold consumes cotton in the bale.'
And so he burned slowly away, haunted by the shipmates with
whom he had served in his youth, and who came nearest, perhaps,
to his vision of what men ought to be. Time had raised them, like
Jack Chase, into demigods, sailing on seas of imagination, and yet
they remained real, images of a kind of men who will always exist,
the cheerful fatalists who take things as they find them, duty or
pleasure, who do the hard work of the world in war and peace and
have always a sharp appetite for pleasure.

Taking things as fated merely,
Childlike through the world ye spanned;
Not holding unto life too dearly,
Ye who held your lives in your hand.

Ye float around me, form and feature:
Tattooings, earrings, love-locks curled;
Barbarians of man's simpler nature,
Unworldly servers of the world.

Here was something that Melville believed in, and it is here that he has something in common with his contemporary Whitman, bending maternally over the wounded during the Civil War. Romantic comradeship was worked up by Whitman into an almost political programme of romantic democracy. For Melville it was a fleeting memory or a visionary ideal which offered some compensation to a lonely heart in a terrifying world. The greatness and the limitations of both these writers are bound up with that moral earnestness and absolute lack of a sense of humour which marked them both and which may perhaps be ascribed to the Dutch blood in the veins of both of them.

[*Penguin New Writing,* 1943]

Louis Couperus

Soon after the last war a number of novels by the Dutchman, Louis
Couperus (1863–1923), appeared in English translations and found
many readers. The best known of them was *Old People and the
Things that Pass*; the most striking, perhaps, was *The Hidden Force*,
of which the English translation, by Teixeira de Mattos, was published by Jonathan Cape in 1922. But Couperus had appeared in
English long before – in 1891, in fact, when his second novel came
out in Heinemann's International Library under the editorship of
the ever enterprising Edmund Gosse. Its original title is *Noodlot*; in
English it was given a rather silly title – *Footsteps of Fate*. Gosse
provided an introduction, headed 'The Dutch Sensitivists', from
which it appears that sensitivism was an attempt, under French
influence, to refine the crudities of realism. In Gosse's *Silhouettes*
there is a gossipy sketch, written many years later, of Couperus,
whom he calls, I think, the representative Dutch novelist.

'The full moon wore the hue of tragedy that evening.' Such is
the opening sentence of *The Hidden Force*, and although it is not the
sort of sentence we should be likely to find at the beginning of a
novel nowadays, it does very well: it at once makes the reader
comfortably expectant of troubles which he is going to enjoy
vicariously. This tragic moon illuminates a languorous evening in
Labuwangi, a town in Java, and the air is full of 'an oppressive
mystery': indeed the atmosphere is quite as oppressive and
mysterious as any in Conrad, but it is evoked by a plainer and
perhaps more detailed, if not more exact, observation. Van Oudijck,
the Resident, is stalking past the villas of the more important towns-
folk – 'faintly lighted, deathly silent, apparently uninhabited, with
their rows of whitewashed flower-pots gleaming in the vague dusk
of the evening'. He is a tall, sturdy man, 'practical, cool-headed,

quick in decision from the long habit of authority', and not allowing enough for the imponderables in the native character. It is not
his nature, we are told, to yield to mystery; he denies it. But we are
assured that the mystery is there: the novelist's task is to convince
us of it.

The Resident is forty-eight, and divorced from his first wife, a
good-looking half-caste, by whom he has had a son, Theo, now
twenty-three, and a daughter, Doddie, only seventeen but a little
ripe for her age. The second Mrs van Oudijck, Léonie by name, is
barely thirty. She has 'the languid dignity of women born in Java,
daughters of European parents', has immense charm, and is a lazy,
shallow sensualist; her pet author is Catulle Mendès. One of her
main preoccupations is clandestine sexual intercourse with Theo,
her stepson. Although, because of her charm, she is not entirely
worthless as a proconsul's wife, she is quite unworthy of the honest
van Oudijck, whose heart, if it were not so much in his work,
would feel even more strongly its isolation. This lonely, capable
man, blinded by dutifulness and by want of imagination to much
of what is going on round him, engages the reader's sympathies
and wins his admiration – unless the reader is one who finds a
cuckold, as such, a joke.

So the centre of the scene is set. Tragedy, we know from the
first, impends: we do not yet guess its nature. 'Mystery', a brooding
melancholy, a vague threat, a 'hidden force', is, we are told, in the
air, is behind the faces and beneath the surface of people and things:
we wait, a little impatiently, for more precision; we are not willing
to have our blood curdled by mere statements, or even by the
gradual and skilful evocation of Dutch society in an admittedly
somehow ominous tropical setting. We are certainly far from any
breezy British convention of colonial life, with its hard-riding,
straight-shooting, boyish man, a pipe between his teeth, and his
'little woman' ordering an early tiffin so that they can be in time
for the gymkhana ... No, the Labuwangi whites are of a different
order. Eldersma, for instance, the district secretary, has, according
to his wife Eva, ceased to be a man: 'My husband is an official.'
Eva herself is a cultivated woman, 'very European', from an artistic
environment at the Hague, where her father is a painter, her mother

a singer. Here at Labuwangi she suffers the isolation of a cultivated
person among the uncultivated, but she has character, she has guts
as well as sensibility, and adapts herself to her surroundings; and
the locals are grateful to her for her gaiety, which they lack, and
forgive her for everything they do not understand – her aesthetic
principles, her liking for Wagner, the arty dadoes in her drawing-
room – and to Eva the lazy Léonie delegates nearly all the social
duties of a Resident's wife. Then there is van Helderen, the con-
troller, and his wife. Apparently quite European, tall, fair and
blue-eyed, van Helderen has been born and bred in Java and has
never been out of it, yet there is something ultra-European in his
manners and tastes. His wife Ida is the type of the white-skinned
half-caste:

> She was full of little mysterious fads and hatreds and
> affections; all her actions were the result of mysterious little
> impulses ... She was absolutely unreliable ... She was always
> in love, tragically.

Such are some of the circle.

It is at a reception at Eva's that we see where trouble is brewing.
Van Oudijck is worried because his relations with the native
Regent, or rajah, are not easier and more agreeable. His relations
with the Regent's late father – a noble, cultivated descendant of
one of the oldest Javanese families – had been perfect: they had
been almost fraternal. But the son, Sunario, the present Regent, van
Oudijck is unable to fathom. Sunario is stiff, aloof, enigmatic,
wholly absorbed in all sorts of superstitious observances and
fanatical speculations, with a reputation among the populace for
sacrosanctity: van Oudijck thinks him unpractical, a degenerate
and crazy Javanese dandy. At the party, where Sunario and his
young wife make a formal appearance, van Oudijck takes him aside
to talk about Sunario's brother, the Regent of Ngadjiwa, who is
gambling and drinking, bringing his family name into disrepute,
and by misrule discrediting the Government. Unless the brother
reforms, van Oudijck explains with tact, he will have to be dismissed, which would bring disgrace upon the family. Outwardly
agreeing, Sunario boils with anger and hatred because this 'low-

born Hollander and infidel' dares to criticize the supremely sacred aristocracy to which he belongs. Later, when Eva's circle indulge in table-turning, the table hints at rebellion and danger, and taps out obscenities involving the name of Léonie van Oudijck. Everybody is made uneasy. Ida thinks she sees a hadji, in white, leaving the garden in the moonlight …

The depravity of Léonie and the tension between the Resident and the Regent grow simultaneously. Léonie, Theo and Doddie go off to stay at Patjaram, which belongs to the de Luces, a half-Eurasian, half-native princely family who have made a fortune out of sugar. Couperus gives a most wonderful account of life at Patjaram, elaborate, leisurely and corrupt, and of Addie de Luce, a son of the house, whose physical beauty he conveys with a disturbing fervour. This seductive animal, with whom Doddie has long been infatuated, is seduced by Léonie under the very noses of her stepdaughter and stepson, Theo, who is also her lover; and she rejoices at her power over both men and at being the rival of a stepdaughter many years younger than herself.

During this sultry, lusciously sensual interlude the storm comes to a head at Ngadjiwa, where, after the erring Regent has publicly disgraced himself, van Oudijck decides to dismiss him. There is a tremendous scene when the mother of the two Regents comes to plead with van Oudijck against his decision. The old princess ends by humiliating herself as greatly as she can imagine: rending her garments and screaming for mercy towards her son, she places the Resident's foot on her neck. But he will not give in. Later there is a patched-up reconciliation, but while van Oudijck is busy congratulating himself on his tact, diplomacy and knowledge of the Javanese, he fails to allow for the hidden force, for 'the hatred which would possess a power of impenetrable mystery, against which he, the European, was unarmed'.

Gradually Sunario avenges the slight upon his house, calling into being the occult powers of which he is master. There are manifestations of what may be supernatural or may be magic forces, and it is on the Residency and its occupants that they are brought to bear – with terrifying effect. They take chiefly the form of inexplicable pollutions. One night Léonie, stepping out of her bath, suddenly finds her naked body being pelted with gobbets of 'something slimy, like clotted blood', apparently betel-stained spittle, discharged at her she knows not whence, and she is driven almost out of her mind. The Resident finds his bed befouled; he lifts a tumbler to drink, and it falls to pieces, or a drink suddenly grows cloudy between the moment of pouring out and the moment of drinking; he hears a persistent, unaccountable hammering overhead. After these happenings have reached a climax, van Oudijck sees Sunario and wins a moral victory over him – or seems to do so, for a very slight gleam of irony is to be seen in Sunario's eyes.

At least the horrors are called off, but the family life of the van Oudijcks has been wrecked by hatreds and jealousies, and the morale of the Resident himself has been broken by the war of nerves, by the hidden force, by 'things stronger than the human will and intellect'. Léonie goes to Europe to tart it in Paris; the Resident abandons his career, which was about to lead to higher things; and the book ends with a visit paid by Eva to van Oudijck living in retirement with a native mistress. At the very end there is a glimpse of that recurrent hadji, grinning at the man who, though he had lived his life in Java, had been weaker than 'That ...'

Such, briefly, and of necessity crudely and sketchily, is the outline of this extraordinary novel. It raises many questions in the mind. The first is why, since it is so dramatic and exotic, it has never been made into a play or film. Ignorance, perhaps. At present it may be too soon or too late to act it, for it raises political matters vast in their implications; and to stress, at this point in history, the differences rather than the similarities between Europeans and Asiatics, or to spread doubts about the part played by Europe in ruling Asia, would be to play into the hands of the Japanese.

Did Couperus intend his novel as a thorough indictment of Dutch rule in Java? I think not, but it would not be surprising to learn that when *The Hidden Force* first appeared in Holland he was accused of such an intention. He does, it must be admitted, put into the mouth of van Helderen some damaging phrases:

... a gigantic but exhausted colony, still governed from Holland with one idea: the pursuit of gain ... a petty, mean-souled blood-sucker; the country sucked dry; and the real population ... oppressed by the disdain of its overlord.

Van Helderen was addressing Eva:

You, as an artist, feel the danger approaching, vaguely, like a cloud in the sky, in the Indian night; I see the danger as something very real, something rising ... if not from America and Japan, then out of the soil of India [i.e. the Indies] herself ...

The truth is that Couperus was touching on something much greater than the life of a Dutch ruling family in Java, with erotic and supernatural variations – and he knew it. But he was out to write a novel, not a political prophecy: he tells his story, he throws out his hints and ideas, and leaves the reader to do the rest. But there is a key passage where he speaks directly enough:

... Java! Outwardly the docile colony with the subject race, which was no match for the rude trader who, in the golden age of his republic, with the young strength of a youthful people, greedy and eager for gain, stout and phlegmatic, planted his foot and his flag on the crumbling empires, on the thrones which tottered as though the earth had been in seismic labour. But, deep in its soul, it was never subjected, though smiling in proud, contemptuous resignation and bowing submissively beneath its fate; deep in its soul, despite a cringing reverence, it lived in freedom its own mysterious life, hidden from western eyes, however these might seek to fathom the secret – as though with a philosophic intention of maintaining before all a proud and smiling tranquillity, pliantly yielding and to all appearances courteously approaching – but deep within itself divinely certain of its own views and so far removed from all its rulers' ideals of civilization that no fraternization between master and servant will ever take place, because the difference which ferments in soul and blood remains insuperable. And the European, proud in his might, in his strength, in his civilization and his humanity, rules arrogantly, blindly, selfishly, egoistically,

amidst all the intricate cog-wheels of his authority, which
he slips into gear with the certainty of clockwork, controlling
its every movement, till to the foreigner, the outside observer,
this overlordship of tangible things, this colonizing of terri-
tory alien in race and mind, appears a masterpiece, a very
world created.

But beneath all this show the hidden force lurks, slumber-
ing now and unwilling to fight ... As for the native, he reads
his overlord with a single penetrating glance; he sees in him
the illusion of civilization and humanity and he knows that
they are non-existent. While he gives him the title of lord
and the homage due to the master, he is profoundly conscious
of his democratic, commercial nature and despises him for it
in silence and judges him with a smile which his brother
understands; and he too smiles ... What is will not always
be ... Dumbly he hopes that God will lift up those who are
oppressed. ... Never is there the harmony that understands;
never does that love blossom forth which is conscious of
unity; and between the two there is always the gap ...

I suppose it might be objected that Couperus is a little too fond of
the word 'mystery'; and that he takes too romantic, too extreme a
view of the incompatibility of the natives of the East Indies and
their white rulers; and that he comes perilously near the claptrap
about East being East and West being West and the twain never
meeting. The answer to that claptrap is that they'd better meet, and
until they do there'll be trouble; and that they must meet on the
ground of their affinities, their common human nature, which is
far more important in the long run than their differences. Couperus
perceived the differences imaginatively and poetically (like Forster
in *A Passage to India*) rather than politically; and it is well to
remember that he was writing of a life now nearly half-a-century
distant. (An English novel about India in 1900 could hardly have
allowed for half of what has happened, internally and externally,
since then.) Van Helderen's hints about something rising, 'if not
from America and Japan, then out of the soil of India herself', were
pregnant. Much has risen. Since 1900 Labuwangi has been through

a political, economic and technical revolution; America and Japan have had much to do with its ideas and habits, and it may have formed ideas of its own. There have been two world wars since the period of *The Hidden Force*. The internal combustion engine whizzes in all directions, on land and sea and in the air, with its enormous thirst for petrol, its speed and lethal power. Propaganda has obtained the use of the wireless and the films, and has become a great part of the art of government. Above all, the Japanese, after intrigues, infiltrations and commercial successes, burst out and seized a great part of Asia, since when they have been spreading their twaddle about 'Greater East Asia' and 'co-prosperity'. Having had a taste of Japanese rule, Labuwangi ought now to be ready to welcome back the Dutch, the whites, almost as brothers.

'No fraternization between master and servant will ever take place,' wrote Couperus: but what if the relationship were to become something other than that between master and servant? I think if Couperus were alive today he would have seen that if the West's present task of 'liberating' many millions in the East is to succeed, it cannot be merely commercial. His 'message' appears to be that exploitation is bound to fail in the long run, and that a cheap, 'democratic' complacency on the part of the practical, pushing Westerner must also fail if he does not allow for what is beneath the surface. A man, a thoroughly just and estimable man, like van Oudijck denies the alien, the unconscious, the uncomfortable, and in the end they break him.

The Hidden Force is valuable for the questions it raises, for its prophetic hints and poetic insight, but primarily it is valuable, and deserves a more recognized place, in that not large class of novels dealing with the momentous impact of Europe and Asia on one another. Its merits purely as a novel are quite out of the ordinary; nor is it the only impressive novel by its author.

[*New Writing and Daylight*, 1945]

George Gissing

It is time that Gissing and his books were reconsidered. He has devoted readers today, but they are too few, for his books have not been easy to get, and his life has still to be written. He has been too much ignored, neglected or misjudged. For this various explanations can be found. Perhaps the most important is that he was a thoughtful novelist, and a man who thinks is apt to be saddened and saddening, particularly if he is not in tune with the spirit of his age. It should be more generally known that although Gissing's novels do not quite make up an English *Comédie Humaine* (as he is said to have at one time intended they should), they are, besides being good stories, an elaborate and illuminating attempt to define the social conditions of English urban life in his own time, and they afford a wider view of society than might be supposed. Largely a personal protest against the trend of the time, they help to show why socialism was bound to grow, why there was bound to be a struggle for a new, if in some ways primitive, form of society in which the sense of community, so largely lost by an industrialized population in the age of *laissez faire*, should be restored, and the frustration of opportunity minimized.

Apart from Gissing's own books and letters,[1] the main sources of information about him include a sympathetic essay by Thomas Seccombe,[2] who also wrote the article on Gissing in the *Dictionary of National Biography*; and the recollections of H. G. Wells,[3] which are lively and valuable, although the two men had such widely

---

[1] *The Letters of George Gissing to Members of his Family,* collected and arranged by Algernon and Ellen Gissing (Constable, 1927).

[2] *The Work of George Gissing.* This is printed as an introduction to Gissing's *The House of Cobwebs* (Constable, 1906).

[3] *Experiment in Autobiography* (Gollancz and the Cresset Press, 1934).

different characters and outlooks. There is a critical monograph by Frank Swinnerton,[1] who examined Gissing's books with care, but hardly conceals his antipathy for their author; and there is an unsatisfactory fiction, *The Private Life of Henry Maitland*, by Morley Roberts.

George Gissing was born at Wakefield in 1857 and died at St Jean Pied-de-Port in 1903. His father, a pharmaceutical chemist, was a man of literary tastes and a botanist of repute.[2] He died in 1870, when Gissing was twelve, and is said to have greatly influenced his son. The small boy had a passion for learning: one morning, in spite of having a fishbone stuck in his throat, he rushed off to school for fear of missing a lesson. Before he was fifteen he won an exhibition at Owens College, Manchester, where he distinguished himself by winning prizes and passing examinations; he excelled in Latin and English. He must have seemed all set for a starry academic career, but a sexual complication intruded: he took up with a young prostitute, so seriously that he wished to reclaim her from her way of living. He failed, got into trouble over a matter of money, and found himself in prison. When he came out, his friends sent him to America for a fresh start: he was not yet twenty.

In America he did some teaching and earned a little money by journalism; he also contrived to read many novels by George Sand at the free library in Boston. After a spell of destitution, during which he is said to have lived for a time on peanuts, he became assistant to an amiable traveller in gas-fittings. By the autumn of 1877 he was back in London, having stayed for a time at Jena, where he read Schopenhauer and Comte. Three years afterwards he dated his letters for a time according to the Positivist calendar.

It is not clear exactly when Gissing married the girl to whom he had attached himself in Manchester; but he did so, she declined, and died in a hospital. His second wife, who, according to Mr Wells, was a servant-girl picked up in Regent's Park, turned into 'a

[1] *George Gissing: A Critical Study,* by Frank Swinnerton (Martin Secker, 1912).
[2] I have before me *The Ferns and Fern Allies of Wakefield and its Neighbourhood,* by T. W. Gissing (Wakefield, 1862), a graceful and scholarly book with pleasing quotations from Gerard and Parkinson.

resentful, jealous scold', and eventually progressed 'through scenes and screams towards a complete mental breakdown'. Between the two marriages there were years of great loneliness, poverty and hard work in London. Gissing eked out a living by tutoring (in 1882 he had no fewer than ten pupils) and by journalism. In 1880 Turgeniev had enquired for someone who would supply a quarterly article of some thirty pages on the political, social and literary affairs of England to the *Messager de l'Europe* published in St Petersburg: Gissing was offered and took the chance of writing it. So far as I know, these articles have never been reprinted.

His spare time was largely spent in reading and writing. One can hardly imagine a more serious reader. In the summer of 1885, when he was at work on *Demos*, he was reading Dante, Plato and Shakespeare, and sent his sister a perhaps slightly priggish list of 'indispensables', all of whom, with the exception of Cervantes, he rejoiced to say he could read in the original:

> Homer, Aeschylus, Sophocles, Euripides, among the Greeks: Virgil, Catullus, Horace, among the Latins: in Italian, Dante and Boccaccio: in Spanish, Don Quixote: in German, Goethe, Jean Paul, Heine: in French, Molière, George Sand, Balzac, de Musset: in English, Chaucer, Spenser, Shakespeare, Milton, Keats, Browning, and Scott.

It is surprising that the list does not include Dickens, with whom Gissing had a lifelong familiarity and whose example, imaged not only in the novels but in Forster's *Life*, was of great importance to him. Towards the end of his life he published an excellent book about Dickens which caused G. K. Chesterton to regard Gissing as 'the best of all Dickens's critics'.

Late in 1879 Gissing had finished his first novel, *Workers in the Dawn*: it was published in the following year at its author's expense – a proceeding made possible by a legacy. As he was only twenty-two when he finished this book, it is, not surprisingly, crude and immature, but Frederic Harrison, who was to be a great help to Gissing, wrote him a long letter saying that he had been deeply stirred and impressed by the writer's creative energy, and that his wife thought there was 'enough stuff in the book to make six novels'. Harrison introduced Gissing to John Morley, who asked him to write for the *Pall Mall Gazette* and the *Fortnightly*, and Morley made Matthew Arnold read the book, but it was not a success, nor were Gissing's struggles much eased. His second novel, *The Unclassed*, did not appear until 1884, although it had been finished in 1882.

Gissing's industry, in spite of the potentially disintegrating tendencies of poverty and loneliness, was immense; he was writing, as he said, 'for bread and cheese'. Between July 1885 and March 1886, for example, he wrote three novels, *Isabel Clarendon*, *A Life's Morning*, and *Demos*; he also read through the *Divina Commedia* and supported himself by teaching: *The Odd Women* (1893) was written in six weeks. All these were three-volume novels. Gissing rejoiced when he saw that, under 'continental influence', the 'old three-volume tradition' was being 'broken through'. If he had lived a little later, his whole approach to novel-writing might have been different, and perhaps less impressive.

Villette is the most thorough exploration of loneliness in English fiction, but some of Gissing's characters, though not physically isolated, live in a solitude as appalling. The solitude of Henry Ryecroft is represented as a form of contentment, but there is something ignobly complacent about it. Gissing's own solitude, and at times his despair, are terrifying, and never more so than in the mid-eighties. In the summer of 1885 he writes to his sister from his rooms in Cornwall Residences, near Baker Street Station and within earshot of the screeching and hissing trains:

> The fact is that this kind of life is too hard, I can't endure it. I grow more and more low-spirited and incapable of continued work. Suddenly in the middle of writing I am attacked by a fearful fit of melancholy, and the pen drops, and I get nothing done. For hours I walk round and round the room and sicken with need of some variety in life.

A few weeks later:

> London is deserted; only some three million and a half people remain to await the coming of next season. All the houses round Regent's Park are shut up, and the sight of the

darkened windows does not make one cheerful. I myself live in utter solitude, it is more than three weeks since I opened my lips to speak to anyone but the servant.

These cries from the heart are utterances of a man who, as *The Times* said after his death, 'valued his artistic conscience above popularity, and his purpose above his immediate reward' – but who had to struggle continually for immediate rewards, which were never large. They are utterances of a man who had not enough money or thrustingness to live as his tastes and abilities required, and who needed a good woman to look after him. As for his artistic conscience, it had reached full development two years earlier, when he was in his mid-twenties. In May 1883 he wrote to his sister Margaret: 'I am growing to feel that the only thing known to us of absolute value is artistic perfection.' Two months later, to his brother:

I am by degrees getting my right place in the world. Philosophy has done all it can for me, and now scarcely interests me any more. My attitude henceforth is that of the artist pure and simple ... In the midst of the most serious complications of life, I find myself suddenly possessed with a great calm, withdrawn as it were from the immediate interests of the moment, and able to regard everything as a picture. I watch and observe myself just as much as others.

And in June 1884, again to his brother:

How I laughed the other day on recalling your amazement at my theories of Art for Art's sake! Well, I cannot get beyond it ... I can get savage over social iniquities, but even then my rage at once takes the direction of planning revenge in artistic work.

In certain artists this planning of 'revenge' is a powerful motive force: they get rid of a disagreeable impression or experience, or a series of such impressions and experiences, by externalizing it in a work of art.

While Gissing's sorrows and sufferings were intense and prolonged – his loneliness, his poverty, his two unfortunate marriages, his enchainment to hard work – he was a man with powers of enjoyment which were not, as both his books and his letters abundantly show, unexercised. He was not a witty or humorous or genial man, but his vital energies could burst out in spasms of gaiety: I say 'spasms' because his gaiety was evidently at variance with his prevailing moods. Austin Harrison noted how his sad and noble face – 'dignified, delicate, sensuous, thoughtful' – would 'flash and light up, and the eyes would beam ... and the misanthrope would become a tempestuous schoolboy, and he would thump the table and positively shout with buoyant exuberance'. Gissing's sister Ellen has spoken of his being at times 'quite boisterous in his merriment', and Mr Wells of his 'ready abundant fits of laughter': I suspect, perhaps wrongly, that at times they were of the hollow kind sometimes called mirthless; support is lent to this suspicion by the rarity and wintriness of the gleams of humour in his novels. Gissing had a strong appetite for life, but it was not in general a playful appetite – though he did notice things like the Weymouth advertisement of pleasure-steamers 'replete with lavatories and a ladies' saloon'.

In the autumn of 1888 Gissing realized a dear ambition and visited Italy. What happiness this meant to him is evident from his letters. He was not merely a classical scholar, he was a passionate classical scholar, and the ancient splendours of Greece and Rome stood for him as examples of how life can be lived in this world, and showed him how different it can be from the life of an indigent novelist in a flat near Baker Street in the eighteen-eighties; those splendours were to him symbols of much that he revered.

It is hardly to be wondered at that Mr Wells, who was a good friend to Gissing, thought him 'horribly miseducated', while Gissing thought Mr Wells (so Mr Wells says) 'absolutely illiterate'. It was not that Gissing looked only back and Mr Wells only forward: it was that when Gissing looked forward and Mr Wells looked back, neither liked what he saw. What worried Mr Wells was that Gissing was 'not scientific' and had had a classical education. This, in Mr Wells's view, had unfitted Gissing to cope with the modern world, and either his nature or his education had made him unable to 'look life squarely in the eyes'. I am not sure what is meant by not looking life squarely in the eyes, but I rather think it means here looking at life from a different standpoint to that of Mr Wells: certainly many of Gissing's readers have thought his view of life anything but indirect. At all events, Mr Wells was led to ascribe Gissing's enduring passion for ancient Rome to an attempt to find compensation for the repressive gentility and respectability of his father's house at Wakefield. Gissing's letters, however, and *By the Ionian Sea* show him as something much more than a pious classicist and romantic amateur of the antique. In 1889, on his return from a visit to Greece, he arrives in Naples and writes: 'Ha, ha! Sunlight and warmth and uproar and palm trees and wine and fruit – Napoli, Napoli! How glorious it is to be here!' This may not be a 'scientific' exclamation, but it is none the worse for that.

In the 'nineties Gissing was not stuck all the time in London: he lived for a time at Exeter, and later at Ewell. In 1897 he again visited Italy, and spent a month in Rome in the following spring with Mr and Mrs Wells. He returned by way of Germany, where he went to stay with his old Jena friend, Bertz, and then settled at Dorking. In May 1899 he was in Paris, where he set up a joint ménage with a Frenchwoman, who had translated some of his novels, and her mother. Unfortunately the elder of these two ladies was a too parsimonious housekeeper, and undernourishment did Gissing the more harm since he had incipient lung-trouble. At the end of 1900 he began his historical novel, *Veranilda*, which he never finished. In the spring of 1902 he was at St Jean de Luz. From there he and 'Mrs Gissing', as she was called, moved to St Jean Pied-de-Port, where he died of pneumonia in December 1903. He was just forty-six. He left two sons by his second wife.

Mr Wells, who was helpfully present at the deathbed, to which he had travelled from England, says that Gissing in delirium

> had passed over altogether into that fantastic pseudo-Roman world of which Wakefield Grammar School had laid the foundations ... 'What are these magnificent beings?' he would say. 'Who are these magnificent beings advancing upon us?' Or again, 'What is all this splendour? What does it portend?'

These utterances at the end of a harassed life have more than pathos; they are awesome, and not less so in view of the statement, communicated to me by a friend of Gissing's, that he

> had no belief in dogmatic religion and was inclined to put all subjects verging on the supernatural on one side. The beauty and glory of the external world were its own justification, but the tragedy of human life could not be explained away. He used to say that he had neither belief in nor desire for a future life, and that the thought of a complete and everlasting rest attracted him more than that of continued existence.

All witnesses agree about the impressiveness of Gissing's appearance – whether the camera, or Sir William Rothenstein (whose fine portrait drawing is reproduced in Mr Swinnerton's book), or Mr Wells, or others who knew him. Mr Wells uses the word 'Viking', and says Gissing was 'an extremely good-looking, well-built man'. Gissing's head has been more than once described as leonine: to Mr Wells it was also 'blond' – but not to Gissing's sister, who called it 'dark auburn', nor to the already quoted informant, who has given me the following account of him:

> Broad-shouldered and powerfully made, he had a leonine head and a profusion of reddish-brown hair surmounting his broad forehead. His sad, rather weary-looking eyes, deep-set under prominent eyebrows, seemed to gaze with pity on all the sorrows of the world and mankind: but the singular sweetness of his mouth belied the tragic bitterness of his eyes. He talked in a low melodious voice, often fast or eagerly, then relapsed into silence and became absorbed in a brooding melancholy.

Another informant who knew him has described him to me as an 'attaching' person. He was certainly attractive to women. The rather too general question, *What sort of men do women like?* has been sensibly answered, *They like the men who like them*: and Gissing, Mr Wells tells us, 'carried the normal expectancy of the male ... to an extravagant degree'. Apart from that, and his good looks, many women must quickly have perceived and been enthralled by his intellectual powers and his serious and benevolent sympathy with suffering and frustration. A surviving friend says that

> notwithstanding his great abilities, he was modest and un-
> assuming almost to a fault and absolutely tolerant of human
> nature and its frailties ... *Human* nature and its past and
> present developments interested him more than scientific and
> philosophical theories.

It did indeed. As early as 1880 he told his brother that he wanted to know the laws by which the mind of man is governed, 'for it is evident that the science of Psychology will soon become as definite as that of Physiology'.[1] There is something prophetic in this allusion to the science of psychology, and I shall have more to say presently about the prophetic vein in Gissing, in connection with his view of his own time.

Among the novelists of the later Victorian era Gissing has an acknowledged place – that is to say, he gets a few more or less conventional and superficial lines in encyclopedias and literary histories. One I have looked at contains a gross error of fact; another the fatuous sentence, 'When not sociological his novels are usually psychological;' they generally speak of 'sombre power'. What they fail to mention, or to stress, is the central point of his work – that it is largely an indictment of the period in which he lived, and particularly of its economic structure, which, in his opinion, too often thwarted the growth of the finer man and woman, and of the finer traits in the more ordinary man and woman. The drawing up of this indictment involved an exposition of suffering, which was identified with the contemporary bogy of 'realism': this became at times almost a term of abuse for those writers who found truth encumbered with too many petticoats and who interested themselves in the anatomy beneath. Zola was regarded as the arch-realist, and often as shocking or salacious; Gissing, whom insular taboos and native fastidiousness deprived of

[1] The eighteen-eighties, be it remembered, were a time of eager scientific enquiry: how eager can be judged by the postscript to an affectionate letter from Olive Schreiner to Havelock Ellis, in which she said (I quote from memory): 'If you come across anything really good about the Higher Apes, be sure and let me know.'

equal candour, was sometimes regarded as a kind of cleaner Zola.

Most of Gissing's novels were published between 1884 and 1900. Earlier, in 1882, Smith Elder told him that *The Unclassed* was 'too painful' to please the ordinary novel-reader and that it treated of scenes which could 'never attract the subscribers to Mr Mudie's Library'. This opinion did not divert Gissing into any resolution to flatter the pride and prejudices, the complacency and narrowness, of the subscribers to Mudie's, most of whom were likely to be depressed by his books. Today, when property and opportunity are more dispersed, we can read Gissing without feeling dispirited or slightly menaced, as the well-to-do subscribers to Mudie's may have felt, by revelations of the underworlds, whether poverty-stricken or shabby-genteel, which largely enabled them to maintain their comfortable or luxurious lives.

'It was her terrible misfortune', we read of Emma Vine in *Demos*, 'to have feelings too refined for the position in which fate had placed her'. This recurrent theme is a reflection of Gissing's view of himself. In him we see a fastidious but energetic man, conscious of his brains, his creative powers, and his faculty of discrimination, and embittered by neither having nor being able to make enough money to do what he wanted to do or live as he wanted to live. His bitterness is not free from self-pity, an emotion he thoroughly explored. Clara Hewitt, in *The Nether World*, has an access of self-pity which is succeeded by 'a persistent sense of intolerable wrong', and then by 'a fierce desire to plunge herself into ruin'. This, we are truly told, was 'a phase of exasperated egoism common enough in original natures frustrated by circumstances'. ('Exasperated egoism', I think, may have had a good deal to do with Gissing's unfortunate marriages.) From observations of this kind, occurring here and there throughout his writings like sulphurous flashes, the reader suddenly gets a clear insight into the torment of Gissing's isolation, into his sense of not belonging closely enough to the community of which he was a member, and of not being needed by it, at least in the way he wished to be needed. 'You are not hiding away from Society because you are unfit for it', says Tarrant in *In the Year of Jubilee*, 'only because you can't live as your equals do'. A plain statement, born of an anguish perhaps only to be understood by those who have experienced its like.

Gissing's years of not being able to live as his equals did are reflected in his manner of writing. His style has been called scholarly, and so it is: his sentences are properly formed and free from extravagance or vulgarity, but they lack also the piercing precision, the intensity, the touch of strangeness to be found in writers, even prose-writers, with a poetic inventiveness or epigrammatic skill. Gissing's pages have steadiness and shapeliness, not brilliancy or exuberance; they are never dull or careless. He was 'one of the extremely rare novelists', said Virginia Woolf in an essay,[1] not, I think, among her best, 'who believes in the power of the mind, who makes his people think'. She spoke also of the passages of description in his books which stand out 'like stone slabs, shaped and solid, among the untidy litter with which the pages of fiction are strewn'. They do; and the books themselves, not merely the descriptive passages, are shaped and solid. But just as Gissing took over, or shall we say inherited, the cumbrous convention of the Victorian three-volume novel (into which he pumped new life), so he took over a conventionality of style. This came easily to him since he wanted to write like a scholar and a gentleman. He recognized the value of easy and graceful manners as a mark of civilization, but in his early and formative years he was constrained by gentility and poverty and isolation, and he had too little experience of the society of persons whose incomes, breeding, education, and habits had given them an easy assurance. Possibly his manner in real life was not free from shyness, stiffness and undue formality; certainly his style is a bit stilted. He tends to write more like a man who wishes to appear to Mudie subscribers as a scholar and a gentleman, than as a scholar and gentleman who writes easily for his equals what has come into his head; in other words, he is highly self-conscious. He is like a man who, dining in the company of others, wishes to be accepted by them as an equal, because he respects and admires them, and who, anxious to avoid appearing gauche or conspicuous, may sometimes be caught glancing furtively round to make sure that he is about to use the right knife and fork. Such a careful man may be preferred to a

[1] *The Common Reader: Second Series* (Hogarth Press, 1932).

self-assured boor.

As I have remarked elsewhere,[1] the Gissing novels do not dazzle or overwhelm, they burn with a clear and even flame that lights up a phase of English social history; and their author has at once an air of conviction and a power of story-telling that lead the reader steadily onwards in that state of bemusement which it is the novelist's first business to induce. In that careful, often oddly formal style of his, he has caught and fixed in countless forms the vulgarity, the materialism, and the social injustice of his late-Victorian days in a manner and on a scale attempted by nobody else. If he often describes drab lives in a monochromatic setting, he is after all writing about England, and it is not because he prefers them; they anger him, they evoke his sympathy, they are types of his own troubles; and he opposes them all the time with his own ideals of civilization; he criticizes the society he explains and describes – a society which was largely uncritical of itself.

Gissing poses in his own way the great and familiar problem which has grown and grown ever since the Industrial Revolution – whether the values of earlier times must be destroyed, and whether man must be reduced by the machine-age to a level unworthy of the better traditions he has inherited. What values? For Gissing they included peace, leisure (not only for a few), culture, real education, good manners, and an adequate standard of living for everybody – peace above all. War, he wrote to his son in 1899, is 'a horrible thing ... Never suppose that victories in war are things to be proud of'. The Boer War – 'this scoundrelly war', Gissing called it – was the culmination of the period in which he had lived and worked, and he did not long survive it. 'This reckless breaking with the fine English tradition', he wrote, 'is a sad proof of what evil can be wrought by inculcating the spirit of vulgar pride and savage defiance'. And a little later, prophetically: 'Who knows what fantastic horrors lie in wait for the world?' Even before the Boer War, he had been more explicitly prophetic. In the last chapter of *The Whirlpool* (1897), there is a conversation between Rolfe and Morton. They are talking of *Barrack-Room Ballads*. 'Millions of men', says Rolfe,

[1] *The New Statesman,* 23 February 1946.

natural men, revolting against the softness and sweetness of
civilisation; men all over the world; hardly knowing what
they want and what they don't want; and here comes one
who speaks for them – speaks with a vengeance ... The
brute savagery of it! The very lingo – how appropriate it
is! ... Mankind won't stand it much longer, this encroach-
ment of the humane spirit ... We may reasonably hope, old
man, to see our boys blown into small bits by the explosive
that hasn't got its name yet.

'We are getting to the end of dreams', as Hardy wrote[1] some years
later, seeing warring nations as 'tickled mad by some demonic
force'.

Peace was a condition of the leisure which Gissing advocated for
others and himself longed for, since it would have enabled him to
be what he thought he wanted to be, instead of a novelist writing
hard for his living. It would have meant the chance to write what
he would most have liked to write, books doubtless nearer to
The Private Papers of Henry Ryecroft, By the Ionian Sea, and *Veranilda*
than to the rest of his work – books of travel or meditation, or of
escape into the classical past of Greece and Rome. Gissing's wistful
image of himself as a refined scholar living in freedom and comfort,
a mild hedonist, a fastidious quietist – his escape-dream – was the
creation of a man of independent mind, energetic and talented,
strongly sexed and greatly overworked, and it may have been
necessary to sustain him; it must have helped him to react strongly
and continuously against what seemed to him the ugliness of his
surroundings, and to 'plan revenge' in the name of Art for Art's
sake. It is by no means to be condemned; it was the formula from
which he built up, in his copious and powerful writing, his protest
on behalf of what he believed to be civilized values.

The Private Papers of Henry Ryecroft, which has been the most
popular of Gissing's books, is by no means the least revealing: it is
a blend of autobiography, rumination, and the escape-dream.
Ryecroft, if you like, is an ostrich who buries his head in the nice
warm sand because he doesn't like the look of the weather; or he is

---

[1] In *Winter Words* (Macmillan, 1928).

the sage – of modestly independent means – who chooses detachment and simple pleasures. The book has been many times reprinted. I think it became popular because, like FitzGerald's *Omar
Khayyam*, it appealed to a combined fatalism and love of pleasure
which is deeply set in the English character but has been strongly
repressed by Puritanism and industrialization. Those whose
consciences were drilled by a severe sense of moral duty, those
whose daily lives were half strangled by the necessity of hard work
in more or less drab surroundings, were able to enjoy by proxy in
both these books – one with its 'Oriental' glamour, the other with
a familiar English setting – the pleasures of reverie and self-
indulgence; moreover, they could understand much of what they
were reading and could at the same time congratulate themselves
on reading 'good literature'. When I was in Japan, I found that
Ryecroft had been much read there in the twenty-five years after
its publication. Its theme of withdrawal from the hurly-burly much
appealed to the intelligentsia of a country caught up in an exceptionally rapid and intensive process of industrialization, a country which
had a long tradition, inherited from China, of the charms of
reclusiveness. In the late nineteen-twenties it was banned by the
Japanese authorities as a propagator of 'dangerous thoughts'. How
pleased, how wryly pleased, Gissing would have been by this act!

If we are justified in taking Henry Ryecroft as his author's
mouthpiece – and it is evident that the 'private papers' are to some
extent autobiographical – Gissing was worried about more than
the way things were going; he was worried about the sorry scheme
of things entire. History, says Ryecroft, is a long moan of anguish,
a long record of injustice; but unlike Hardy, who questioned
Providence, Gissing questions mankind itself about its follies and
miseries. In his novels he enters into them and displays them, for,
just as a touch of madness is necessary to a poet, so a novelist must
be able to lose himself in common follies: directly the novelist
stands aside from his fellow-beings and says, 'But they're acting
like lunatics,' he is in danger of ceasing to be a novelist and becoming
a philosopher. Gissing in the role of Ryecroft could stand aside and
indulge the luxury of detachment which the hard-working novelist
could not afford. Ryecroft says that his worst trouble is 'wonder at

the common life of man': it seems to him incredible, oppressive, haunting. 'What lunatic', he asks, 'ever dreamt of things less consonant with the calm reason than those which are thought and done every minute in every community of men called sane?' The ringing grooves of change rang too loud for Gissing, so Ryecroft picks on science as the greatest insanity. Science, he says, is to be hated and feared, because he sees it as something that will destroy all simplicity and gentleness of life, and all the beauty of the world; that will restore barbarism under a mask of civilization; will darken men's minds and harden their hearts; and will bring vast conflicts in which mankind's laborious advances will be lost in 'blood-drenched chaos'. It seems a little hard that science should be held to darken men's minds, since its aim is the opposite. And if history is an anguished moan of injustice, is there so much to lose by change? No, it is not from science that Gissing–Ryecroft stands apart, but from the fierce unreasoning energy of the mass of mankind, 'tickled mad' – from action, in short. He admits, indeed, that it is as idle to quarrel with science as with 'any other force of nature', but he will stand apart, he will find his own salvation in detachment. In reading a Gissing novel, however much one is absorbed in the story, one is apt to be haunted by a Ryecroftish emanation of the author, and this may be adduced as evidence that Gissing is a less perfect artist than he might have been.

If one were asked which is Gissing's best novel, one might reply that he cannot be judged by any single novel, partly because some of his work is below his best level. A fair estimate of his achievement as a novelist could be formed by reading, besides *A Life's Morning*, at least the two great 'proletarian' novels, *Demos* and *The Nether World*; the tender *Thyrza*; *New Grub Street*, so true to its title; *Born in Exile*; *The Odd Women* and *In the Year of Jubilee*, if only for their portraits of women; *The Whirlpool*, which a little foreshadows *Howard's End*; and *The Crown of Life*. Gissing said in a letter (July 1886) that the writers who helped him most were French and Russian, and that he had 'not much sympathy with English points of view'.[1] The latter statement is rather vague, but he gave

[1] Thomas Seccombe called Gissing 'an honest, true-born, downright ineradicable Englishman'.

it as a reason for predicting that he would scarcely be popular with 'the mob', which was daily growing in extent and influence. I think his lack of popularity with 'the mob' may rather be ascribed to his thoughtfulness and lack of heartiness.

Though Gissing lacked heartiness he did not lack heart, and one outstanding virtue of his novels is his portraiture of women, which is various and full of deep understanding, emotional and intellectual. There is the lonely woman, like Virginia Madden, the secret drinker in *The Odd Women*; there are the beauties in love – Isabel Clarendon, Sidwell Warricombe in *Born in Exile*, and Beatrice Redwing in *A Life's Morning*; there are the 'new' women like Rhoda Nunn in *The Odd Women* and Beatrice French in *In the Year of Jubilee*; there is the coarse monster, Clem Peckover, in *The Nether World*, who has been compared to La Cibot in *Le Cousin Pons*; there is the honourable, right-minded, decent old working-woman, Mrs Mutimer, in *Demos*; there is the autocratic old parvenue, Lady Ogram, in *Our Friend the Charlatan*; there is a whole gallery of designing middle-aged middle-class women and innocent young working girls. There are explorations of the destinies of women happily and unhappily married, of girls and women battling alone, of women pursued and pursuing, jealous or resigned, women neglected and ill-treated, female idealists and female beasts; of the tenderest sisterly love (notably in *Thyrza*), and even of a homosexual intensity, as when Stella Westlake writes to Adela Mutimer (in *Demos*), 'I wait for you like the earth for spring'. The tirades on the one hand against ill-natured and ill-behaved women, the championship on the other of virtuous women, the indignation, the pity, the sympathy, suggest that Gissing, like Hubert Eldon in *Demos*, 'could not remember a time when he had not been in love'; and it was apropos of Hubert Eldon that he remarked that 'a reckless passion is a patent of nobility'. The nobility in Gissing sought for nobility in women, but was too often confronted with its opposite. He saw and approved the beginnings of the emancipation of women, but felt that 'one of the supreme social needs of our day is the education of women in self-respect and self-restraint'. The women he admired had a sense of responsibility to themselves, to their lovers, husbands and children, to society generally; the women he disliked were only out for what they could get and gave themselves disagreeable airs. About marriage Gissing was sensible, and certainly looked its disadvantages 'squarely in the eyes': 'Not one married pair in ten thousand', he wrote, 'have felt for each other as two or three couples do in every novel.' He could make a masterly analysis of an unhappy marriage, like that of Reardon in *New Grub Street*, and for a happy marriage could prescribe, as at the end of *In the Year of Jubilee*, conditions not easily attainable.

On the whole Gissing's male characters are much less various, less subtle, and less interesting than his women. He goes deepest with those more or less socially and sexually frustrated and tormented heroes – Waymark in *The Unclassed*, Kingcote in *Isabel Clarendon*, Grail in *Thyrza*, Peak in *Born in Exile*, Reardon in *New Grub Street* – who represent variations on himself. It would be hardly too much to say that while Gissing saw men in general as reflections of himself in distress, he saw and loved women as separate and varying entities.

Mr Swinnerton, who has carefully discussed Gissing's novels under the two general headings 'The Proletariat' and 'Studies of Temperament', draws attention to the interaction in some of them between members of the leisured and unleisured classes, and rightly says that in some respects this interaction weakens the 'singleness of impression'. Gissing was not alone in treating of such interaction, but shows himself acutely conscious of the social transitions of his own day, the changing pattern of urban life in an industrialized civilization, that final breaking-up of the structure of an older society and its standards, the prevalence of irresponsible capitalism and aching poverty, which precede a new and more or less socialistic reintegration: in that consciousness lies one of his chief claims to fame. I have said nothing of his short stories, which are of minor importance, though some of them are effective.

When James Payn, who was reader for Smith Elder, saw the manuscript of *A Life's Morning*, he was 'enthusiastic'.[1] He serialized

---

[1] But insisted, according to Morley Roberts, that Gissing should make a drastic change in the dénouement. Roberts says Gissing was enraged, but was driven to make the change by 'Payn and poverty'. Its nature can easily be guessed.

it in the *Cornhill*, and it was published in three volumes in 1888. It is an uneven book, with a story basically hackneyed and in the convention of its period – the story of a 'pure' young virgin to whom true love comes in the shape of a radiant hero, but whose path is crossed by a designing villain. This basic theme has often been presented as crude melodrama, but as a theme it is not to be sneered at: the resolve of a young woman to keep herself intact, physically and spiritually, for the man she loves, must always have dramatic possibilities. Gissing's treatment of this theme is encumbered by the convention of the Victorian three-volume novel, but it transcends certain crudities, such as those of coincidence and renunciation, for which Payn has been blamed.

Wilfrid Athel, the hero, has his weaknesses, and Dagworthy, the villain, his better nature – indeed, with his aspirations towards culture and 'the finer things in life', Dagworthy is an embryonic Gissing hero. Emily Hood, the central figure, is no milk-and-water miss. She is more articulate than some of Gissing's good girls, and the intensity of her feelings is unusual and exciting. 'Self-consciousness', says Gissing, 'makes of life itself a work of art', and Emily's aesthetic approach to life has a touch of Pater's 'new Cyrenaicism' about it; she has something of that 'kind of passionate coldness' which he tried to define. 'The task before her, a task of which ... she was growing more and more conscious, was to construct an existence every moment of which should serve an all-pervading harmony.' She 'made the pursuit of beauty a religion, grew to welcome the perception of new meaning in beautiful things with a spiritual delight'. The chatter about Gissing's 'realism' has missed his aestheticism: what could be more Paterish than his dictum, again apropos of Emily, that 'it is the art of life to take each moment of mental joy, of spiritual openness, as though it would never be repeated, to cling to it as a pearl of great price, to exhaust its possibilities of sensation'? Emily's motives are explained as 'but the primary instincts of womanhood exalted to a rare perfection and reflected in a consciousness of exceeding lucidity'. Not only in her obsession with Athel, her fear of Dagworthy and her firmness with him, but in her love for her father and her gentleness with her dilapidated mother are these instincts seen in play. The reader shares her thoughts, knows her from the inside, and can trust her to behave, in any given situation, as he could expect her to behave. She is a created being.

It is in accordance with common experience that Emily's kind of beauty should 'address itself with the strangest potency to an especially vehement nature here and there' – that is to say, to Dagworthy. Now villains are apt to be more interesting than heroes; Dagworthy is fuller-bodied than Athel, and indeed we should have been fully assured of his potential heavy-handedness without being told that he had once, in a fit of rage, 'all but pounded' another man 'to a jelly'. As for this hard Yorkshireman's violent and obsessive passion for Emily, it puts one in mind of Bradley Headstone in *Our Mutual Friend*. Such passions remind one of Crabbe's[1] saying about happy marriages: 'They are not frequent, but they may be found.' They are apt to lead those whom they possess into courses quite as tortuous as Dagworthy's. From a mid-twentieth-century point of view, Dagworthy is perhaps insufficiently explored by his author, but it must be granted that the morning scene in the allotments, and the cognate happenings, are compelling. It is relevant to recall Anatole France's saying to the effect that the symbol of love, instead of a little boy with a bow and arrow, might better be a headless bull.

'The more I see of Surrey,' said Gissing in a letter to his sister, 'the more convinced I am that it is the ideal of English rustic scenery.' This was in August 1885, when he paid a visit to the Frederic Harrisons at Elstead, and was writing the first chapter of *A Life's Morning*; but the set-up at The Firs, Wilfrid Athel, Beatrice Redwing, and all the leisured-class parts of *A Life's Morning* seem to be derived as much from Meredith as from life.[2] They are so presented as to seem mainly in a different key to the rest of the book. The lively common Cartwrights, for instance, are wonderfully

---

[1] Gissing found Crabbe 'particularly interesting'. Crabbe's verse stories, he wrote, 'anticipate in a remarkable way our so-called "realistic" fiction'. *Letters*, p. 222.

[2] Gissing had first met Meredith as reader for Chapman & Hall. In 1885, when he was writing *A Life's Morning*, he thought Meredith great and incomprehensibly neglected. In the 'nineties he visited Meredith several times at Box Hill.

true and natural, they live and breathe; but Athel is rather a stuffed shirt – albeit a shirt of quality, by no means unskilfully stuffed – and his language (even allowing that he had an Italian mother) is often, by naturalistic standards, turgid and false; we know what he meant when he said to Emily, 'The empire of my passion is all-subduing,' but we can't hear him saying it. When Emily's father, on the other hand, expresses a wish to see Holborn Viaduct before he dies – and whenever he speaks, acts, or refrains from speaking and acting – we believe in him and are moved far more by the pathos of his existence than by the supposed glamour of Athel's. Mr Hood is an embodiment of the Gissing axiom that 'indigence is the death of the soul', an illustration of the truth that 'men and women go to their graves in wretchedness who might have done noble things with an extra pound a week to live upon'. So insecure was poor Hood's footing in the community that he was deprived of it by the loss of his top hat: that he should have had to wear one at all seems today grotesque.

If we object, as we should be justified in objecting, to the inequality given to this novel by the stylization of the upper-class characters (a stylization not consequent upon long and intimate knowledge) and the naturalness of, for example, the Hoods and the Cartwrights, we must admire Gissing for grappling with the over-lapping of classes, making it dramatic, and illuminating it with his sympathies. Into his feeling for Emily went much of the essential Gissing.

I should not be surprised if Dunfield were identifiable, topo-graphically as well as socially, with Wakefield. Banbrigg, Hebsworth, the Heath, and the remains of Pendal Castle may reasonably be taken to correspond to local places, and both interiors and landscapes may well have been drawn from local models. The view from the Cartwrights' upper windows ('of the extensive cattle-market, of a long railway viaduct, and of hilly fields beyond'), the heath, the quarry, the allotments, are seen with a familiar eye; and the view that met Dagworthy after his sleepless night is worth singling out:

The smoke of the mill-chimneys, thickening as fires were coaled for the day's work, caught delicate reflection from the sky; the lofty spire of the church seemed built of some beautiful rose-hued stone. The grassy country round about wore a fresher green than it was wont to show; the very river, so foul in reality with the refuse of manufacturers, gleamed like a pure current.

It seems a pity that Gissing did not more indulge this feeling for landscape: his sketches of landscape are generally not so precise. His love for the countryside was 'passionate' (the word is Rye-croft's), but it appears rather as a city-dweller's love for what was not urban squalor than as a particularized affection: it was none the less a passion, one of the several that helped to make him so good and various a novelist.

[Published as an Introduction to a new edition of
A Life's Morning, 1947]

Edward FitzGerald

When one begins to enquire into the life and character of FitzGerald it appears that the records are abundant, but not as full as they might be. For example, some of his letters have not been published in full and some have not yet been published at all. It also appears that his interpreters have not been free from bias. The best one tended to take a high moral tone about FitzGerald's detachment from the life of his time, and his latest biographer, an American, seems bent upon ironing out FitzGerald's eccentricities. He assures us, on no evidence but that of high spirits, that FitzGerald was a 'perfectly normal' boy. I think this opinion would have surprised FitzGerald himself, who said of his family, 'We are different from other people,' and 'We FitzGeralds are all mad.'

I wish we knew more about FitzGerald's parents, about his feelings towards them, and about his childhood. His father and mother were cousins, Anglo-Irish and very well off; his mother was said to be the richest commoner in England. She was a handsome and perhaps rather imperious woman who lived in great style, a little aloof, it seems, from her children. Of his father it is difficult to get a clear picture. What is clear is that the father was not content with his fortune: he tried to increase it by speculation, and eventually went bankrupt.

It would be interesting to know what FitzGerald thought about his parents, but there are not many clues. In his letters he scarcely mentions his father, but there is one passage that is slightly critical of his mother. It occurs in a letter to Fanny Kemble, written when FitzGerald was in his sixties. He recalls that when he was a child his mother used sometimes to come up to the nursery, 'but we children', he says, 'were not much comforted. She was a remarkable woman, as you said in a former letter: and as I constantly believe in

outward beauty as an index of a beautiful soul within, I used sometimes to wonder what feature in her fine face betrayed what was
not so good in her character. I think (as usual) the lips: there was a
twist of mischief about them now and then, like that in – the tail of
a cat! – otherwise so smooth and amiable.'

It looks as if there was some kind of strength in his mother and
some kind of weakness in his father that disturbed him, but this
may be only guesswork. What is certain is that his own life shows
from the first a strong pull against his mother's showy worldliness
and against his father's futile pursuit of gain. It was not long after
he came down from Cambridge that he plumped for a more or less
reclusive life. 'Such things as wealth, rank, respectability,' he said,
'I don't care a straw about.' He had already formed a strong distaste
for polite society, and he sent a message to Thackeray, with whom
he was on intimate terms of friendship, to say that Thackeray was
never to invite him to his house, as he meant never to enter it –
apparently because he thought he might meet strangers there. It
seems clear that this was not the behaviour of a 'perfectly normal'
young man, but of one acutely conscious of being different from
other men.

A convenient refuge in the nineteenth century for the cultivated,
unworldly, mildly eccentric man was the Church, and but for one
important obstacle, FitzGerald might have been one of those
country parsons who made such idiosyncratic contributions to
English literature in his time, men like William Barnes, Charles
Tennyson Turner, and Hawker of Morwenstow. He did make his
contribution, more important than theirs, but it was unsanctified,
for the fact is that he had an early tendency to agnosticism.

To be up at Cambridge in the later eighteen-twenties, for an
undergraduate at all serious, was to be exposed to a great deal of
moral earnestness on the subject of the Christian religion. Fitz-
Gerald's own brother John, for example, turned into a keen lay
evangelist, so enthusiastic that while preaching he was liable to
take off his boots and whistle. At Cambridge, FitzGerald's friend
John Allen, a clergyman's son who in due course became a clergyman himself, was tireless in his efforts to turn FitzGerald's scepticism
into faith. Allen was a serious person. He had difficulty in getting

out of bed of a morning, and to correct that little weakness spent a good deal of time invoking the aid, or perhaps one might say the leverage, of the Deity. He even exchanged his umbrella for an alarm clock, but where prayer had failed, this machine was not more effective. Not that Allen gave up the struggle against self-indulgence, as this typical entry in his diary makes plain: 'At tea began course of amendment by leaving off butter.' When anything went wrong, Allen used to say, 'How admonitory!'

This excellent man seemed to come near converting his friend, but FitzGerald boggled at miracles. 'If you can prove to me', he wrote to Thackeray in 1831, 'that one miracle took place, I will believe that he is a just God who damned us all because a woman ate an apple'. As it turned out, FitzGerald stuck to what he called his 'dark views', but this did not prevent him from being tolerant of other people's religious inclinations (unless they were High Church), or from sometimes going to church, or from believing in the value of religion. In his early thirties he was much impressed by the preaching of a friend of his brother's, whose sermons, he said, shook his soul; and at the age of forty he drew up a proposal for liturgical reform to counter Romanizing tendencies. But as he grew older his dark views became more fixed, and must have incurred some local disapproval. When, on one occasion, this disapproval became vocal, it drew from him a steam-roller-like rejoinder some-what in the style of Dr Johnson. The rector of Woodbridge had called on FitzGerald to say he was sorry he never saw him at church.

'Sir,' replied FitzGerald, 'you might have conceived that a man does not come to my years of life without thinking much of these things. I believe I may say that I have reflected them fully as much as yourself. You need not repeat this visit.'

FitzGerald's agnosticism and fatalism are crystallized in the *Rubáiyát*. Nowhere does he lose his temper with God, as Housman does, but there is one stanza which urges God to accept forgiveness from man – a stanza, by the way, which Mrs Hardy read aloud to Hardy on his deathbed. It is a curious fact that this stanza is the outcome of a mistranslation from the Persian.

It is easy to exaggerate FitzGerald's reclusiveness. In fact he made a good many little excursions from his Suffolk headquarters, especially when young, yet it must be admitted that he did develop into a somewhat solitary eccentric. We see him, as he grew older, walking into Woodbridge wearing an old Inverness cape and a flowered satin waistcoat, with slippers on his feet and a handkerchief tied over his hat; in cold weather trailing a plaid shawl, or in hot weather walking barefoot with his boots slung on a stick. At home he generally wore an Oblomov dressing-gown, slippers, and a top hat, and he seldom took off his hat except when he wanted his handkerchief, which he kept inside it.

His way of life was simple. He was practically a vegetarian, he delighted in little things, in bright colours and pleasant noises, and always he showed a complete indifference or distaste towards worldly ways and values. There is a pleasant story about his being in a gathering of people one evening, and among them was a snobbish man who kept talking of his important friends, all of whom seemed to have titles. FitzGerald listened for some time with an appearance of deep dejection. At last he got up, lighted a bedroom candle, and standing at the door, with the candle in his hand, he turned, with a look of hopeless melancholy, and said, 'I once knew a lord, too, but he's dead.'

FitzGerald's letters give plenty of pictures of his seclusion, and they often have this same tinge of humorous melancholy. 'Oh,' he wrote, 'if you were to hear "Where and oh where is my soldier laddie gone" played every three hours in a languid way by the chimes of Woodbridge Church, wouldn't you wish to hang yourself? On Sundays we have the Sicilian Mariner's Hymn – very slow indeed. I see, however, by a handbill in the grocer's shop that a man is going to lecture on the Gorilla in a few weeks. So there is something to look forward to.'

Naturally, as FitzGerald grew older, he grew more conscious of his isolation, and the correspondence he so persistently kept up with his friends was hardly adequate to keep him in touch with them. In 1866, for instance, he wrote his usual Christmas letter to Carlyle and asked to have his annual remembrances made to Mrs Carlyle. Carlyle replied that his wife had died in the previous April.

There is no plainer indication of FitzGerald's detachment from the world than his attitude to politics. He did once make, in 1838, a striking pronouncement on this subject. It occurs in a letter to Thackeray, and what makes it striking is that it expresses an opinion which is widely held in this country today but can hardly have been common in the eighteen-thirties. 'I will exalt your name,' he wrote, 'if you will contrive to persuade me that we have nothing to fear from the domineering Russia. It is not the present fuss about her that makes me tremble, but I have always been afraid that she was the Power kept in pickle to overwhelm Europe just as men were beginning to settle into a better state than the world has yet seen. If she were out of the question, we should do very well.' A statement like that is rare in FitzGerald: on the whole, it was his habit to turn a deaf ear and a blind eye to politics. For a man of his temperament, in his position and in his time, it was much easier to do that than it would be in an age of constant anxiety like our own. He once gave his landlord instructions, when he was living in lodgings, that in case anyone called about his vote, the caller was to be told that Mr FitzGerald would *not* vote, advised everyone to do the same, and 'let the rotten matter bust itself.'

In fact, FitzGerald did have a political attitude of a kind: he was what would later have been called a Little Englander. He thought that a nation with great possessions was like a man with great estates, liable to incur more trouble than profit. (Perhaps he was thinking of his father.) He thought it would be a good thing if England were to give away some of her possessions overseas before they were taken from her. He wished that the English were a little, peaceful, unambitious, trading nation like the Dutch. He had a persistent conviction that England's best day was over, and that there was no way of arresting her inevitable fate. 'I am quite assured', he said, 'that this country is dying, as other countries die, as trees die, atop first. The lower limbs are making all haste to follow.' 'Sometimes,' he said, 'I envy those who are so old that the curtain will probably fall on them before it does on their country.' It is not very clear upon what he based these conclusions, or precisely what he meant by the curtain falling.

FitzGerald was inclined to be a praiser of times past, and he had a bee in his bonnet about the Suffolk squirearchy of his day. He held a romantic view about the fine old English gentleman, and his landowning neighbours failed to measure up to this idealized figure. They were a petty race, he said. 'They only use the earth for an investment; cut down every old tree; level every violet bank; and make the old country of my youth hideous to me in my decline – so I get to the water, where friends are not buried nor pathways stopt up – I am happiest going in my little boat round the coast to Aldeburgh, with some bottled porter and some bread and cheese, and some good rough soul who works the boat and chews his tobacco in peace.' This seems almost like a paraphrase of the most hackneyed quatrain in the *Rubáiyát*: all we have to do is to substitute a mast for the bough, and a bottle of porter for the jug of wine, and add a little cheese to the bread; and the enigmatic 'thou', singing in the wilderness, is seen to be a congenially rough soul chewing tobacco in the North Sea.

To go back to this belief of FitzGerald's about the decline and fall of England. It no doubt did come partly from the cutting down of trees and the stopping up of rights-of-way. I think also that he had an intuitive understanding that he was a privileged person in a favoured place and time, and that it is seldom in this world that the peaceful time and the favoured place and the private income are all found together. So intelligent a man must have been conscious of the great changes, the expansive industrialism, going on in his own time. 'England cannot expect long', he wrote in 1842, 'such a reign of inward quiet as to suffer men to dwell so easily to themselves.' Perhaps also there was some biological reason for his belief that England's day was over. A man who feels that there is something terminal about his own existence may easily envisage the world as failing with him. That is why old men commonly mistake change for decay, and why they enlarge upon the decline in manners and morals and the poor prospects of the world they soon expect to leave. Now FitzGerald was not young for long: even in his middle thirties he appeared to Crabbe's grandson like a grave middle-aged man. This may have been because he was lonely, melancholy and frustrated; but he seems to have been an old soul, and possibly this had something to do with his heredity and with the in-breeding of the FitzGeralds.

There had been men somewhat like FitzGerald before his time, and there is one earlier writer in particular whom FitzGerald in many ways resembles: it is a curious fact that each of them is chiefly remembered by one poem and a great many letters. The writer I mean is Gray, and the resemblance is worth exploring a little. FitzGerald made a distinction between taste and genius, and was responsible for the saying that 'Taste is the feminine of genius.' This is an autobiographical remark: FitzGerald laid no claim to genius, regarded himself as a man of taste, and knew himself well enough to recognize the feminine aspects of his own mind and character. It is evident that he found his aphorism equally applicable to Gray. Both men were admirers of Dryden's prose, and speaking of Gray's admiration for Dryden, FitzGerald calls Gray 'that man of taste, very far removed, perhaps as far as feminine from masculine, from the man he admired'. In another place FitzGerald says, 'I always think that there is more genius in most of the three volume novels than in Gray: but by the most exquisite taste, and indefatigable lubrication, he made of his own few thoughts, and many of other men's, a something which we all love to keep ever about us.' Does that not apply just as well to Fitz-Gerald's *Rubáiyát* as it does to Gray's *Elegy*?

If we look at certain criticisms of Gray, made before FitzGerald was thought of, the resemblance between these two men becomes even clearer. Take, for instance, Dr Johnson's pronouncement after he had made what he called 'a slight inspection' of Gray's letters. 'What has occurred to me', he said, 'is that his mind had a large grasp; that his curiosity was unlimited, and his judgment cultivated; that he was a man likely to love much where he loved at all, but that he was fastidious and hard to please.' The same opinion might be formed after a slight inspection of the letters of FitzGerald. Then there is a remark of Hazlitt's about Gray's letters which would apply just as well to FitzGerald's: 'He pours his thoughts out upon paper as they arise in his mind; and they arise in his mind without pretence, or constraint, from the pure impulse of learned leisure and contemplative indolence.'

Like Gray, FitzGerald cherished his learned leisure and his contemplative indolence. 'It is a misfortune', said Gray, 'which, thank my stars, I can pretty well bear.' The difference between their feelings about leisure is the difference between the eighteenth century and the nineteenth: whereas Gray made no bones about it, FitzGerald felt guilty about it, and sometimes made excuses for it. Nowadays, I suppose, he would be classified as a drone, but civilization has come to a pretty pass when work is thought of in terms of man-hours, because there are no such things. We need a few reminders that leisure is the only soil in which certain flowers can grow, and that because a man is so fortunately placed as to be able to use his own brains in his own time, he need not be instantly stigmatized as a social outcast. One would not advocate a whole nation of FitzGeralds, but a nation which allows a FitzGerald to exist.

But there it is: in the nineteenth century there was a tendency to preach up work for work's sake. No doubt there were people who regarded FitzGerald's life as culpably selfish, and there are many today who would do the same: but 'selfishness', as Wilde happily remarked, 'is not living as one wishes to live, it is asking others to live as one wishes to live'.

If a community is to be called civilized, it must support persons who have the leisure, as well as the ability, to cultivate their taste; and anybody who has attempted to do that knows that a lifetime is not long enough for the job. FitzGerald cultivated his taste in painting, in music, and in literature. He formed a habit of buying odds and ends of pictures, and they gave him great pleasure, even if they were not always what he wanted them to be. 'My Titian is a great hit,' he wrote; 'if not by him, it is as near him as ever was painted.' His connoisseurship seems to have been a little erratic. 'If it is not by Gainsborough,' he wrote of another picture, 'who the devil is it by?' And he treated pictures rather cavalierly; he was apt to touch them up, or even to chop them up; he cut one picture in half and made two pictures of it, and was very pleased with the result. Less questionable than this proceeding was his arrival at the important point where he could say, 'I like pictures that are not like nature. I can have nature better than any picture by looking out of my window.'

As for music, FitzGerald had been a member of a musical society at Cambridge, and was soon regarded as a creditable pianist. He used, later on, to entertain himself and others at the piano, or at a small organ, on which he played snatches from Mozart, Beethoven and Handel. There exists a drawing of him by his friend Charles Keene, showing him crouching over this instrument and looking as solitary as a man at his prayers. He also composed. None of his songs and other compositions has been published, but they exist in manuscript. They probably have the faults of a literary man's music; they are said to be 'dated' and to contain structural weaknesses. FitzGerald's friend, Archdeacon Groome, said that he was a great lover of the old English composers, especially William Shield. Recalling that the figure of Handel in Westminster Abbey held a scroll in his marble hand bearing the first bars of 'I know that my Redeemer liveth', FitzGerald suggested that Shield should also hold a scroll, and that on it should be written the first bars of 'A flaxen-headed ploughboy'. FitzGerald probably knew that Shield began his career as apprentice to a boat-builder, a fact that would have pleased him.

FitzGerald read a great deal and had the leisure to assimilate and think about what he read. What is known of his taste in books – and much is known – of course helps in the understanding of his character. He knew eight languages. English was his mother-tongue; Latin, Greek and French he was taught when young; Italian, Spanish, Persian and German he acquired later. The range of his reading was wide, and where he surrendered himself to the writer, he was the perfect reader, because his response was both emotional and critically reasoned; but he had strong antipathies, wilful blind spots, capricious dislikes. Arthur Benson hit a nail on the head when he remarked that FitzGerald's critical judgment was much affected by his feeling of personality. For instance, FitzGerald never tired of Virgil, but 'why is it', he asked, 'that I can never take up with Horace – so sensible, agreeable, elegant, and sometimes even grand?' It may have been that he just couldn't like the personality of Horace – or it may even have been that he didn't like the personality of somebody who doted on Horace, some old prig, perhaps, at school or at Cambridge: but it would be a tricky business trying to account for his likes and dislikes. He greatly enjoyed the

novels of Dickens, Thackeray, Wilkie Collins, and Trollope, but
he could not stand Jane Austen or George Eliot. He loved Shakespeare but disliked Milton. He discovered Blake for himself as
early as 1833. He liked Lamb more and more as he grew older, and
'Daddy' Wordsworth, as he called him, less and less. He liked the
earlier but not the later work of Tennyson, Browning he abhorred,
and his rejoicings over the death of Mrs Browning ('No more
Aurora Leighs, thank God!') drew in due course a well-known
piece of vituperative versification from her widower. FitzGerald
liked nothing better than *Don Quixote*, the romances of Scott, the
letters of Madame de Sévigné, and above all the poems of Crabbe.
This isolated man of leisure lived so long and so intimately with the
books he liked best, that the writers became part of his life. When
he speaks of 'my dear Madame de Sévigné', it is almost as if he is
speaking of someone as real to him as his friends, as Thackeray or
George Crabbe the younger.

I have already called FitzGerald lonely, melancholy and frustrated. The cause of his feeling like that was simply, I believe, his
consciousness of being different from other men. For instance,
although there were women for whom he felt affection, an affection
in which there was sometimes warmth and tenderness, there is no
evidence that he was ever carried away by his feelings for any
woman. It is true that when he was twenty-six he met a young
woman, Elizabeth Charlesworth, the daughter of a Suffolk parson,
with whom he contemplated marriage; but the contemplation
seems to have been purely cerebral. There is no indication that he
ever made any declaration of love, let alone proposed to her. In
a letter he described her as 'very pious, but very rational, healthy,
stout, and a good walker'. Love has some strange ways of showing
itself, but it would be too much to accept that as the language of
passion. In a letter written at this time he says, 'I am ashamed of
living in such ease; and really think I ought to marry ... that I may
not be more happy than my fellows.' One can hardly think of a
more extraordinary motive for marriage. Either this remark was a
joke, or it was another way of saying that he was already acutely
conscious of being different from the ordinary, active, ambitious,
and averagely sensual man, and had been wondering whether by

marrying he might not be able to reduce the difference.

At this time, in fact, his feelings were strongly engaged in another quarter. At the age of twenty-four he had met, on a journey to South Wales, William Kenworthy Browne, a boy of sixteen, for whom he conceived what has been rightly called a romantic friendship. Browne was the son of a Bedford alderman, fond of riding, shooting and fishing, sensible and cheerful. He became a captain of militia, a country gentleman, and the father of a family. FitzGerald said Browne was 'quick to love and quick to fight – full of confidence, generosity, and the glorious spirit of youth'. We know that people are often attracted by their opposites, and that they sometimes tend to idealize them. Browne was the complete extravert, and there was more than a little hero-worship in Fitz-Gerald's feeling for him. The friendship lasted for a quarter of a century, and only came to an end with Browne's death. FitzGerald has left a deeply moving account of his visit to Browne's deathbed. It seems reasonable to conclude that FitzGerald would have liked the friendship to be closer than in fact it could be; and it was almost certainly a feeling of frustration that caused him at times to be irritable and sarcastic with Browne, and afterwards to be very sorry for it.

Before his friend's death, and at a time when FitzGerald was nearing fifty, he took what was for him the rashest of steps: he married. His friend Bernard Barton, the Quaker poet, left a daughter Lucy, who was of about the same age as FitzGerald. FitzGerald seems to have considered it his duty to provide for her, as she had been left very badly off, and he seems to have made Barton some promise that he would do so. It looks as if Barton and his daughter, or FitzGerald himself, regarded this as a promise of marriage; it is difficult to discover any motive that FitzGerald could have had for marriage with her except a wish to do what he felt must be the proper thing. He does not seem to have expected happiness to result from it, and Browne was not alone in trying to dissuade him: even Lucy Barton herself asked him to break off the engagement if he felt that the marriage would not make him happy; but he persisted. Lucy had, on the face of things, much to gain – financial security, for instance; and, for what it was worth, the status of a married woman, of a woman married to a man of means and of a higher social standing than her own. Now Lucy, as FitzGerald said later, was 'brought up to rule', and this judgment seems to accord with somebody else's description of her, according to which 'her features were heavy, she was tall and big of bone, and her voice was loud and deep.' She evidently looked forward to getting her husband out of his bachelor ways and his eccentricities, and expected to influence him into conforming with the social conventions that she cherished. She hoped that he would pay calls, receive visitors, and dress for dinner. What a hope!

The wedding-day did not show FitzGerald in any haste to be ruled or reformed. He turned up in a slouch hat, looking like a victim being led to his doom, and during the wedding-breakfast only spoke once. This was when he was offered some blancmange. He looked at it, and then waved it away with a gesture of disgust, saying as he did so, 'Ugh! Congealed bridesmaid!'

After a fortnight they separated for five weeks, and after a few months parted for good, because they were quite incompatible. FitzGerald made Lucy a proper allowance, and that was that. He admitted later that he had been stupid to take so wrong a step as to marry, and that having taken it he had shown what he called a want of 'courageous principle' in not making the best of it.

It was perhaps after the death of Browne that FitzGerald used, as he wrote, 'to wander about the shore at Lowestoft at night, longing for some fellow to accost me who might give some promise of filling up a very vacant place in my heart'. This vacant place was filled when FitzGerald was fifty-five and he fell in with a young fisherman called Joseph Fletcher, generally known as Posh. Posh was then twenty-four, and therefore as widely separated from FitzGerald by age as by temperament and class. It has been rather unkindly said that a good deal of sentimentality was wasted over this sea-lion. Hero-worship was certainly lavished upon Posh, and FitzGerald tended indeed to rave about him. Posh, he said, had simplicity of soul, justice of thought, tenderness of nature. Posh was a gentleman of nature's grandest type. Posh was the greatest man he had known. Posh was 'as good an image of the mould that man was originally cast in, as you may chance to see in these days', he was 'a man of the finest Saxon type, with a complexion *vif, mâle et flamboyant*, blue eyes, a nose less than Roman, more than Greek, and strictly auburn hair that any woman might sigh to possess'. This is enthusiasm, but is it sentimentality? FitzGerald was so constituted that his deepest affections could only be called forth by an image he had formed of a man whose good looks were the outward aspect of a noble character, a man the reverse of introspective, a man active, simple, hardy, faithful and affectionate, with some degree of intelligence. The nearest to this image had been Browne, and it is significant that Posh reminded FitzGerald of Browne, both in looks and character. 'I seem to have jumped back', he said, 'to a regard of near forty years ago; and while I am with him feel young again, and when he goes shall feel old again.' I do not see sentimentality in that, but I do see a certain pathos. I see a man cut off by heredity, temperament and habit from some of the elementary pleasures of ordinary life; and a man conscious that he is on the threshold of old age and that there is much that he has missed; and I see this old soul enchanted by a young man who seems to him to embody the energies and hopes that alone can make life bearable, and that may make life splendid. FitzGerald had Posh's portrait painted and hung it up beside those of Tennyson and Thackeray as if to show that Posh's 'greatness', though different from theirs, was not inferior.

So far as can be judged, Posh, finding himself on a pedestal, kept his head tolerably well, and he does not seem to have exploited FitzGerald as he no doubt could have done if he had been of a baser nature – and if, be it added, FitzGerald himself had been less crotchety and set in his own ways. Posh thought FitzGerald very odd – 'a master rum un', was his phrase – but he was no doubt flattered to have been singled out for favour. FitzGerald was useful to him, and, as is well known, set him up with a herring lugger called the *Meum and Tuum* (known locally as the *Mum and Tum*). I dare say he even felt a certain tolerant affection for FitzGerald. But the relationship foundered, as such relationships are apt to do, because FitzGerald expected too much of him. Possibly FitzGerald expected an intenser and more constant emotional response than Posh was capable of: he certainly expected too high a standard of conduct in certain directions. The aristocrat, the autocrat, in Fitz-Gerald expected deference to his wishes; he expected reliability and punctiliousness of a kind that used to be drilled into the upper middle classes and was not as a rule characteristic of the working class. FitzGerald was annoyed because Posh drank too much at times and broke his pledge not to do so, and because Posh was careless about keeping his accounts and paying his debts: Posh, for his part, resented FitzGerald's interference in his affairs and managing attitude towards him. They remained ostensibly friends, but not close friends. In 1906, more than twenty years after Fitz-Gerald's death, Posh's fortunes had declined and he was beach-combing at Lowestoft. Somebody who had sought him out at this time said, 'I don't like the man because notwithstanding all FitzGerald's kindness to him – and he gave him a grand chance to prove himself, at least, something like what FitzGerald imagined – he is ungrateful, and blames FitzGerald for "spoiling" him.' Posh died in a local workhouse in 1915.

FitzGerald's charm captivated a variety of people. 'So kind he was,' said a woman who had been his housekeeper, 'not never one to make no obstacles. Such a joky gentleman he was, too.' His kindness was not all in personal relationships: for instance he paid a doctor a fixed sum every year to visit the poor. But if we are to take a comprehensive view of his character, we must admit that, like his mother, he was not wholly amiable. Crabbe's grandson had the impression that FitzGerald was 'a proud and very punc-tilious man'. He could in fact become aloof and haughty and rather formidable in manner, and although he was easily annoyed by a want of politeness in others, he was not always a model of civility himself. Once when a Woodbridge neighbour greeted him with a genial 'Good morning', FitzGerald replied, 'I don't know you' – simply because they had never been formally introduced. On another occasion he asked a man to dinner, but the guest, when he presented himself, was not admitted, so he went home in dudgeon. The next day he had a note from FitzGerald saying, 'I saw you yesterday when you called, but I was not fit for company, and felt that I could not be bothered.' That is what comes of living alone. One cannot help feeling that if he had worked out some *modus vivendi*, some kind of compromise, with his wife, that sort of thing need not have happened. How far he had drifted, how much he had become what used to be called a crotcheteer, can be judged from a painful scene in which, long after their separation, his wife was involved. FitzGerald was walking in Woodbridge with Posh when he saw his wife approaching. He held out his hand and was about to greet her when he suddenly changed his mind. 'Come along, Posh!' he said, and hurried away without a word to Lucy. A sense of guilt, a sense of shame, a fear of questions and explanations, a sudden panic, might easily make a man behave like that, but such behaviour is not urbane, and whatever poor Lucy's shortcomings, it seems hard that she should have had to suffer what was certainly a private humiliation and presumably a public one as well.

His oddities of behaviour came partly from solitariness: a lonely man may easily and mistakenly come to feel that he is answerable to nobody but himself for his actions. They came also perhaps from a natural and no doubt hereditary taint of arrogance. And they have been attributed to his feminine characteristics, one of which was alleged to be the desire to dominate a situation, to show a momentary power at whatever cost. FitzGerald himself several times applied the word 'ladylike' to himself. 'I am an idle fellow,' he wrote, 'of a very ladylike turn of sentiment, and my friendships are more like loves, I think.' It has been said of him that his deepest instinct was the need of affection. With it there went the need of admiring and looking up to the real or potential source of affection. This double need was felt most strongly in regard to Browne, and later to Posh, who seemed to FitzGerald to resemble Browne. But it would be a mistake to take a narrow view of FitzGerald's capacity, his talent, for friendship. His reputation rests partly on the fact that he was a close friend of three men so eminent and so different as Tennyson, Thackeray and Carlyle. It is possible that some feminine power of adaptation enabled him to win and hold the affections of men so different, but to say that is to suggest that he put on some kind of act. It seems much more likely that they loved him because he did not put on any act, because he was simply and always 'dear old Fitz' – a lovable old oddity whom they could not think of as an ambitious literary rival, who never wanted to

make use of them or exploit them, whom they could trust, and
who was, as a friend, wonderfully constant and faithful. To both
Thackeray and Tennyson he gave material help, and he is believed
to have given Tennyson in his early and difficult days three hundred
a year for some years. In his youth, Thackeray was his most
intimate friend, and there is an ebullience in the letters they then
exchanged which makes them rather tedious to read, as if energy
were being misdirected. As Thackeray and Tennyson became more
and more men of the world and more famous, they became, to
FitzGerald, buried in the country, more and more, so to speak,
pen-friends; and as he gets older one can feel more and more that
he is writing not so much to real people as to his remembered
images of people as he had formerly known them.

We find FitzGerald carrying on a perennial correspondence
with some people, Frederick Tennyson for example, with whom it is
hard to think that he had much in common – but he must have had
a rare gift for perceiving and responding to the best in different
people. Of his attachment to Carlyle, Arthur Benson wrote:

> It is an interesting friendship because so unequal. It shows
> that respect, and affection, and sincerity are the true levellers
> of all differences. Two men could hardly have been selected
> whose temperaments were not only so dissimilar, but to each
> of whom the faults of the other's intellect and character
> would have been naturally so repugnant. The gentle-
> hearted sceptic and the puritan prophet. Yet both had an
> eye for humanity and simplicity; and upon these qualities
> their mutual regard was based.

There is a story which illustrates both the difference between
FitzGerald and Carlyle and FitzGerald's notable disinclination to
push his own writings, even into the notice of his friends. Just
thirteen years after the *Rubáiyát* had first been published, Charles
Eliot Norton paid a visit to Carlyle, and happened to speak of his
admiration for the poem. Carlyle, said Norton afterwards, had
never heard of it.

> He asked me whose work it was, and I told him what I
> had heard, that the translation was made by a Reverend

Edward FitzGerald, who lived somewhere in Norfolk, and spent much time in his boat. 'The Reverend Edward Fitz-Gerald?' he said in reply. 'Why, he's no more Reverend than I am! He's a very old friend of mine – I'm surprised, if the book be as good as you tell me it is, that my old friend has never mentioned it to me.' I told him I would send him the book, and did so the next day. Two or three days later ... he said, 'I've read that little book you sent me, and I think my old friend Edward FitzGerald might have spent his time to much better purpose than in busying himself with the verses of that old Mahomedan blackguard.' I could not prevail on Carlyle even to do credit to the noble English in which FitzGerald had rendered the audacious quatrains of the Persian poet; he held the whole thing as worse than a mere waste of labour.

It is easier to understand how FitzGerald got on with a man like Charles Keene, who shared his interest in sailing, and in old books, old music, and old pictures. But here again a curtain of silence concealed the *Rubáiyát*. After Keene had known FitzGerald for some years, he happened to mention him to William Bell Scott. Scott, according to Keene, jumped off his chair. 'Do you *know*˙ him?' he said. 'Why, Ram Jam (some wonderful Persian name he gave it) is the most quite too exquisite work of the age.' This was more than twenty years after the poem had been published.

Of the *Rubáiyát* Arthur Benson wrote rather sententiously at the beginning of the century that 'it is not to be feared that this subtle murmuring voice out of the East will win any notable influence in the busy world of the West'. I should say that it has had in this century not merely a notable but an enormous influence both in this country and in America and that its influence continues active. I have sometimes wondered if any bibliophile has ever undertaken to collect editions of the *Rubáiyát*. If they were all got together they would constitute a museum of taste, largely bad taste, in book production. Years ago one used to see in drawing-rooms the most horrible little editions about the size of a patience card and bound in floppy suede of the colour that Herbert Spencer called 'impure

purple'. There were also large quarto editions with coloured illus-
trations sometimes of an unspeakable ugliness and gaudiness. But
these books were read, and so were the cheaper and more portable
editions; and new editions continue to appear from time to time
in the bookshops. I glanced at one the other day, and when I left
the bookshop I got on to a bus. In front of me a woman was sitting
with a large square of printed artificial silk tied over her head. It
was brightly coloured, and of a dubious oriental design with a good
many minarets and palms, interspersed with mottoes scribbled in a
wavering writing, perhaps to suggest some Middle Eastern script.
If one has the habit of reading, one cannot help reading whatever
may happen to be printed on other people's headgear, and without
much effort I managed to decipher one of these inscriptions. And
what did I read?

Yet Ah, that Spring should vanish with the Rose!

Yes, it was that old Mahomedan blackguard again, and as the bus
proceeded, and I was able to hazard a guess at my fellow-passenger's
age and profession, I wondered if in some fold of her headgear one
might not discover an even more fitting quotation. For instance,

Ah, take the Cash, and let the Credit go;

or

My Clay with long Oblivion is gone dry.

The subtle murmuring voice out of the East has come to seem
rather unsubtle because it is now much hackneyed – but then so is
Gray's *Elegy*, and it is not a fault in a poem that it appeals, over a long
period of time, to the common as well as the uncommon reader.

The theme of the *Rubáiyát*, according to FitzGerald, was 'a
desperate sort of thing, unfortunately found at the bottom of all
thinking men's minds: but made music of'. Its message is agnostic,
epicurean and fatalistic; its form is pleasing to the senses and to the
imagination. It came into existence, in FitzGerald's version, at a
time when the hold of Christian dogma upon English minds was
weakening and doubt was growing; it became widely known in the
English-speaking world at a time when people were ripe for a reminder that pleasure is not wicked but agreeable; that what must be,
must be; and that mankind, being ignorant of the ultimate purpose,

if any, of the universe, had better make hay while the sun shines. Why did not FitzGerald write more? He gave the answer to that question in a letter to Bernard Barton as early as 1842. 'I know', he said, 'that I could write volume after volume as well as others of the mob of gentlemen who write with ease; but I think unless a man could do better, he had best not do at all: I have not the strong inward call.' He knew his limitations as a man of taste, not of genius, built more to enjoy than to create. Finding that he lacked the strength and scope, and probably the ambition and perhaps even the inclination, to undertake or carry out creative writing on the scale, for example, of that of his friends, Tennyson, Thackeray, and Carlyle, he devoted himself to enjoying and discriminating between the works of others. Even his *Rubáiyát* owes its existence to his enjoyment of another man's work.

There is no more sense in reproaching him retrospectively for not writing more than in reproaching him for his idleness. To do either is to misunderstand his nature, which was all of a piece. 'This visionary inactivity', he said, 'is better than the mischievous activity of so many I see about me.' There was something Oriental about him. As an Orientalist he was only a wonderful amateur, but in his way of life and his attitude to life in the bustling nineteenth century he was more like some ancient Chinese or Indian sage or poet than a modern European. One could not have expected him to travel in the East; travelling, he thought, was a vanity, because the soul remains the same. But if he had read more widely and deeply in Asiatic literature, his quietism and non-attachment might have become free of the sense of guilt, and he might have become less melancholy and less conscious of frustration.

When FitzGerald was alive, there were people in Suffolk who called him 'dotty' and 'soft', and perhaps harder things as well, but I imagine that Suffolk now takes a proper pride in having harboured the living FitzGerald and in holding his bones now that he is dead. If he still has detractors, let them read the epitaph he chose for his grave,

It is He that hath made us, and not we ourselves.

[Delivered as a lecture at the Aldeburgh Festival, 1948. Published in *Orpheus* 2, 1949. Reprinted in *Tribute to Benjamin Britten* (1963)]

William Hickey

At the age of sixty the retired lawyer from Calcutta had settled in the village of Beaconsfield. He found it, after the splendours of his years in the East, a 'trifling' place. One of nature's bachelors, he gardened a little, rode or walked every day, and made excursions to London, but found the local society very limited. Menaced by boredom and annoyed by headaches and his old trouble, internal spasms, he found himself living much in his crowded, his 'strange and varied' past, and so hit upon a plan for filling up the 'painful vacuum' of the present: he would write his memoirs. This task must have taken some time, from 1809 onwards. The manuscript peters out in the middle of a list of names, and the writer himself fades from view, supposedly dying, apparently intestate, in lodgings at Camden Town in 1830, just before his eighty-first birthday.

With a real or professed modesty of a kind unfamiliar today, William Hickey declared that his memoirs could not be in any way interesting to persons unacquainted with him, and he reminded any strangers into whose hands they might fall that he had only written them to amuse himself and kill time. It is clear, all the same, that the impulse that drove him to write was that of a creative artist; he wanted to make a lasting picture of his vanishing life, he did make it, and to his picture-making he brought unique qualifications. A writer in the *Athenaeum* once called Hickey a typical man of his time: he may have been typical in his absorption of claret, but he was individual in his effusion of ink.

It is relevant to notice what Hickey was not. He was not a religious man. Plainly more interested in the solid comforts of this world than in the putative rewards and punishments of the next, he could speak of death as 'the remorseless tyrant'. He could make a drunken exhibition of himself in the Haymarket in the white habit of a nun, or, years later, accompany a party of rowdy drinking companions to church. If later he felt ashamed it seems to have been only because he had not been true to his sense of social propriety. Even when he speaks of conscience as an 'old and faithful monitor' it is difficult to feel that conscience is for him much more than a synonym for that same social sense. It was an all-ruling Providence, he observed, which had furnished mankind with the useful sugar cane, but that same Providence, he could observe elsewhere, seemed almost to have dealt unjustly by the flying fish: its workings upon that creature verged upon the questionable. With great candour he tells how he robbed his father; he admits that it was disgraceful, but does not use words like sin or crime. Hickey, then, was not religious, not a moralist, not a thinker, not a writer, nor a reader, nor an aesthete. Susceptible to the appropriate emotions when confronted with impressive scenery he could note how the rising sun ('the glorious orb') gave 'luxuriant' tints to a 'stupendous' mountain: and if mountains were fairly high he had learned to apply to them the epithet 'romantic'. Such comment seems hardly more than the social tribute of a bow, or than those little polite effusions of praise for a good dish, a bottle of wine, a garden, or a piece of music – 'as pretty a spot as I ever beheld', 'some of the sweetest duets I ever heard' – which, when they occur in his memoirs, seem to make the sociable Hickey audible, almost visible.

He was a man of the world with a strong constitution and a clear head, who, as his deceived and disappointed father told him when he was nineteen, wished to do right, was not without sensibility and generosity, but had no resolution or control over his passions. His youthful recklessness might have ruined him, but resolution gained the upper hand. Born in 1749, Hickey was the eighth child of a love-match between an Irishman and a Yorkshire girl. His father became a prosperous London lawyer with convivial habits and a distinguished circle of acquaintance. One of William's godfathers was a publican; at five the child was 'a complete pickle', and Pickle he was accordingly nicknamed; before he was fourteen he was accustomed to drinking champagne, port, claret, strong ale and punch, was 'in high favour as a fine forward youth', and had spent a good deal of time in a fast set haunting taverns and brothels, which fostered his appetite for women and wine but put him off gambling. What would now be considered precocity was less likely to be thought so in his time, when, for example, a boy of twenty could be in command of an East Indiaman, and when the expectation of life must have been much less long than in this age of better hygiene and wholesale 'scientific' slaughter.

Hickey admits that up to the age of thirty he was beyond measure extravagant and thoughtless. 'Cheerful companions', he says, 'and lovely seducing women always delighted me and frequently proved my bane;' and again, 'Dear, lovely woman, I never could resist.' In short, he was a playboy of abounding energy. He 'made good', but was luckily never transformed by age or the pressure of circumstance into a too sober, too perfect citizen: unless the pickle in him had retained its savour, he might have become too dull to write his memoirs. His character, as he consciously or unconsciously presents it, is extraordinarily likable, and this is not because he presents himself in a rosy light. He is never, as Mr E. M. Forster has remarked, pretentious or insincere, never concerned to draw lessons from his failure or success. Not for him the riddle of the universe or the discrimination of fine shades of appearance or feeling; he is too little imaginative, too much of a worldling and materialist. Living for many years in Asia, he shows a wonderful, if unusual, want of curiosity about the civilizations of its indigenous peoples. While his judicial contemporary in Bengal, Sir William Jones, opens up new fields of knowledge for the West, Hickey is contentedly busy with his social and professional round, his native mistress, his imposing houses (furnished 'in such a style as gained universal approbation'), his princely boat and his sixty-three servants.

Englishmen did not make the long and hazardous voyage to exile in India in those days to explore exotic cults and customs; if India afforded scope for honourable careers, it was, at the lowest, 'that common receptacle of all abandoned and undone men', and the Company's service, at worst, 'the last resource of ruined profligates'. India was a hopeful hunting-ground for fortune-hunters, men like that Mr Moore who, after eighteen months at the Residency of Rungpore, had acquired so overgrown a fortune as to be enabled to return to England with all his family, get into Parliament, and buy a fine estate in Essex: 'by what means such wealth was so suddenly acquired,' Hickey comments, 'he best knows.' Luck had a part to play. Of the fortune-hunters whose lives Hickey often wonderfully depicts, many struggled against the climate, against disease, against time, against their own temperaments, against other men's hostility, against the law, against a thousand hazards, not least those of the voyage home – again and again a great ship full of men and treasure is lost without trace. The whole phase of acquisitive imperialism which the memoirs reflect is summed up in the epitaph upon the tombstone of a certain Dutch gentleman at Sadras, on the coast of Coromandel:

> Mynheer Guldenstack lies interred here,
> Who intended to have gone home next year.

Hickey was luckier, and attained Beaconsfield.

If anybody announces, 'Selfishness never has been amongst my numerous faults,' the opposite is likely to be true. Hickey said it, yet it does not seem false; a selfish man would have taken better care of his own interests and less of other people's; Hickey was a faithful, generous and considerate friend. Vanity he admits, and a bent for ostentation. He comes peacocking home to London at one point in 'gay India coats' of scarlet and spangled lace, and an old friend shames him by pretending to mistake him for the Lord Mayor's trumpeter. He admires the 'man of fashion' and shows an emulous dandyism. He wishes always to appear well bred, but it would have been against a later standard of manners for a guest, dining with a parsimonious host, to 'bounce up', as Hickey once did, show plainly his distaste for what was offered him, take his hat and depart. Because he has 'always been rather prone to profuseness', and likes and needs, wherever he may be, to move in 'the first society', his sticking to a high and showy standard of living is seen to be an essential function of his character. His candour against himself frees his expressions of self-esteem from any taint of complacency. He thought himself and shows himself truthful, believed himself to have been, at least when young, of 'a mild temper and tender nature', and was naturally drawn to what he called 'plain, straightforward integrity', wherever it might occur.

Hickey's creative gift is not that of a conscious artist. The sustained freshness of the first volume is later intermittent. He does not by any means always solve one of the autobiographer's greater problems, which is to decide what is likely to seem almost as interesting to the reader as to the writer: he is not selective enough. He begins, he continues, he glows, is excited or amused by his memories, excites and amuses the reader, then lapses and turns at times into an old Beaconsfield bore from Bengal; then 'Pickle' is in eclipse. He continues, but he does not end; his temple of memory is not so well proportioned as his house in Calcutta. His style is plain enough. If it never surprises by a fine excess or a special grace, it never offends by uncouthness. It has the formal propriety and dignity of his day, when custom and ceremony try to hold in, and keep failing to hold in, human weaknesses, robust energies, temperaments inflamed by too much wine. It has a prevailing affability; Hickey might easily have been censorious more often, and when he does show contempt, it is withering; those Portuguese sailors, for instance, who, panic-stricken in a storm at sea, scrambled for a crucifix brandished by a priest, and tore it to pieces, are not called cowards or fools or knaves, but 'miserable enthusiasts'; while they were trying to save their souls, their more stout-hearted fellows were trying to save the ship.

It would be difficult to exaggerate the nautical interest of the memoirs. To a later age Hickey brings home the delays, the dangers and the discomforts of sea voyages in the eighteenth century – especially the discomforts. Hickey is not the only writer to have done this, but he does it in a way of his own. If, he explains, a passenger were housed on the gun deck, the use of dead lights in bad weather made a black-out, but although they kept out the daylight they did not always keep out the sea. Then there were the 'horrid screeches' of children, or, what was just as bad, their 'vociferous mirth'; one must expect to be poisoned by a variety of stinks, and annoyed by the perpetual creaking of bulkheads and the noise of the rudder working. Even if one were in the round house, frequent noises were made by seamen upon the poop, especially when they were working the spanker boom; and then, since the cooped-up poultry were fed twice a day, there was the 'consequent pecking', which was likewise 'extremely unpleasant'. In 1782 Hickey had louder noises to endure than creaking and pecking. It was in June of that year that he sailed from the Tagus for India in the *Raynba de Portugal*, in company with Charlotte Barry, his ostensible and amiable wife. His account of the horrors and dangers of this voyage has a kind of blunt eloquence which makes it the most sustained and dramatic piece of descriptive prose he ever wrote. The Hickeys did not arrive at Madras until the following March, having been delayed not only by the elements but having been held in a largely delightful internment at Trincomalee by the French under Suffren.

To read Hickey's account of Suffren would be enough to make it plain why he has been compared to Smollett, Fielding and Defoe: he has more than an eye for character, he has the power of presenting it alive. His portrait of Suffren is one of his best; there is something great and good about this man, something of Nelson's ability and charm; and Hickey does not simply tell us this, he shows it to us. He is always delighted by idiosyncrasy, and by a 'quiz', whether it be Doctor Bonynge, the Jamaican planter, whose son justifiably described him as 'the most *outré* and extraordinary old quiz', or the eccentric but humane and noble Mr Justice Hyde in Calcutta, who was sworn at by a drunkard as a 'damned old quiz, in his stiff formal periwig, with his confounded folio volumes of chicanery'. In each instance it is important that Hickey remembers not only what he himself thought, but what other people said; and it always happens that his eye for detail gives value to his memoirs as what has come to be called social history. For instance, when General St Leger said he wanted to smoke, Hickey thought he must be joking, 'not supposing so elegant a man could ever have been in the habit of using so vulgar a herb'; and when Hickey led St Leger to Arthur Forrest, who was caught in the clandestine enjoyment of a cheroot, Forrest's embarrassment was as great as St Leger's joy at discovering a fellow vulgarian with whom to indulge in a pipe or 'sagar'. In Hickey's gallery of portraits the two most important, besides his own, are those of Bob Pott and Charlotte Barry, the two people he loved best. Pott was a playboy and pickle like himself, but unmaturable; Charlotte the mistress who acted perfectly the part of a wife – a paragon of women. They were charming, and Hickey has made their charm immortal. What writer could have done more?

The memoirs have now been reissued, but not in such a form as to make them most easily accessible to a new generation of readers. The publishers might consider the desirability of preparing a portable Hickey made up of selections, helpfully and succinctly introduced, and as little annotated as possible. It is near forty years since the memoirs began to be prepared for publication. The editor, a director of the firm which published the book, omitted some parts which he, no doubt rightly, thought dull, and left in some which are perhaps hardly less dull; other parts again, owing to the freedom of the language, he thought unfit for publication. It may be, since freedom of language is more possible today than it was in 1913, when the first volume of the memoirs was first published, that the taboo could be relaxed for a more shock-proof reading public. Hickey is in the first class of English memoirists and deserves to be presented to many intelligent readers who would be daunted by four volumes even if they knew of them, but who, once acquainted with him, would find out how much they had missed.

[Review of *Memoirs of William Hickey*, edited by Alfred Spencer, *The Times Literary Supplement*, 3 June 1949]

Olive Schreiner

General Smuts, who knew Olive Schreiner, thought she was like Emily Brontë – 'a flame', he said, 'which burnt too fiercely'. Both women were daughters of poor clergymen living in remote places. Each was to earn her living by teaching. Each first wrote under a man's name, had a powerful imagination, and is chiefly remembered by one highly original book. But there would be little point in pursuing the comparison further: it would soon break down.

Everybody who knew Olive Schreiner agrees that she was intense and lively, with big, expressive eyes, a quick mind, and a warm heart. Her figure was stocky, she did not dress well, and she does not seem to have bothered about veils, gloves, and ornaments: she was interested in trying to improve the world, not in trying to look elegant. Yet there is a photograph of her as a young girl which is all grace, alertness, and charm; and something radiant and noble shone out of her face even when she was physically worn out at the end of her life.

Olive Schreiner's name is chiefly remembered in connection with her novel, *The Story of an African Farm*. To have written a novel that is still being read after more than seventy years – that in itself is a step towards immortality. *The Story of an African Farm* was one of the very first sustained pieces of imaginative writing to come out of what used to be called 'the Colonies'. This intense and original work, with its unfamiliar subject-matter and its excited style, was written by a solitary, half-educated girl living at an enormous distance from England. And yet it was very much of its time, the early eighteen-eighties. Besides reacting strongly to her surroundings, Olive Schreiner had begun to grapple fiercely, and all by herself, with ideas that were then being discussed far away by persons with enquiring minds and advanced opinions. Perhaps it would be more exact to speak of Olive Schreiner's 'ideals' rather than her 'ideas', because the reformer and propagandist in her eventually got the better of the thinker and artist.

What else did she write? There is an early novel, and also a long, unfinished one, both published after her death. This long one is called *From Man to Man*, and she spent about forty years *not* finishing it. It contains some striking scenes and passages; like all her work it is full of feeling – and preaching; it deserves to be better known: but it is unwieldy and half-formed, like a huge block of stone from which a sculptor has failed to release the heroic figures he knows it to contain. She also published allegories, and a number of pamphlets and essays on political and social themes.

Her life is to be thought of in terms of struggle rather than of happiness. Her father was the son of a shoemaker near Stuttgart. He came to England to be a missionary, and married the daughter of an English dissenting minister. Gottlob Schreiner was a poor man, good, unworldly, somewhat innocent. His wife was small and managing – no doubt she had to be. They went out to the Cape in 1838 and carried on their missionary work round about Basutoland. Mrs Schreiner gave birth to a good many children, of whom I think eight survived. One of Olive's sisters was famous as a social worker, and her brother William was an eminent lawyer who became Prime Minister of the Cape Colony.

Olive was born in the Wittebergen, a wild and mountainous region, so rugged as to make the Brontës' Yorkshire, scenically at least, seem almost as tame as a suburb. The place was exposed to violent thunderstorms, and between the Schreiners' primitive dwelling and their primitive church rose a lightning conductor. Olive said later that her childhood was bitter and dark, and it is known that her mother was repressive and even cruel to her. I have just been reading a book by Marion Friedmann, a South African psychologist, who explains all Olive Schreiner's writings as a lifelong protest against her mother, unconsciously identified by Olive with all authority, whether human or divine, and all oppression. Olive Schreiner suffered grievously from asthma, a complaint which is thought in some cases to be connected with an unsatisfactory relationship between a child and one of its parents.

From a very early age this particular child had an unsatisfied craving for affection. If that craving had been satisfied why should she have rebelled, even in childhood, as she did, against conventional standards of belief and behaviour?

At sixteen she took the first of a series of posts as a governess on lonely farms. At seventeen she became engaged for a short time to a man about whom little is known. Nobody seems to know exactly why the engagement was broken off, or precisely what effect the shock of his behaviour had in helping to form her forceful views about the wrongs done to women.

When she was twenty-six she went to England, taking with her the manuscript of *The Story of an African Farm*. After being rejected by three publishers it was accepted by a fourth on the advice of his distinguished reader, George Meredith. It appeared in 1883, was soon reprinted, and was much talked about. She became a celebrity, but she aroused disapproval as well as admiration: at a lending library near the Crystal Palace the lady subscribers made such a fuss that the librarian burnt the book. Since then it has been reprinted over and over again. It has a place of its own in English literature, and a pre-eminent place in South African literature. Her novel brought her, among other things, an intimate friendship with Havelock Ellis. She was in sympathy with Ellis's pioneering, scientific approach to sexual problems, although she herself held rather soulful and exalted views about love. She found in Ellis understanding and sympathy, but they evidently did not find in each other any sure grounds for the hope of a lifelong partnership.

It might have been expected that having made a name in London she would have followed up her success. But she was incapable of exploiting social opportunities, or of calculating her literary advancement, or indeed of settling down to steady work. She was made dreadfully restless by asthma and the emotional frustration and tension which apparently caused it, and after a few years she went back to Africa, perhaps mainly in the hope of better health. There, when she was nearly thirty-nine, she married a man seven years younger than herself, Samuel Cronwright. They had to face two uncomfortable possibilities: first, that she must be expected to grow old sooner than her husband; secondly, that he might find her too fidgety and highly strung to live with. And did he stop to think that he was in danger of being regarded as only the appendage of a celebrity? They decided to be known as Mr and Mrs Cronwright-Schreiner – but that did not make them equal.

Her marriage brought her at least some respite from loneliness, but the state of her health obliged her husband to move about with her instead of staying in one place, and when she gave birth to a child – her only child – it lived only one day. Little more than ten years after her marriage she wrote to Ellis saying that although she had not lost any of her faith in 'the possible beauty and greatness of human nature', her personal life had become 'crushed and indifferent' to her.

In 1913 she returned to England, still in search of health. She spent the war years in London. She was lonely, and she was turned out of at least one hotel and refused admission to others because of her German name. In the spring of 1920 her husband at last came to England from South Africa. When he called at her address an old woman came to the door, and he asked if he might see Mrs Cronwright-Schreiner. There is something terrifying about the answer he got. 'Don't you know me, Cronwright?' she said. He had failed to recognize his own wife, she had been so aged by her sufferings. Soon after this she returned to South Africa, but her husband did not go with her. She died in South Africa a few months later, in December 1920.

At a very early age she made the sad discovery that narrowness, hypocrisy, intolerance, and other disagreeable qualities can flourish under an outward show of conventional piety. Olive Schreiner reacted violently, and seems to have been driven towards the strange superstition that science might succeed better than religion in making us behave better towards one another. Her agnosticism seems quaintly old-fashioned, calling up pictures of earnest tea-parties in the 'eighties, with high-minded exchanges about evolution, socialism, and free love. But there was a real need for emancipation in many directions, and it took courage to preach it.

Although professing to be an agnostic, she lived a more Christian life than many who call themselves Christians. She remained an ardent believer in mercy, pity, and peace. In one of the last articles she ever wrote she said that there are two things we can do, and those are to get rid of all desire to see evil come to those who have injured us or others, and to help the weak and oppressed.

An early decision of hers was that the position of women in society in those days was unjust. She thought it unendurable, and became a strong feminist – a suffragette, it has been said, before the word was ever invented. Her book *Woman and Labour* was an important influence upon the movement to gain more freedom, more scope, and more happiness for women in their work and in their social and personal life. She was always rebellious, and where she found evidence of injustice, selfishness, cruelty, and violence she attacked them with courage. She was always – one might say she was automatically – on the side of the weak and the oppressed. She was against nationalism, imperialism, and war. She was against any kind of racial discrimination. When anti-Semitism showed itself in South Africa, she at once attacked it. At the time of the South African War, which she thought unnecessary and unjust, she had the courage to be a pro-Boer, and to write and speak in public and in private explaining why: she was bravely backed up by her husband. On the other hand, the existence of colour prejudice in South Africa made her a champion of the African and coloured peoples: she believed that there should be no racial or political discrimination against them.

Her life was one long resistance movement, and even if it can be shown that this resistance movement was neurotic in its origin and motive power, that does not invalidate it. She may have shown herself aggressive against aggression, but her ideals were not contemptible – they were compassionate and humane. The influence of her life and writings must have been fairly wide, and sometimes deep; it is still going on. Her longing for more soundness and sweetness in human relationships was profound and life-giving. Her existence was troubled, her writings were spasmodic and imperfect, but she was a generous nature and she will not be forgotten.

[*Listener*, 24 March 1955]

Leonard Woolf

One of the best-informed obituary articles about Leonard Woolf spoke of him as a many-sided man with a perfectly integrated personality. It also said that his autobiography was a masterpiece and the outstanding autobiography of our time. This opinion was presumably based on the first four volumes, because the fifth and last volume has only just appeared. Perhaps the greatest compliment that has been paid to the book came from E. M. Forster, who spoke of the 'absolute honesty' of the first volume. It isn't often that an autobiography is praised for honesty, and I can't remember any previous one ever having been praised for absolute honesty.

Anybody intending to write about his own life might well pin up a list of things to be avoided – vanity, self-complacency, self-delusion, untruthfulness, boasting, vindictiveness, too much self-justification, and, perhaps above all, taking for granted that what interests himself is bound to interest other people. How well did Leonard Woolf avoid these things? So much better, surely, than most autobiographers that this alone puts his book in an un-crowded class. His own guiding principles are to be found in the second volume, called *Growing*:

> The only point of an autobiography is to give, as far as one can, in the most simple, clear, truthful way, a picture, first of one's own personality and of the people whom one has known, and secondly of the society and age in which one has lived.

Like himself, his book has charm, dignity, a dry humour, and the absence of self-pity that goes with stoicism. I should think few women could read with indifference his account of the perpetual strain of his married life, during which he was always alert to guard his wife against the dangers of her mental instability. Any-body interested, not only in Virginia Woolf but in the art of biography, or in the evolution of an independent man, who had close experience of colonial administration in the days of the British Empire, of socialist politics over the last fifty years, and of being a distinguished publisher for almost as long, is likely to find this, to a great extent, a most engaging book, and to feel that he is being taken into the confidence of the writer as if he were an equal. What has been said about the book so far, in public and private, shows that the rare personality of Leonard Woolf, his plain speaking in good, straight, unaffected prose, the story he has to tell, and the development of his opinions, are fascinating enough to float the reader over any passages where the subject-matter may possibly seem unimpelling.

I have mentioned the development of Leonard Woolf's opinions. I might have said the development of his emotions, because this Cambridge-bred rationalist was never aloof or detached; he was an emotional, even a passionate man, and knew it. Off he went as a young man to Ceylon, and there became a diligent, conscientious, capable servant of the Crown. He went there as what he calls 'an unconscious imperialist', but emotion, perhaps more than reason, turned him against imperialism. Back to England he came, a newly fledged Liberal, but the emotional shock of a close-up view of poverty in Hoxton turned him from a Liberal into a Socialist. His passions, he says, were always especially aroused by injustice, and among them were anger and disgust.

How lucky it is that he lived long enough to round off the story of his life. If one says that the fifth and last volume is evidently the work of an old man, that doesn't mean that it shows any failure in reasoned argument or in clarity and precision of language. There's nothing senile about it, in the clinical sense. What most plainly shows it to be an old man's work is its prevailing tone of dis-illusionment. Nothing can be more deeply wounding than the disillusionments of a child or an adolescent, but the disillusion-ments of an old man are old scars, slowly formed over the wounds of a long lifetime.

To speak of disillusionment is not to speak of pessimism.

Leonard Woolf loved life and enjoyed many things right up to the time of his last illness. But he did feel, and had reason to feel, like most people who can recall the atmosphere in the early years of this century and who were living above the poverty-line, that the kind of hopefulness or confidence which largely imbued life in Western Europe before 1914 became, from then on, hardly tenable and eventually impossible. He felt that civilization, in his sense of the word, had largely declined and had on a large scale been destroyed, and he gives his reasons for this opinion. He came to feel that his own efforts to work for a better world had been wasted:

> Looking back at the age of eighty-eight over the fifty-seven years of my political work in England, knowing what I aimed at and the results, meditating on the history of Britain and the world since 1914, I see clearly that I achieved practic-ally nothing. The world today and the history of the human anthill during the last fifty-seven years would be exactly the same as if I had played pingpong instead of sitting on com-mittees and writing books and memoranda. I have therefore to make the rather ignominious confession to myself and to anyone who may read this book that I must have in a long life ground through between a hundred and fifty thousand and two hundred thousand hours of perfectly useless work.

He defines the purpose of that work as having the direct object of influencing men's minds and so of altering the course of historical events. Perhaps his political work might have had more effect if he had aimed at influencing men's emotions rather than their minds: it is a mistake often made by reasonable men, that they think they're addressing their equals when they're really addressing their inferiors.

Can it be true that in his political work Leonard Woolf 'achieved practically nothing'? Only, I think, if he was more ambitious and more idealistic than appears. He seems to have invented the League of Nations, and if that came to nothing, because of cynicism and coldly competitive nationalism among governments scrambling for power, surely to have designed such a castle in the air at least proves him a remarkable architect.

What he doesn't seem to have allowed for in his book is the extent of the influence of his life and his writings, not least of his autobiography.

This makes me think of two lines of Emerson's:

> Nor knowest thou what argument
> Thy life to thy neighbour's creed hath lent.

I should have thought that all that work for the Fabian Society and the Labour Party, all that journalism, both political and literary, for the *Political Quarterly*, for the *Nation*, and for the *New Statesman*, all the fruitfulness and range of Leonard Woolf's work as a publisher, all those personal relationships, all that passion for justice, all the noble and impressive examples of his personality and behaviour in everyday life, at home and abroad, must have had a wide and lasting effect on other people, tending, one might hope, to make some of them just a shade more tolerant or imaginative, just a shade more thoughtful. But perhaps that's mere sentiment, and his own verdict may be more realistic.

Can one say that there are in his autobiography any striking new ideas? On the whole one is more impressed by him as an interpreter than as an originator, but sometimes he sets out a theory which seems new and important. Such is his notion that all occupations, professions, and individuals 'create around themselves a kind of magnetic field':

> Everyone walks through life, materially and spiritually, enveloped in a magnetic field of his own personality which gives to everything and everyone entering the field a magnetized reflection of his ego, a meaning and value which he alone in the world feels and understands. Occupations and professions, even institutions, acquire the same kind of magnetization ... The psychology of this occupational hallucination or self-deception is shown most obviously and commonly in the enormous, sacred importance which the vocation and everything connected with it acquire in the eyes of those who practise it.

This notion, with its development in the pages that follow, seems to me something that really can make one see oneself and other people in a new and clear, if decidedly chilling, light.

No wonder Leonard Woolf was disillusioned. He believed toleration to be at the foundation of all civilized life and society, and considered that in the last thirty years there had been 'more horrors, misery, and barbarism than in any other thirty years of recorded history'. Why, then, did he persist in what he calls those 'two hundred thousand hours of perfectly useless work'? Because he thought that although, as he says, 'in the eye of God or rather of the universe' (and it is amusing to see him shying away from the word 'God' and endowing the universe with, of all things, an eye):

in the eye of the universe, nothing human is of the slightest importance; but in one's own personal life, in terms of humanity and human history and human society, certain things are of immense importance: human relations, happiness, truth, beauty or art, justice and mercy ... Though all that I tried to do politically was completely futile and ineffective and unimportant, for me personally it was right and important that I should do it, even though at the back of my mind I was well aware that it was ineffective and unimportant. To say this is to say that I agree with what Montaigne, the first civilized man, says somewhere: 'It is not the arrival, it is the journey which matters.'

It was from that last phrase that he took the title of the last volume of his book, *The Journey not the Arrival Matters*. Montaigne, of all writers, was one of the most congenial to him. I remember once remarking to him that I had deliberately put off reading Montaigne until I was almost middle-aged, because I felt that one mightn't be able to appreciate him properly when one was young and headstrong. The memory of the look he gave me reminds me a little of what he says in his first volume about the look he saw at times in the eyes of Virginia and Vanessa Stephen when they were young. Their silence and quiet appearance, he says, were like those of a seemingly quiet horse, but if you look carefully, 'you observe at the back of the eye of this quiet beast a look which warns you to be very, very careful ... a look of great intelligence, hypercritical, sarcastic, satirical.' I'm afraid he thought me not fully aware that a proper grasp of Montaigne was a basic necessity in the education of a civilized man.

Most of the taboos which used to inhibit autobiographers have collapsed. They can now discuss in public what used to be thought private – the failings, for instance of their parents, nearest relations, and friends, and can be frank about sex. The most striking candour in Leonard Woolf's book is about his wife. Long before the first volume appeared, it was common knowledge that Virginia Woolf had killed herself. It is now common knowledge that she had twice previously attempted to do so, and in the fifth volume there is a straightforward account of her end.

Naturally this is distressing to read, and no doubt some will think that it shouldn't have been published. A few people still believe in distinguishing between what is public and what is private. But if it's painful to read about Virginia Woolf's precarious sanity, it's heartening to read of her husband's unrelaxing care of her, and of her acknowledgment, in her last words, of the happiness of her married life, which she called 'the greatest possible'. Her suicide can be seen as an act of self-sacrifice. 'Without me you could work,' she said in the note she left for him, and it may be that unless she had left him he wouldn't have been able to write the story of his life: he certainly couldn't have written it in the way or perhaps on the scale he did write it.

Though candour in print is now allowed, one taboo is still strong. People will write about what they do, or would like to do, between the sheets, but not about what they do among their balance sheets: it would be a bold autobiographer who would expose his overdraft in public. This taboo was set aside by Leonard Woolf, and he lets us into the penetralia of his book-keeping. In his third volume, *Beginning Again*, he does this, he says, to show the effect of his and his wife's earnings upon their writings and their lives. For instance, they started the Hogarth Press in 1917 on a capital of forty-one pounds, fifteen shillings and threepence, and in 1921 it looked as if Mr and Mrs Woolf couldn't count on earning more than twenty-three pounds a year between them by writing novels.

Perhaps this sort of frankness is not too difficult for an old man who has had to worry about money in earlier years and no longer has to worry about it.

We all have to think about money – the wherewithal, the necessary – and its importance became clear to Leonard Woolf when he lay in bed as a child, as he describes in his first volume, and realized that his father was dying and comparative poverty would result. 'From my twelfth to my twenty-fourth year,' he says, 'we had to be extremely careful of every penny.' Apart from that perhaps it's fair to link Leonard Woolf's concern with money with his being a Jew. His appearance and character were inseparable from his Jewishness. I've heard it said that he looked like some Old Testament prophet. Which? Jeremiah, perhaps. Leonard Woolf's energy, his stoicism, his good judgment, his imagination, his respect for learning and for art and literature, his loyalties to persons and ideas – these are virtues not necessarily Jewish, but in him they do seem characteristically Jewish. So, I think, does his fastidiousness, and certainly his unending diligence.

> To work and work hard was part of the religion of Jews of my father's and grandfather's generations ... There is, I think, or there was, a tradition consciously or even unconsciously inculcated in Jews that one should work and work hard, and that work ... is a proper, even a noble, occupation for all the sons of Adam.

Although a man of great qualities – wisdom, honesty, humanity, and so on – Leonard Woolf had, I'm glad to say, his weaknesses or blind spots. He could be much irritated sometimes by others who differed from him, and so proved themselves incapable of seeing reason. Another weakness was that his antipathy to established religions seemed to make him quite blind to their civilizing influences and to the good they have done and continue to do. His atheism or agnosticism, or whatever it was, struck me as being narrow – as narrow as, say, Calvinism. Then he had a distaste for those who take their own social position, power, and privilege for granted, and this could blind him to their merits. A bias against such institutions as monarchy and aristocracy may be justifiable, but may become absurd. I remember, in a friendship of forty years, a few occasions when, in my opinion, he allowed prejudice to get the better of reason and toleration. For example, he refused to allow any merit to a man generally known to be of uncommon ability and intelligence.Why? Because this man, whom he had never met, happened to be of royal blood. And I remember his total refusal to tolerate praise of a writer of acknowledged talent, because, although she had rebelled against upper-class parents, she was thought by him to have behaved too much like the offspring of such parents.

I don't know if I've spoken of him and his book with the critical detachment that might be shown by somebody who never knew him. It's unlikely. In the mid-nineteen-twenties he published my first book, and, from that moment, he and Virginia Woolf treated me not merely as an author but gave me, so to speak, a chair at their table. He was one of several men of his generation, each old enough to have been my father, for whom I've felt a constant admiration, respect, and affection, and I see no reason to deny that I think his book as admirable, as lovable, and as completely out of the ordinary as he was himself.

[Review of *The Journey not the Arrival Matters*, broadcast 14 October 1969, and published, slightly abbreviated, in the *Listener*, 4 December 1969]

Francis Kilvert

Thirty-five years ago nobody had ever heard of Francis Kilvert, except members of his family and a few aged country-folk or their descendants. Today it seems hardly necessary to explain who he was, because he has come to be recognized as one of the best of English diarists.

Kilvert's presentation of country days and ways in mid-Victorian times is just as lifelike as what we find in novels of the period, but as it is factual, and apparently perfectly truthful, and full of well-observed detail, it gives, in a different way to that of the novelists, an invaluable picture of day-to-day existence. His Diary gives more than a picture, it creates an atmosphere, and evokes what would now be called a life-style.

The Diary is much more than a source of social history. Like the eminent novelists of his time, Kilvert was an artist. He was a prose writer of distinction, and while writing entertainingly about a variety of other people, he paints a self-portrait of a fascinating man whom readers of the Diary get to know with a special intimacy. A proof of his power to fascinate those who read him is that the Kilvert Society, which has now been flourishing for nearly a quarter of a century, has more than six hundred members and keeps on growing.

Francis Kilvert, like Thomas Hardy, was born in 1840. He was one of six children of a country parson, the rector of Hardenhuish, near Chippenham in Wiltshire. His father, the Reverend Robert Kilvert, augmented his stipend, like a good many other country clergymen in those days, by taking in pupils. One of his pupils happened to be Augustus Hare, who later became known as a writer of guide books and as a copious, name-dropping, and gossipy writer of memoirs. It is now fashionable to seek out instances of what is

called the seamy side of Victorian life, and Hare has left it on record
that life among the boys at Hardenhuish Rectory was not entirely
decorous:

> The first evening I was there, at nine years old, I was com-
> pelled to eat Eve's apple quite up – indeed, the Tree of
> knowledge of Good and Evil was stripped absolutely bare:
> there was no fruit left to gather.

The boys, according to August Hare, were 'a set of little monsters'.
As for the rector, he was ultra-Evangelical, a dry scholar, very hot-
tempered, entirely without originality, and with no knowledge
either of the world or of little boys. He punished his pupils fero-
ciously and unjustly for exceedingly slight offences; living under
this reign of terror they learnt nothing useful, and spent much time
learning by heart the Psalms and the Thirty-Nine Articles.

That was how Hare remembered life in the 1840s at Hardenhuish Rectory, but Kilvert later looked back upon it as what he
called his 'sweet old home', so perhaps the rector segregated his
sons from his pupils and gave them a less unpleasant time. From
there Kilvert went to a school near Bath kept by his uncle, another
parson, and then up to Oxford. He was ordained when quite young,
and spent a year acting as curate to his father, who had moved to
the neighbouring parish of Langley Burrell.

At the age of twenty-four he went as curate to the Reverend
Richard Lister Venables, the vicar of Clyro in Radnorshire. Mr
Venables was more a man of the world than Kilvert's father, and
he had even travelled in Russia and had written a book about it,
which was published by the ever-distinguished firm of John Murray.
He was kind to Kilvert, so was his sympathetic and understanding
wife, and so were many people in the neighbourhood, both of the
landowning and the labouring class. The surroundings of Clyro are
beautiful, and Kilvert was highly responsive to the landscape and
to the Border people. Not quite Welsh and not quite English, they
have a delightful character of their own, and round about Clyro
they grew as fond of Kilvert as he was of them. Altogether the
seven years he spent there seem to have been the happiest of his life.

At the age of thirty-one he went back as curate to his father in

Wiltshire for another four years. He was then presented to a remote living in Radnorshire, and in the following year to that of Bredwardine, on the Wye in Herefordshire, not far from Clyro. Soon after this he married a young woman called Elizabeth Rowland: he was thirty-eight, she was twenty-two, and he had known her for three years. They went off to Scotland for their honeymoon and returned to an affectionate welcome from his parishioners at Bredwardine in a downpour of rain. This saturated the triumphal arches erected for the occasion, but did nothing to dampen the presents and speeches, and the warm-hearted villagers took the horses out of the carriage and themselves drew it to the vicarage.

Within a couple of weeks Kilvert was dead. He had died suddenly of peritonitis, no doubt the result of a ruptured appendix – those were the days before appendectomy. He was only thirty-eight, and the year was 1879. He was buried there at Bredwardine, and his young widow went home to Oxfordshire and her father, did good works in the parish, and lived on for more than thirty years. She had hoped to be buried beside him, but left her demise a little too long. Two maiden ladies had been inserted, one on each side of her late husband, so poor Mrs Kilvert had to be deposited in a distant extension of the churchyard. It always seems to me that this circumstance might have furnished a motif for an ironical poem by Hardy.

Speaking of Hardy reminds me of a descriptive passage in Kilvert's Diary, which may well be called Hardyesque. In August 1873 Kilvert travelled up with Mr and Mrs Venables to a remote village in Radnorshire where a fête was being held.

> While the athletic sports were going on, I wandered away by myself into congenial solitude for a visit to the ruined Church of Llanleonfel ... The ruined Church tottered lone upon a hill in desolate silence. The old tombstones stood knee-deep in the long coarse grass, and white and purple flowers nodded over the graves. The door stood open and I went in. The window frames and seats were gone. Nothing was left but the high painted deal pulpit bearing the sacred monogram in yellow letters. Some old memorial tablets bearing Latin inscriptions in remembrance of Marmaduke

Gwynne and his family were affixed to the East Wall. The place was utterly deserted, there was not a sound. But through the ruined windows I could see the white tents of the flower show in the valley beneath. I ascended the tall rickety pulpit and several white owls disturbed from their day sleep floated silently under the crazy Rood Loft on their broad downy wings and sauntered sailing without sound through the frameless east and west windows to take refuge with a graceful sweep of their broad white pinions in the ancient yew that kept watch over the Church. It was a place for owls to dwell in and for satyrs to dance in.

It is long since the Church has been used, though weddings were celebrated in it after it was disused for other services. There is a curious story of a gentleman who was married here. Some years after his marriage his wife died, and it happened that he brought his second bride to the same Church. Upon the altar rails she found hanging the lace handkerchief which her predecessor had dropped at the former wedding. The Church had never been used nor the handkerchief disturbed in the interval of years between the two weddings.

That evocation of a solitude shows how fitting it is that Kilvert's gravestone was inscribed with the words 'He being dead, yet speaketh': through his Diary he not only speaks, but speaks with a living voice.

When the Diary came to light it was found to have been written in twenty-two notebooks, closely written in a conventional hand, with no margins, perhaps for economy's sake. It had apparently been kept continuously from January 1870 until five months before his wedding in 1879; but there were two large gaps, each of six months. The MS had been inherited by Kilvert's widow, and she is said to have destroyed the missing portions because she thought them too private and personal about herself. Not only about herself, perhaps. The first of them almost certainly contained some allusions to Kilvert's infatuation in Wiltshire with a handsome girl called Etty Meredith-Brown. We know she was handsome because we have a photograph of her and also a description of her by Kilvert:

> At 4 o'clock Miss Meredith-Brown and her beautiful sister Etty came over to afternoon tea with us and a game of croquet. Etty Meredith-Brown is one of the most striking-looking and handsomest girls whom I have seen for a long time. She was admirably dressed in light grey with a close fitting crimson body which set off her exquisite figure and suited to perfection her black hair and eyes and her dark Spanish brunette complexion with its rich glow of health which gave her cheeks the dusky bloom and flush of a ripe pomegranate. But the greatest triumph was her hat, broad and picturesque, carelessly twined with flowers and set jauntily on one side of her pretty dark head, while round her shapely slender throat she wore a rich gold chain necklace with broad gold links. And from beneath the shadow of the picturesque hat the beautiful dark face and the dark wild fine eyes looked with a true gipsy beauty.

We know that rather more than a year later Kilvert parted from this young woman with what he called a clinging embrace and passionate kiss, because there is an entry in the Diary which tells us so, an entry which perhaps escaped either his widow's eye or her scissors. We know from her photograph that Mrs Kilvert, however amiable she may have been, was extremely unlike a ripe pomegranate, and it seems probable that she could not view with equanimity either her late husband's amorous confessions or the prospect of their being read by strangers. The second missing portion of the Diary presumably contained an account of Kilvert's courtship and his engagement to herself, and it is disappointing not to have it.

After the printed Diary had become famous, an old lady who had been brought up in what was already beginning to be called the Kilvert Country – that is, the border region of Herefordshire and Radnorshire – and who had been alive in his time was asked, 'And what did your family think of Kilvert?' 'I don't suppose they thought of him at all,' she rather snubbingly replied. 'After all, he was only the curate.' Only the curate! Now he is immortal, and they are forgotten.

There were legions of country curates in mid-Victorian days. We have it on the authority of Gladstone that, during the time when Kilvert was growing up, quite half the undergraduates at Oxford and Cambridge were reading for Holy Orders. Naturally curates, like other human species, were of widely varying characters and interests. No doubt some of them kept diaries, and no doubt most of these were of very slight significance, full of ephemeral trivialities: most diaries are like that. I cherish a typical entry from an ordinary diary, kept in the present century:

> Another miserable wet day, even wetter than yesterday. It is earnestly hoped that it will be less wet tomorrow.

Kilvert never wrote like that. It does seem wonderfully lucky that at least this one diary of exceptional interest and quality was kept in the 1870s by one country curate, and was eventually made public in the form of printed selections from what Mrs Kilvert did not put in the fire. It is equally lucky that she did not put it all in the fire. I was told by a member of the Kilvert family that there was always an understanding among them that Mrs Kilvert did not wish the Diary to be preserved. Thanks to the initiative of a more imaginative and intelligent person, a nephew of Kilvert's, now long dead, the process of editing it for print became possible.

Something must now be said about the editing of diaries, and of this diary in particular. Experience suggests that few diaries are worth printing, and very few indeed worth printing in full. If Kilvert's Diary, even after the amputations by his widow, had been printed as it stood it would have filled nine volumes, and such a bulky and expensive book by a man nobody had heard of could hardly have found a publisher, let alone enough public libraries or private readers to buy it: but Jonathan Cape launched the Diary, at a time when the Second World War was coming up. An editor's responsibility, in abridging a diary, is to concentrate what seems most characteristic of the diarist and his world and most likely, for one reason or another, to be of special or general lasting interest. There are always persons who suggest that some of the editor's omissions must have been of a scandalous or pornographic nature. This is not true of Kilvert's Diary: what was left out of it was mostly trivial, repetitive, or judged not to be of special value. What was printed can be now read not in nine but in three volumes, or still further abridged in one volume in paperback.

Can one speak of 'the diary' as one speaks of 'the novel' as a literary form? If so, it is a most difficult form. A diary is so personal that its effectiveness is specially dependent upon the private character, and particularly the honesty, of the writer. A poem, a play, or a novel can or must be imaginative, invented, fanciful, indirect, but a diary is direct. The diarist speaks in his own person, mostly about what has just happened, a few hours or even a few minutes before, and of its immediate effect upon himself and others. So does a reporter, but a diarist is quite different. A reporter is subservient, as a rule, to an editor; he is looking for news of what he supposes to be of instant public interest, which generally seems to mean something as horrible or depressing as possible: but a diarist is independent, and is recording, as truthfully as he can, private matters, or a private view of public matters, which he presumably supposes may be of future or even of continuing interest.

A diarist living in close touch with persons of great political, social, artistic, or scientific position, or distinction, or influence, may well feel that what they do or say in private may be worth recording; a careerist might want to keep in his diary a proud and self-justifying account of his arrival on each successive rung of the ladder to fame and fortune; but the motives of either of these cannot be much like the motives of an obscure country curate in mid-Victorian England. For whom would such a man as Kilvert be keeping a diary? Was it for the benefit of his descendants, if he should ever have any? (In fact, he left none.) Was it to re-read in his old age? (In fact, he died in his thirties.) Was it because he had something sensational to record or confess? He made no such claim. Kilvert could not, I think, be called introspective or introverted, but he did once ask himself, in his Diary, why he was keeping it. This is what he wrote:

Why do I keep this voluminous diary? I can hardly tell.

Partly because life appears to me such a curious and wonderful thing that it almost seems a pity that even such a humble and uneventful life as mine should pass altogether away without some such record as this, and partly too because I think the record may amuse and interest some who come after me.

There is the point. Everyday life did not seem to him ordinary or humdrum; even what he called the humble and uneventful seemed to him 'curious and wonderful', therefore enjoyable. His responses to it were evidently more alert and sensitive than those of the people around him. He wanted to record it, to give it a lasting shape, to communicate it to others, to entertain them. This was the impulse of an artist.

One stormy afternoon in March, a hundred years ago, he was out in the hills near Clyro, when the dark clouds suddenly and dramatically began to roll away as he was looking across to the Black Mountains. He describes in some detail the dazzling revelation of white snow in a burst of sunlight in the clear blue sky:

> I never saw anything to equal it, I think, even among the High Alps... The sudden contrast was tremendous, electrifying. I could have cried with the excitement of the overwhelming spectacle. I wanted someone to admire the sight with me. A man came whistling along the road riding upon a cart horse. I would have stopped him and drawn his attention to the mountains but I thought he would probably consider me mad. He did not seem to be the least struck by or to be taking the smallest notice of the great sight.

There is a curious parallel to this in another diary, an earlier one than Kilvert's. In fact it was written by a woman who lived not a hundred but a thousand years ago. She was Japanese, and her name was Sei Shōnagon. With a Kilvert-like attention to detail, she gives a beautiful account of raindrops sparkling on chrysanthemums and spiders' webs in the early sunshine of an autumn morning. 'I was greatly moved and delighted,' she says. 'Later I described to people how beautiful it all was. What most impressed me was that they were not at all impressed.'

This ancient diary was translated by that famous poet and orientalist, Arthur Waley, and it was from him that there came one of the greatest compliments yet paid to Kilvert. When Waley was on his death-bed in 1966, and in great pain, the book he wished to have read to him was Kilvert's Diary. After his death a passage was found sidelined in pencil and against it he had faintly written 'Like Chinese poem.'

What sort of man was Kilvert? His sensibility did not make him an aesthete or dilettante. He shows no knowledge or taste at all in architecture, painting, or music: one might say that his Diary is about people in a landscape; and surely that is mainly what makes a good diary – human interest in a particular environment, and a zest for life in the diarist. Kilvert's social status was that of a gentleman in Holy Orders, an educated man without private means. As a Churchman he had evidently been formed by his Evangelical father, but was ahead of his father in his ecumenical tendencies: he was capable of slipping into a Roman Catholic church to pray for Christians to be united. In those days a country parish was still a close community, and as a parish priest Kilvert was dutiful, devoted, and much loved.

His social and political views seem to have been conventional and unquestioning. He knew when local people had no blankets or boots or not enough to eat, and minded, and tried to help them, but except from hearsay he knew little, it seems, of industrial and urban miseries. He was conventionally patriotic, expressed no doubts about imperial expansion, and did not question the accepted ideas of the propertied class in which he moved as easily as among their tenantry. His status, his opinions, and his religion evidently gave him a sense of security, or at least of continuity. If he had no money, at least he knew where his next meal was coming from. A countrywoman whose mother had known and revered Kilvert once told me that when he had a chicken for his dinner he used to set aside half of it to take to some poor person who would be glad of it. This rather suggests St Martin bisecting his cloak for the beggar.

What did Kilvert look like? We have his photograph in profile. He is seated on a chair, wearing a clerical black frock-coat and floppy trousers, practical boots, a white bow-tie, and a thick dark beard which is virtually a mask. His thick, dark hair is shiny with pomatum. The camera may not lie, but it can anaesthetize a sitter, and the face is all but expressionless. The nose is short and straight, the eyes are averted from the camera, and appear small. We know there was something troublesome about his eyes, but not whether it was temporary or permanent. His sight was excellent, but at one point he believes that a girl is fond of him in spite of what he calls 'my poor, disfigured eyes'. What did he mean? Did he have just then, perhaps, a stye, or something like conjunctivitis? There is no sign of disfigurement in the photograph.

An old cousin of Kilvert's remembered him as 'very sleek and glossy and gentle, rather like a nice Newfoundland dog'; and he must have had an attractive voice. His father, after listening to him in church one morning, said, 'As you were preaching there came back upon my ear an echo of the tones of the sweetest human voice I ever heard, the voice of John Henry Newman. No voice but yours ever reminded me of him.' But Kilvert's dulcet voice and glossy sleekness did not make him a softy. He was a considerable athlete, not that he was interested in sport, but he was a vigorous walker in the Welsh hills and mountains. In fact he had great energy and vitality. For most people, whether in Victorian or any other times, life is largely an endurance test, but Kilvert wrote in his Diary, 'It is a positive luxury to be alive.'

It may have been; but the situation of a young and healthy man with natural appetites, hedged in by the taboos of a non-permissive society, and in no position to live, like some Victorians, a double life, even if he had wanted to, was not easy. When Kilvert, in his Clyro days, wanted to marry a gentle girl of his own class called Daisy Thomas, he was headed off by his intended father-in-law, not because of his character but because he was a penniless curate without apparent prospects. Having described the interview, which is as good as something in a novel, he admits that at the time he had only one sovereign in his possession, and he owed that.

Kilvert was extremely susceptible, and was always in love with somebody. A few years ago Richard Hoggart remarked that 'Kilvert had an enormous capacity for love in all sorts of aspects – for sensuality, for tenderness, for regard and affection ... a sort of love flowed from his finger-ends.' He was obviously attractive, in a magnetic sort of way, and knew it. 'It is a strange and terrible gift,' he wrote, 'this power of stealing hearts and exciting such love.' He did excite love and affection among all sorts of people, old and young, and notably in very young girls. Like his contemporary, Lewis Carroll, Kilvert doted on young girls. He idealized them, sentimentalized over them, and responded so warmly to their play-fulness that, even by present-day standards, he seems indiscreet. If there had been anything sinister in his attentions to them he would hardly have written so candidly in his Diary about his feelings. He could certainly have said, as Lewis Carroll once did, 'I am extremely fond of children, except boys.'

From his bedroom window in Clyro he had a view of a wooded hillside with a white farmhouse at the top, and when he looked up at it he used to think of a dairymaid who lived there. What he writes about her is not at all like a Chinese poem. Half erotic, half religious, it is a sort of Pre-Raphaelite rhapsody:

> The sun looks through her window which the great pear tree frames and lattices in green leaves and fruit, and the leaves move and flicker and throw a chequering shadow upon the white bedroom wall, and on the white curtains of the bed. And before the sun has touched the sleeping village in the shade below ... he has stolen into her bedroom and crept along the wall from chair to chair till he has reached the bed, and has kissed the fair hand and arm that lies upon the coverlet and the white bosom that heaves half un-covered after the restlessness of the sultry night, and has kissed her mouth whose scarlet lips, just parting in a smile and pouting like rosebuds to be kissed, show the pearly gleam of the white teeth, and has kissed the sweet face and the blue veined silky lashed eyelids and the white brow and the soft bright tangled hair, till she has unclosed the sweetest eyes that ever opened to the dawn, and risen and unfastened the casement and stood awhile breathing the fresh fragrant mountain air as it blows cool upon her flushed cheek and her half-veiled bosom, and lifts and ruffles her bright hair which

still keeps the kiss of the sun. Then when she has dressed and prayed towards the east, she goes out to draw water from the holy spring, St Mary's Well. After which she goes about her honest holy work, all day long, with a light heart and a pure conscience.

Such fanciful reveries are rare in the Diary, which mostly tells of things seen and heard, not imagined. Kilvert was always out and about. He was constantly asked out to dinners and picnics, croquet parties and archery parties at local country houses, and was evidently a welcome guest. Most of his time was taken up with 'villaging', as he called it, walking all round the parish to visit often remote dwellings, to comfort the old and the sick and the poor and the mad and the lonely. Their lives were often grim, and there are tales of suicides and murders. Memories went back a long way. He used to talk to a veteran of the Peninsular War, and help him to dig up his potatoes; people would tell him anecdotes of Charles II or Cromwell; and old Hannah Whitney in Clyro could remember talk of persons born in the early eighteenth or even the late seventeenth century, and could repeat their tales of the fairies in which they believed.

In the early part of the last century, before the Oxford Movement and the Evangelical revival had got under way, the Anglican religion had sunk, in some country places, into an extraordinary state of neglect. Kilvert now and then heard reminiscences of this:

Crichton said that old Boughrood Church was a most miserable place. The choir sat upon the altar and played a drum.

Then in Dorset:

The Vicar of Fordington told us of the state of things in his parish when he first came to it nearly half a century ago. No man had ever been known to receive the Holy Communion except the parson, the clerk, and the sexton. There were 16 women communicants and most of them went away when he refused to pay them for coming ... At one church there were two male communicants. When the cup

was given to the first he touched his forelock and said,
'Here's your good health, Sir.' The other said, 'Here's the
good health of our Lord Jesus Christ.'

One day there was a christening and no water in the font.
'Water, Sir!' said the clerk in astonishment. 'The last
parson never used no water. He spit into his hand.'

Kilvert was not pompous about his religion, and has some lively
anecdotes about mishaps or eccentricities in church and about a
most remarkable hermit whom he calls the Solitary. And there is a
charming little story about a child:

The Bishop of Worcester, who is singularly spare and
attenuated, was staying in a house. He observed a child looking at him very attentively for some time, and when the
Bishop left the room the child asked, 'Is the Bishop a spirit?'
'No, the Bishop is a very good man, but he is not exactly a
spirit yet. Why do you ask?' 'Because,' said the child gravely,
'his legs are so very thin, I thought no one but a spirit could
have such very thin legs.'

Kilvert was not always stuck in one place. He visits London,
Oxford, the Isle of Wight, Cornwall, Bath, and Bristol, and we
know he visited Switzerland and France. In good repute among the
local clergy, he was so well thought of at a higher, episcopal level
that he was offered the chaplaincy at Cannes, which seems an
unusual preferment for an unworldly and inconspicuous country
parson. His diary at Cannes, in what would then have been to him
an unfamiliarly grand, worldly, and cosmopolitan society, would
have been worth having, but his heart would not have been in it.
Cannes was, so to speak, in the Augustus Hare country, and Kilvert
had lost his heart to the country people round Clyro and Bredwardine. Perhaps that was why he declined the offer.

Kilvert had a lively interest in poets and poetry, and the Diary
has some interesting allusions to Wordsworth, and a valuable
account of a visit to William Barnes in Dorset. He also wrote
poetry himself, but his poems are quite without the sharp focus of
his prose; they are soft-centred, and in form and diction show the

typical weaknesses of the conventional minor verse of his time.

A man so fond of people and of chronicling their sayings and doings is unlikely to be perfectly solemn, and there is a good vein of humour in the Diary. There used to be a most delightful railway along the Wye Valley between Hereford and Brecon, and here is a delightful account of an old lady, Mrs Dew, making an outing by train from Whitney-on-Wye to Hereford and proving rather a trial to her son, a clergyman:

> At Whitney station Henry Dew and his mother, old Mrs Dew, got into the train to go to Hereford. They wanted to go second class but one carriage was full of farmers and another was full of smoke generated by the two captains, so they went first class and paid the difference. While Mrs Dew was standing upright in the carriage, the train snatched on suddenly, throwing her back breathless into her seat. The station master threw in a parcel of blankets after them and away they went, leaving on the platform a brace of rabbits which they were to have taken to the Frederick Dews. The rabbits were sent after them by the next train, but being insufficiently addressed and unable to find Mrs Dew they came back by the train following.
>
> Meanwhile Mrs Dew in Hereford had been much discomposed and aggrieved because her sons Henry and Frederick would not allow her to spend more than an hour and a half at Gethin's the upholsterer's, a time in which Henry Dew said he could have bought the whole town. He declared he never was so glad to get away from anywhere as from Gethin's shop where young Gethin and four shopmen were all serving Mrs Dew on the broad grin. Then Mrs Dew bought a large bag of buns and sweets for her grandchildren at Ayston Hill, the young Frederick Dews, but in the excitement of parting she forgot to leave the bag and brought it to Whitney. Then to crown all she was nearly driven over and killed by an omnibus in Broad Street. The omnibus came suddenly round a corner and she holloed at the driver and the driver holloed at her, the end of it being

that she was nearly knocked down by the pole. Her son Henry saved her and told her she was not fit to go about Hereford by herself. She said she was. He said she thought she was ten years old and could go anywhere and was as obstinate as she could be. While they were arguing a cab came round the corner and nearly knocked the old lady down again. 'There,' said her son, 'there you go again. Are you satisfied now?'

That might almost be a sequence from some farcical film. Mrs Dew, by the way, had the unusual distinction of having been kissed by Coleridge when she was a baby, of having had a sonnet addressed to her by Wordsworth, and of having broken off an engagement to one of Wordsworth's sons.

In various parts of the Diary there are scenes, incidents, anecdotes, and characters which would have done very well in some novel by Trollope or Dickens or Hardy, and there is a remarkable set-piece about the death at Worcester of a relation of the Kilverts, about her will, and about what Kilvert and his parents found when they went to her house near the Cathedral to attend her funeral, and to find out how she had disposed of her property, and whether they had benefited, and to what extent, by the will. This is a wonderfully vivid scene from mid-Victorian life, told with that skill which proves Kilvert a prose writer of real accomplishment, with a sense of drama, of character, and of irony. If there is one thing about his prose which is conspicuous it is that not a word is wasted, there is no padding, all is clear and orderly. His father may have been a dry old scholar, but Francis Kilvert was no doubt given by his father a proper grounding in Latin; he was taught how to put a sentence or a sequence of sentences together; and his own feeling for words, his delight in finding the right words to shape and colour what he wanted to say, and his delight in life, save him from ever being dry or dull.

Throughout the Diary there are exact and beautiful pieces of description – not 'fine writing', but perfect writing. It was said by the late Humphry House that Kilvert's 'great virtue is the power of conveying the physical quality of everything he describes', and at times one is reminded that he lived in the same era as the French Impressionists. Here is his 'great virtue' in a single sentence:

> The lurid copper smoke hung in a dense cloud over Swansea, and the great fleet of oyster boats under the cliff was heaving in the greenest sea I ever saw.

Kilvert had the good fortune to live in parts of the English or Welsh countryside which had, and still have, special beauties, and to be unusually aware of them. His England had its wrongs and its troubles, but the countryside did have a deep and ancient quietness which has gone for ever. Living before that horrible invention, the internal combustion engine, before the telephone, the radio, the aeroplane, and the pop festival, he experiences and continually fixes in words that marvellous lost peacefulness. If he had known that he was enjoying the great privilege of living in the last few remaining years of tranquillity he could not have taken more care to describe it.

Sometimes, on a quiet day in summer or autumn, the sort of day when any commonplace diarist would have felt that nothing whatever had occurred to write about, Kilvert would give a detailed account of what was to be seen or heard. Here is an example. April, 1870. It is Easter Eve in Clyro churchyard, and people are decorating the graves with primroses and other spring flowers:

> More and more people kept coming into the churchyard as they finished their day's work. The sun went down in glory behind the dingle, but still the work of love went on through the twilight and into the dusk until the moon rose full and splendid. The figures continued to move about among the graves and to bend over the green mounds in the calm clear moonlight and warm air of the balmy evening...
> At 8 o'clock there was a gathering of the choir in the church to practise the two anthems for tomorrow... The moonlight came streaming in broadly through the chancel windows. When the choir had gone and the lights were out and the church quiet again... as I walked down the churchyard alone the decked graves had a strange effect in

the moonlight and looked as if the people had lain down to
sleep for the night out of doors, ready dressed to rise early
on Easter morning. I lingered in the verandah before going
to bed. The air was as soft and warm as a summer night, and
the broad moonlight made the quiet village almost as light
as day. Everyone seemed to have gone to rest and there was
not a sound except the clink and trickle of the brook.

Five years later, on an afternoon in May, Kilvert is at home in
Wiltshire:

As I came down from the hill into the valley across the
golden meadows and along the flower-scented hedges a great
wave of emotion and happiness stirred and rose up within
me. I know not why I was so happy, nor what I was expecting, but I was in a delirium of joy, it was one of the supreme
few moments of existence, a deep delicious draft from the
strong sweet cup of life.

By a complex of lucky chances, one man, evolved by a particular
civilization, in a particular place and time, a man who had a healthy
appetite for life and who was uncommonly articulate, left on record
how the strong sweet cup of life tasted to him. By another tangle of
lucky chances, we can escape into his lost world, now almost as
remote as the world of a Chinese poem, though still just within
living memory, and we can enter into it so closely that it seems to
become part of our own experience.

[Read to the Royal Society of Literature, 19 July 1972. Published in *Essays by
Divers Hands*, 1975]

Admirations

II

Poets

Christina Rossetti

From time to time English literature is enriched by the work of several members of one family. There were the Brontës, for instance; then the Rossettis; and in our own day there are the Sitwells. There were three grown Brontë sisters and one brother; two Rossetti sisters and two brothers; one Sitwell sister and two brothers. In the case of the Rossettis, only one brother and one sister were important: William Michael Rossetti was rather a dull fellow, and Maria Rossetti is little remembered today.

A striking fact is that each of these little family groups produced one of England's best women poets – I mean Emily Brontë, Christina Rossetti, and Edith Sitwell. Apart from these three, there has been only one poetess of the first rank in England, Mrs Browning, and one in America, Emily Dickinson. A good many people must have wondered why it is so rare for women to write good poetry, and a good many theories must have been put forward in explanation. I think it would be generally agreed that a woman's mind and character are much less likely to be turned to poetry, and successfully turned, than a man's; that poetry is simply an art to which the special gifts of women, who excel in so many things, are not as a rule adapted. Feminists, on the other hand, may argue that women are often capable of writing good poetry, but have not yet been long enough or fully enough emancipated to prove it. Against this we might suggest that only a spiritual or emotional emancipation was needed to produce Emily Brontë, Mrs Browning or Christina Rossetti.

Let us consider Christina Rossetti more from the biographer's point of view than the literary critic's, and that may bring us a little nearer to understanding how she and her work came into being. She was born in 1830 and died in 1894. Her father was an

Italian, a poet, a revolutionary patriot, something of a scholar, and, although a Roman Catholic, something of a freethinker. Her mother was half Italian and half English, but of a decidedly English rather than Italian type of person and character: she was a devout member of the Church of England. It is necessary to stress these religious details, because religion was of paramount importance in Christina's life. We cannot say that Christina was formed more by her father than by her mother, or *vice versa*; but we know that she was specially devoted to her mother, to whom her first childish verses were addressed and to whom she remained always closely attached. I think we might be justified in saying that while Christina may have derived from her father much of the ardour of her temperament, as well as her lyrical impulse, her mother probably fixed her devotional tendencies in accordance with the teachings of the Church of England. This fixation formed Christina's mind to a great extent and imposed a rigid discipline on whatever impulsiveness, warmth and rebelliousness she may have inherited from her purely Italian father.

The Rossettis were poor, and as a young woman Christina worked for two or three years as a teacher, but she always lived with her family and had always that sense of comparative security which comes from being poor with the people one loves instead of being poor by oneself. She never made much money out of her poetry: for many years her income from her work was something less than £40 a year. But if money was not very important to Christina Rossetti (except that there was enough of it to enable her to write), her health, or rather her want of health, must be carefully considered.

She was fairly healthy as a child, but at the age of puberty she became what in those days was called 'delicate'. She was supposed to have angina pectoris, and then she was supposed to have been cured of it. Then she had an awful cough which lasted for years, and was thought likely to send her into what was known in those days as a decline – what we should now call tuberculosis. It has often been remarked that the swan-like neck of the typical Pre-Raphaelite beauty shows obvious signs of goitre: when Christina was just over thirty, she developed an exophthalmic goitre. This not only altered and for a time quite spoilt her good looks, it left her plump and with lasting heart-trouble. And then in the end she died of cancer. You may wonder why I dwell on these clinical details. The reason is, as her brother William explained in a memoir he wrote of her, that nobody can understand her who does not understand that she was a constant invalid, and sometimes so ill that the thought of death must have been uppermost in her mind or at least never long absent from it. Death indeed is a main pre-occupation in her poems. I am not a doctor, but I doubt if there was much understanding a century ago of the endocrine glands. It seems obvious now that one of Christina's chief troubles was hyperthyroidism, and this would explain to some extent the intensity of her temperament. Possibly if modern science had been able to diminish the secretions of her thyroid gland, her poetry might have run much thinner or dried up altogether.

So much for religion and health: now we must consider the subject of love, which, as we can tell from her poems, was, apart from God and death, her main concern. When Christina was seventeen, a minor Pre-Raphaelite painter called James Collinson fell in love with her, wished to marry her and was refused. Now Collinson had been brought up in the Church of England, but before meeting Christina he had been converted to the Church of Rome. This is thought to have been her reason for refusing him: perhaps it was not so much the idea of marrying a Roman Catholic that worried her, as the idea that there might be difficulties as to which faith her children should be brought up in. Having been refused, Collinson returned to the Church of England, proposed to Christina again, and was accepted. He then, after a while, went back to the Church of Rome, and Christina broke off the engagement. These manoeuvres took something under two years. Whatever respect we may feel for the fidgety conscience of Collinson, there is no doubt, as Christina's brother said, that he struck a staggering blow at her peace of mind on the very threshold of her life as a woman. For a mid-Victorian girl so intense, so deeply feeling, the disappointment, and perhaps the humiliation, cannot easily be measured.

Years later, when Christina was over thirty, her long and intermittent acquaintance with another man ripened into love. From a distance he appears more lovable than Collinson. His name was Charles Cayley and he was then about forty. He was an unworldly and absent-minded scholar, of sweet and simple character, a philologist and a translator of Dante, who had also written some verses of his own. In course of time he so far withdrew his mind from unworldly matters as to propose marriage to Christina. She loved him deeply, but thought it necessary to enquire into his religious views. She found them wanting, though it is not quite clear in what way. Cayley did not, like Collinson, keep skipping backwards and forwards between the Church of England and the Church of Rome. He had been brought up in the Church of England, but apparently he doubted whether Protestant Christianity was the absolute truth, and may have thought that other religions were just as valid and just as admirable as Christianity. At all events, Christina refused him. If he had been an ardent lover, he might have overcome her scruples; if she had married him, she might have been too absorbed by household cares to go on writing. But it is no good saying 'if': Christina's last chance of marriage was gone. She remained on affectionate terms with Cayley, but her deepest energies went into poetry and piety.

Taking a general view of Christina Rossetti's poetry, we might say that it is musical and melancholy. It is certainly easier to understand in the light of the main facts about her life, which I have just attempted to sketch for you. It does not lend itself easily to critical analysis; it is lyrical and instinctive, subtle and simple. Sir Walter Raleigh, one of her critics, thought her almost impossible to criticize. He thought that she owed her unique position among English writers to a simple loyalty to her own experience and vision, and that in this she was comparable to Jane Austen. We have seen what that experience was: it was the experience of a woman of deep feeling who was frustrated in love and continually oppressed by illness, and whose heart and mind were subjected to a religious discipline, but who could not help singing; her sensuousness, her playfulness, her longings and regrets, her dreams and fears and fantasies, all found expression in her poetry. She has been called morbid, and if it is morbid not to take an easy way out of one's difficulties, not to accept life on the cheap and easy terms that are good enough for most people, not to compromise, not to be ashamed to be sad and admit it; if it is morbid to be oppressed by the vanity of human wishes and worldly shows, well, then, she *was* morbid, and morbid in good company. But in reading her, we do well never to lose sight of the religious discipline which causes her to strike often a strong and stoic note. For instance, in one of the sonnets called 'Later Life', she says:

> When I was young I deemed that sweets are sweet:
> But now I deem some searching bitters are
> Sweeter than sweets, and more refreshing far,
> And to be relished more, and more desired,
> And more to be pursued on eager feet.

And she is confident of ultimate repose and reward, even though the road winds 'uphill all the way'. 'I am no summer friend', she says, 'but wintry cold':

> For I have hedged me with a thorny hedge,
>   I live alone, I look to die alone.
> Yet sometimes when a wind sighs through the sedge
> Ghosts of my buried years and friends come back,
>   My heart goes sighing after swallows flown
> On sometime summer's unreturning track.

The poems of Christina Rossetti which are among her most vivid, moving and enduring are those in which she sighs after 'summer's unreturning track'. Her regrets and frustrations were wonderfully fruitful in poetry.

I would like to end by quoting, not one of the most familiar of her lyrics, but the last four stanzas of the poem called 'Dream Love', which seems to me to convey a pleasure almost physical:

> Young Love lies dreaming
>   Till summer days are gone –
> Dreaming and drowsing
>   Away to perfect sleep:
> He sees the beauty
>   Sun hath not looked upon,

And tastes the fountain
  Unutterably deep.

Him perfect music
  Doth hush unto his rest,
And through the pauses
  The perfect silence calms:
Oh poor the voices
  Of earth from east to west,
And poor earth's stillness
  Between her stately palms!

Young Love lies drowsing
  Away to poppied death;
Cool shadows deepen
  Across the sleeping face:
So fails the summer
  With warm delicious breath;
And what hath autumn
  To give us in its place?

Draw close the curtains
  Of branchèd evergreen;
Change cannot touch them
  With fading fingers sere:
Here the first violets
  Perhaps will bud unseen,
And a dove, may be,
  Return to nestle here.

[*Listener*, 29 August 1946]

C. P. Cavafy

Most of those English readers who had heard of Cavafy by the mid-nineteen-twenties must have owed the pleasure to E. M. Forster. An essay in *Pharos and Pharillon* was devoted to this poet – 'a Greek gentleman in a straw hat', it may be remembered, seen in the streets of Alexandria, halfway between his flat and his office, pausing where 'kings, emperors, patriarchs have trodden the ground', and 'standing absolutely motionless at a slight angle to the universe'. Some account of his poetry was given, together with some translations which showed it to be unlike anybody else's, and the whole essay, so fresh in matter and manner, was a whetter of curiosity.

In the same far-off decade it was possible to buy in Athens and Alexandria a voluminous anthology of modern Greek poetry. Like some others it was fatuously comprehensive, and memory calls up specimens from a good many poetasters who had dipped their pens in honey and were much too ready to rhyme *louloudia* with *tragoudia*. Among them one came suddenly upon a small portrait of Cavafy, with an aloof air, a sad moustache, and the appropriate high collar of the nineteen-hundreds: beneath it was a short biographical note, and beneath that, like wrought gold, some of his poetry.

This reviewer had the honour of receiving from Cavafy copies of two volumes of his poems, printed in Alexandria – those of 1905–1915 and 1916–1918. Cavafy (1863–1933) took care to arrange his poems according to the dates of their composition, and some-times to annotate them with the dates of the real or imagined happenings which they commemorate. He was obsessed with the flight of time. A meditative poem called 'Since Nine O'Clock' ends with the lines:

> Half past twelve. How the hours have passed.
> Half past twelve. How the years have passed.

The two strains in Cavafy's poetry (or, as Mr Rex Warner calls them in his introduction, 'main sources of inspiration') are bound up with considerations of place and of specified epochs. Alexandria is the centre of his world, and his strongest feeling for Greek traditions seems to begin where what Mr Forster has called Public School Greece leaves off. A poet has his obsessions, and this non-heroic, non-political, non-topical, and essentially non-popular poet's imagination drew its nourishment from the scattered Hellenistic world with its mingling of races and cultures, from anecdotes and legends of Seleucid kings and Byzantine emperors, from Antioch and Alexandria, from records and memories, and, in his own life, from homosexual love affairs. There is much learning in Cavafy, and Professor John Mavrogordato, in his footnotes, indicates some of the literary sources. He has also given a list of those works on Cavafy, published in Greek since the poet's death, which are necessary to a full study of his life and writings. Above all, he has given us this most welcome English version of an extraordinary Mediterranean poet.

Demetrios Capetanakis, that gifted Greek poet and critic who died in England in 1944, singled out as a characteristic of modern Greek poetry 'the attitude of absolute freedom in facing Death with courage', and found examples of this attitude in Cavafy. Other characteristics of Cavafy's poetry are much more obvious. There is his sense of continuity, which seems to steep in the same ambience all his remotest and nearest evocations of Levantine life. Cavafy is like that old mirror which

> had seen, and seen,
> In the many years it had been
> In existence, thousands of things and faces;

and he has that kind of serene disillusionment and spiritual urbanity that is only to be found in old, noble, and corrupt civilizations. Uniquely mingled with his sense of history, or with his personal mythology of history, is his erotic intensity, and this is inseparable

from his candour and directness. He had the courage of his own
bias:

> Delight and perfume of my life for me, that
> I rejected
> Every indulgence in habitual loves.

A poem commemorating the consummation of a 'lawless pleasure'
touches upon a slight sensation of guilt and anxiety that followed it,
and ends:

> But for the artist how his life has gained.
> To-morrow, the next day, or years after will
> be written
> The lines of strength that have had their
> beginning.

Life has gained, and art has gained, and how can any gain be greater?
'Days of 1896' alludes to a puritanical community which 'had all
its values wrong' because it failed to allow for physical beauty or
the courage that does not hesitate to set

> The pure flesh that gives
> Pure pleasure to man

above worldly success and conventional ideas of honour and
reputation.

The sensuality of many of Cavafy's poems, though open, is
never crude. It is transmuted into poetry, exalted by the thought or
memory of pleasure, and by pleasure made fruitful for art and for
irrepressible and ever new pullulations of life itself. The tinge of
melancholy that imbues his work may be ascribed in part to his
acute sense of the transience of beauty and pleasure, to his detachment, and above all to his pervasive consciousness of time passing
– but not like a 'winged chariot'; behind every Cavafy poem time
can be heard ticking, not so much like a clock as a time-bomb.
His melancholy can flower as a kind of impassioned pity, as in the
early lines about the solitary old man who sits with a newspaper,
thinking of his missed opportunities, and who absurdly trusted
Prudence, with her false promise of 'Plenty of time. Another day.'

The originality and poetic force of Cavafy's collected poems are known outside the Greek-speaking world, but the modesty of Professor· Mavrogordato's note on his translation must not be allowed to obscure his great care and ingenuity or the service he and his publisher have done to literature by making these versions of the poems generally accessible to the English-speaking reader.

[*New Statesman*, 7 July 1951]

F. T. Prince

Mr Prince's merits as a poet have won him the recognition of other poets and of that small public which both reads and discriminates among contemporary writers of verse. He has been drawn upon by anthologists, and reviewers of varying weight, advancing their claims as talent-scouts or literary tipsters, have praised him. It is to be hoped that the publication of this volume, his second, will extend a reputation already established.

'Soldiers Bathing' is possibly the most impressive English poem associable with the Second World War. It appears here in a revised version and contains memorable statements of which the directness may suggest Wilfred Owen. For example, a sudden relaxation brings to the soldier a momentary forgetfulness of

> His hatred of the war, its terrible pressure that begets
> A machinery of death and slavery,
> Each being a slave and making slaves of others

and the dreadful assertion that

> Because to love is frightening we prefer
> The freedom of our crimes.

The compassion is worthy of Owen, but Mr Prince has attained a largeness of vision hardly within the scope of Owen, who died young and whose fellow-feeling was not discernibly strengthened by a Christian mysticism like that of Mr Prince. A dignitary of the Church was quoted the other day in the papers as having spoken of moral squalor and a want of intelligibility in verse today: he might be heartened by the nobility and lucidity of 'Soldiers Bathing'. The poem evokes a blessed evening interval in wartime, when soldiers, battleworn, are free to bathe playfully in a warm and tranquil sea; they are transfigured by the moment, by their own feelings, and by the poet's perception. He recalls a drawing by Michelangelo of a comparable scene, and another of a fiercer scene by Pollaiuolo, and in an instant all comes into focus in the light of history, of human nature, of the Redemption – of the knowledge (which is not the same as understanding)

That some great love is over all we do.

In a sense all Mr Prince's poems are love poems. A group of them here are classified as such: in their strict forms, their imagery, their intricate thought and emotion, they have a seventeenth-century air and yet a newness, and they tend to reverberate in the mind's ear:

And so we too came where the rest have come,
To where each dreamed, each drew, the other home
From all distractions to the other's breast,
Where each had found, each was, the wild bird's nest.
For that we came, and knew that we must know
The thing we knew of but we did not know.

There is also a group of translations from St John of the Cross, in which Mr Prince has 'tried to reproduce the effect of the Spanish rhythms in the stanza of Crashaw's *Weeper*', besides some early poems, including the two exquisite African flower-pieces, 'The Babiaantje' and 'The Moonflower'.

Two long and powerful pieces conclude the group of love poems. Both are concerned with the love of the unattainable or with an unattainable love. 'The Old Age of Michelangelo' is a passionate and crystalline conception of its subject – a spirit

Which is an infinite sea of love

and which sees itself, in a sustained image, as a Zeus unable, for want of wings, to seize the beloved being and so to

gain or regain
The sole pure love, and fence it with my wings.

This eloquent poem ends on a most telling note of pathos. A not wholly unrelated theme is that of 'Apollo and the Sibyl', in which the aged Cumaean Sibyl, alone,

And now a low brown person, shrinking slowly to a bag of
   skin,

dreams and ponders on all that she has forfeited by not accepting
the love of Apollo, until she is at last only a voice in a cave

                – And the sky opens
Like a fan its vault of violet light, unfolding,
A wide and wingless path to the impossible.

These poems have something definable in a word and especially
rare in an age when meanness and self-pity are literary fashions:
the word is splendour.

[Review of Soldiers Bathing,
London Magazine, August 1954]

R. S. Thomas

R. S. Thomas is Welsh, was born in Wales, and is the rector of a country parish there. He has published in Montgomeryshire three books of poetry: *The Stones of the Field* (1946), *An Acre of Land* (1952) and *The Minister* (1953). He has now united the three books, discarding some poems and adding new ones to make *Song at the Year's Turning*. He is a regional poet of much more than regional interest. His poetry is born of a sympathy and a struggle with his fellow-countrymen. A poet is liable to be a kind of exile in his own country or time: the consciousness of difference, and the effort to communicate it, may provide his motive power as a poet.

It is needful for a serious writer to try and measure his own limitations; it must be his hope and it may be his luck to transcend them. Much of the verse offered to editors and publishers, and some of the verse they cause to be printed, is deformed by the inability of its authors to harmonize what they intend to say with their way of saying it, or to convince even the well-disposed reader that it is worth saying. Looking for poetry, that reader is often confronted with feeble or facile or bardic posturings, empty rhetoric, strainings after effect, reach-me-down diction, turgidity, false simplicity or false complexity. Mr Thomas's poems never look as if they were saying something more important than the things they do say, but the significance of what he has to say is not invariably matched by the way he says it. There are moments when his lines are a shade prosy. Mr Betjeman tells us of the influence of Yeats upon Mr Thomas; this poet may have been helped by Yeats towards an admirable, colloquial directness without wholly guarding against momentary slackenings of tension that a short poem is unlikely to be able to afford. But Mr Thomas, we feel, is never bluffing; he is ours sincerely; he takes us directly into a world of his own. In that world he knows his way, or, when he does not know it, explores it without arrogance or prejudice. At first sight it appears a narrow world, but, illuminated by him, it is seen to be not so narrow. His unities of time, place, and action, and his integrity (to use a hackneyed word) distinguish him from the dipping, mobile, occasional, versatile kinds of poet. They make his poems cohere in an unusual way; it is as if they were all parts of a single poem. It might be difficult for an anthologist to single any of them out; few of them look like 'anthology pieces'; they are more like successive entries in a diary that traces the development of a single experience or phase of experience. Only the poetry itself can define this experience, but it can be indicated.

Mr Thomas's poems are a country priest's response to the atmosphere and look of his parish, and more especially to his parishioners; they are the product of his exploration of their lives, of his understanding and compassion as a man and as a priest. As much could be said of the prose of an earlier clergyman in Wales, Francis Kilvert, but Kilvert's Diary lacks the element of conflict that produces poetry. Living in a non-industrialized environment, Mr Thomas sees and hears natural phenomena, perceives their effect upon those beings who live nearest to them, and is conscious, as a townsman cannot be, of the fertility and fruitfulness of the soil and of the beauties of growth. At the same time he is deeply troubled by the apparently stunting and impoverishing effect upon the human spirit of wringing a living from the soil by incessant hard work. But if his toiling peasants, he seems to say, are thus spiritually gnarled and emotionally starved, if they do not show in their lives the exuberance, joyfulness, playfulness, spontaneous warmth or passion of nature, that is not only the fault of grubbing about in stony ground, it is a consequence of the puritanical and life-denying Welsh tradition of Calvinistic Methodism that has done much to form them. The long and dramatic poem called 'The Minister', which was written for broadcasting on the Welsh Regional service, tells of what happened to the Reverend Elias Morgan, B. A. Fearing beauty and 'nature's truth' he 'fell', as Mr Betjeman puts it, 'to railing against sin and leaving out charity until his heart was twisted and he died defeated by his own fierce creed':

> Is there no passion in Wales? There is none
> Except in the racked hearts of men like Morgan,
> Condemned to wither and starve in the cramped cell
> Of thought their fathers made them.
> Protestantism – the adroit castrator
> Of art; the bitter negation
> Of song and dance and the heart's innocent joy –
> You have botched our flesh and left us only the soul's
> Terrible impotence in a warm world.

The peasantry of whom Mr Thomas writes are a survival, almost an anachronism. His living among them and his involvement with them link him with older poets and isolate him from his contemporaries among English poets, but there is nothing remote or sentimental or what is called 'nostalgic' about him; he is deeply engaged with actualities. Round the obscure, small village spins 'on slow axis' a world 'vast and meaningful', everything matters, the transient is seen in the light of the eternal. The man in the field, 'gaitered with mud', is also human, and although

> the eyes,
> Fuddled with coldness, have no skill to smile,

the man's speech has in it 'the source of all poetry'. However parched, frustrated, indifferent, or hostile a man's nature may be, he is still a man, never to be despised, never beyond salvation. The Christianity of this poet is implicit, not paraded, but there are moments when it shows itself directly and powerfully, as in the poem 'In a Country Church':

> To one kneeling down no word came,
> Only the wind's song, saddening the lips
> Of the grave saints, rigid in glass;
> Or the dry whisper of unseen wings,
> Bats not angels, in the high roof.
>
> Was he balked by silence? He kneeled long,
> And saw love in a dark crown
> Of thorns blazing, and a winter tree
> Golden with fruit of a man's body.

In whatever direction this poet develops, he is likely to be solitary, singular, quite apart from what is merely fashionable, and happy in the exactness of his senses. He sees how

> the snow made room
> On the sharp turf for the first fumbling lamb;

he sees, hears and feels

> the hissing swarm
> Of winged oats busy about the warm stalks.

[Review of *Song at the Year's Turning*,
London Magazine, March 1956]

John Betjeman

The public success of this book has given special pleasure to those who have been declaring a strong bias in favour of its author since the days of *Mount Zion*, more than a quarter of a century ago. He has now caught and held the attention of many for whom the very word 'poetry' had become a synonym for ennui. This break-through, a triumph for poetry as well as for Betjeman, has no doubt been made much less difficult by his emergence as a public personality, visible, audible, likable, and a champion and defender of things which, though neglected by many, have a continuing place in English affections and the English conscience – the Anglican faith, for instance, and that great national treasure, the parish churches. By various means he has succeeded in touching a host of poetry-contemners, amusing them, making them clearer to themselves, and enlarging and enriching their views of their common inheritance in the country they inhabit as well as of poetry itself. Two of our most outstanding national fortes are mechanical inventiveness and poetry, and it is good to see one helping the other, as when broadcasting and television, by enlarging the poet's audience and projecting the poet's personality, give to poetry new scope and new audiences. These media have given a new impetus to the poet as entertainer – Dylan Thomas, for instance. (Annoying, though, that we shall never see Tennyson or Chaucer on the evening screen, or Skelton, or Burns.)

The poetry of Betjeman is a wonderful antidote to a diet of headlines. But it is not wholly palatable to those who think it obligatory for a poet to hold the same views as later and younger poets about the matter and manner of poetry, or who think that to cherish what is inherited is sentimental and blameworthy, an escape from present responsibilities and a refusal to share anxieties about the future. Betjeman, remaining true to the revelations of an intensely impressionable childhood and to values then inculcated, cannot be expected to compromise with what seems to him unworthy of them. The pealing of church bells which excited his early hearing and which haunts his work has prevailed over other sounds, and he writes as a Christian, with a sense of good and evil and of the inadequacy of human complacency, and trying to cultivate faith, hope, and charity – uphill work, at times, in what has been called the century of the common man. Betjeman is not satisfied that man should be common or should try and enforce commonness. His whole work is a celebration of what is rare, personal, choice, wayward, unstandardized. His poetry is *sui generis*, euphonious, intelligible, witty, tender, sad, and funny. It has a range of human interest that may seem puzzling to less feeling natures, and a variety and exactness of observation that obviously startle unexercised eyes, ears, and imaginations.

Betjeman's progress from a small audience to a large one is characteristic of a creative original. Evidently at Oxford, if not earlier, his gifts were appreciated and encouraged by a few of his contemporaries. Others were ready to write him off as flippant, precious, affected, out of touch with his time, or simply cracked. And even now, the idiosyncrasy of his attitude to persons, places and things seems still to cause much misunderstanding. Nothing could be stupider than to suppose that to write playfully, teasingly, or ambiguously is to write as a humbug with tongue in cheek: this is an honest and consistent poet, and all his poems, even those which seem to irritate some readers, belong together as parts of a deeply felt and singularly chanted declaration about life. But there is never any scarcity of solemn prigs even among those whom an expensive education might have been expected to loosen up, and there are always plenty of inelastic minds incapable of acclimatization in that borderland where solemnity and playfulness intermingle. Some of these have long been disconcerted to find Betjeman finding beauty in what they supposed ugly, value in what they believed worthless, pathos in what they had not noticed at all, and apparently even larking about with ecclesiastical, and therefore sacred, themes. To them it is perhaps not much good explaining that one only bothers to tease those one has an affection for, that one can afford to be jocund about what commands one's devotion, and that where there is wit there is bound to be the *play* of wit.

Betjeman's intense Englishness may be a limitation but it is not a weakness. His rootedness in tradition, his susceptibility to his environment, his sense of belonging to it and his affection for it, and his ability to draw nourishment from varied, neglected, or supposedly infertile strata of social life and history, have done much to make his poetry possible. It is true that his nuances and his profusion of precise and specialized detail might quickly madden a translator. But already, no doubt, bespectacled students in Sendai or Seattle must be having an enjoyable time, trying to crack conundrums on every page, raising questions, compiling notes, planning glossaries, and worrying out the significance of allusions to hymnology, bell-ringing, suburban etiquette, or branded domestic commodities, before trying to hunt out and sort out real or supposed influences of, say, Tennyson, Calverley, J. M. Neale, Crabbe, Butterfield, John Meade Falkner, Sir Ninian Comper, John Piper, Dr E. E. Bradford, or novels about public school life.

Even those who are prepared to accept that the Englishness of this poet and the nature of the things that move him must exclude from his work evidence of direct concern with nuclear fission, space travel, the Beat generation, Zen, 'abroad', 'foreigners', race riots, or other cognate themes, even they are sometimes disturbed by his habit of looking fondly backward (which they call 'nostalgia') and by what they regard as his class-consciousness. It is perhaps worth remarking that Betjeman's recognition of some of the achievements, merits, and charms of the nineteenth century follows properly on the natural reaction of the Bloomsbury generation, born in mid-Victorian times, against Victorian values. The Betjemanian rehabilitation of Victorian architecture, and his delight in the surviving lights and shades of Victorian and Edwardian life, have restored a balance of judgment and have had an unprecedented influence on English taste. As for the charge of class-consciousness, those who advance it seem chiefly galled by the piece called 'How to get on in Society'. This is a light and fanciful mockery of the false refinement of those who talk of the 'lounge' and the 'toilet'. It may seem to imply an attack upon the standards of those who seem to Betjeman to be spoiling England by a want of good judgment. He has the right to attack them. But in these lines he does seem to lay himself open to a charge of pharisaism, and to be flattering in a rather uncomfortable way the vulgarity of those who think superiority lies in the acceptance or mastery of a system of petty verbal taboos. All the same, the *vers de société* of a classless society would not seem to promise much fun – or much pathos. And it is for the music of his variations on the funny and the pathetic, and for his ability to give them dignity and at times the touch of terror, that this poet is being and seems likely to go on being re-read.

[Review of *Collected Poems,*
London Magazine, March 1959]

Charles Tennyson Turner

After Tennyson's brother Charles had rebuilt the church at Grasby in Lincolnshire, where he was the settled incumbent, a sonnet was composed in his honour. It was the work of the Reverend Richard Wilton, and was entitled 'On the new Church Spire at Grasby, in connexion with the Poetry of Charles Tennyson Turner'. Not a powerful piece, it rejoiced that the spire would last for ages, and that beneath it had grown 'another structure, not of stone', which would 'lend its beauty to the aftertime' and make Grasby famous.

It cannot be supposed that Charles Turner's poetry is widely known today, but it has special virtues, and it deserved to be made newly accessible. The two editors, Mr John Betjeman and Sir Charles Tennyson, have made an almost perfect selection from it, representing rather less than one-third of the whole, which consists almost entirely of 342 sonnets. They have provided a sympathetic introduction to this gentle and retiring poet, a photograph of him, and a reproduction of a contemporary view of Grasby. And the format of the book is altogether pleasing.

Turner has always had devotees. Those who take up this selection must surely find how well the two editors have done their work. Only very few of the more memorable sonnets are missing. A claim could be made for 'The Wood-Rose' (No. 192 in James Spedding's edition of *Collected Sonnets* by Turner, published in 1880) with its quick movement of dragon-flies 'glimpsing about the rosy sprays':

> Light, flitting forms, that haunt our ponds and wells,
> Seen, lost and seen, along the reedy brink.

And among the sonnets on religious themes is one memorable for
its mild and touching deploring of excess in the cult of Mariolatry.

The picture of Turner that emerges from what he himself wrote
and from what has been written about him – by Hallam Tennyson,
for example, by Canon Rawnsley, by Spedding, by Sir Harold
Nicolson, and by the present editors – is of a modest man, simple,
devout, and sensitive. He had his weaknesses: his delight in little
things, which can be called childlike, does at moments verge on
slightness. But the poet who, when young, had won applause from
Coleridge, and who retained the admiration of Alfred Tennyson,
is seen to be a perfect miniaturist and perhaps something more.
His freshness and exactness of observation are such that even
within the strict limits of the sonnet (limits which he would at times
deliberately and effectively overstray) he seems to be minting
something new. And it is risky to suppose that small themes treated
with a charming tenderness can only lead to a namby-pamby kind
of poetry. Alfred Tennyson thought his brother's tenderness comparable with that of the Greek Anthology; and it is interesting to
learn that Charles, reading his poems aloud, had a voice of 'grandeur'
and 'deep organ tones' – and a Lincolnshire accent stronger than
Alfred's.

As a poet he seems to have another affinity which could not have
been known to himself and could hardly have been noted in his
own time; it is an affinity with the *haiku* poets of Japan. Again and
again, usually in a line or two, Turner's exact evocation of something observed and poignantly felt seems to bring one to the very
edge of deeper emotion, to reminders of loss or longing, illusions
of peace, or perceptions of mortality:

> The low of oxen on the rainy wind,
> Death and the Past, came up the well-known road.

or

> The white-arm'd girls in dark blue bathing-gowns,
> Among the snowy gulls and summer spray,

or

> The moonrise seems to burn a golden oil,
> To light a world of plenty, while it shows

The woodland, listening in its dark repose.

These are accents that go with what Charles Turner himself called 'old ruralities', with the quiet world of the now lost English countryside, but they are not the less true for that, nor the less personal to this poet, nor the less worth preserving and remembering.

[Review of *A Hundred Sonnets, The Times Literary Supplement,* 23 December 1960]

Thomas Pringle

A few weeks ago I saw in *The Times Literary Supplement* a brief notice of a new biography of Thomas Pringle (1789–1834), published in Cape Town by the distinguished publisher Balkema. The reviewer called Pringle a 'writer and reformer'. So he was, but I thought he could more fittingly be described as 'poet and reformer', and I wrote to the editor to say so. Coleridge, I remarked, had declared a poem by Pringle to be 'among the two or three most perfect lyric poems in our language', and I said I thought Pringle deserved to be better remembered than he is.

I then took down from my shelves a copy of *The Poetical Works of Thomas Pringle: with a Sketch of his Life*, by Leitch Ritchie, published by Moxon in 1839. This copy came from a barrow in the Farringdon Road more than thirty years ago. I don't believe it is a very rare book, but I have always thought it a pleasing object. It is handsomely bound, and contains the armorial bookplate of a Scottish gentleman, which indicates that it was No. 238 in the section of his library occupied by poetry. The frontispiece is an engraved portrait of Pringle.

One would guess, if one knew nothing about him, that he was a lightweight in body, with a character of sense and sensibility. His rather large eyes show, or seem to show, not so much a 'fine frenzy' as a power of seeing and telling the truth. On the title page there is a romantic engraving of an African landscape with figures grouped in the radiance of a setting sun, and in the middle of the book is a full-page engraving, after C. Landseer, to illustrate one of Pringle's poems.

Not having seen the new life of Pringle, I don't know whether it has new things to say or whether the author has done any special research. As a poet, Pringle is interesting as a lesser Romantic, reacting, in the spirit of his eminent contemporaries, to a completely new environment, at that time almost as remote as some distant world. His peculiar importance is that he was the first English-speaking poet to live and write in South Africa.

Pringle came of a family of Border farmers in the region of Kelso, where he was sent to the grammar school; he went on from there to Edinburgh University. An accident in infancy made him lame for life, but he was no weakling, and his early hatred of oppression caused him to organize and lead a body of forty or fifty young men in a protest demonstration in Edinburgh. He married, tried to make a living by literary journalism, and then decided to go to South Africa (1820) with a party of emigrants.

After two years of real pioneering in the hinterland of Algoa Bay he went to Cape Town, where he successfully ran a school and a paper, but he stood up to the tyrannical governor, Lord Charles Somerset, who tried to impose censorship, and this ruined him. He left the Cape for London in 1826, became secretary of the Anti-Slavery Society (and also editor of the annual *Friendship's Offering*), and was killed by tuberculosis in 1834, aged forty-six.

That very sketchy outline of his life can give no idea of his courage and energy. Again and again the facts show him putting matters of principle – his belief in justice, freedom, and humane treatment for all human begins, irrespective of race – above his personal comfort and well-being. As a reformer, he worked with and won the respect of Wilberforce, Zachary Macaulay, and Clark-son; as a poet, he is especially esteemed in South Africa, though his enlightened views on racial justice differ greatly – to put it mildly – from those of the present régime there.

The whole subject of English colonial literature, comprising that of the former Empire and the Commonwealth, and merging with that of recently emancipated countries where English is written, has at last been recognized as important, and promoted to the rank of an academic study. The University of Texas, in particular, has formed a large library of relevant printed and manuscript material, which is no doubt being progressively en-larged and classified.

It has, I notice, besides the Moxon *Poetical Works*, Pringle's

Ephemerides (Smith, Elder, 1828), and his prose narrative, *African Sketches* (Moxon, 1834). It also has, edited by Pringle, *The Anti-Slavery Album: Selections in Verse* (Howlett and Brimmer, 1828); *Some Account of the Present State of the English Settlers in Albany, South Africa* (Underwood, 1824) and *Narrative of a Residence in South Africa* (Moxon, 1835).

Perhaps Pringle's first appearance in an anthology was in *Albyn's Anthology* in 1816, when he was a clerk in the Scottish Records Office. A contribution to *The Poetic Mirror* was praised by Scott, with whom he became acquainted. And I have a note that two of Pringle's poems are to be found in *The Bow and the Cloud* (1834), a collection of prose and verse by various hands, 'illustrative of the Evils of Slavery', the proceeds of which were to be devoted to 'the West Indian Negroes'.

But I am not a bibliographer, and much as I admire Pringle's energies as a humanitarian and 'reformer', am chiefly interested in his poetry. What of the poem that Coleridge praised so strongly? This is 'Afar in the Desert'. It is strange that it has not more often appeared in anthologies, whether of Romantic or of nineteenth century verse, or of English poetry in general. It is written in the first person, ostensibly Pringle, who rides away into the African wilds with a 'silent Bush-boy' on foot beside him, and a gun in his hand.

It is hardly a desert into which he rides, because there are allusions to water and forests, but it is a solitude – and an escape. Away from regrets, the sorrows of exile, and human wickedness:

> ... scenes of oppression, corruption, and strife –
> The proud man's frown, and the base man's fear, –
> The scorner's laugh, and the sufferer's tear, –
> And malice, and meanness, and falsehood, and folly,

he begins to feel 'freedom, and joy, and pride'. Those were the days of plentiful big-game, and perhaps he was the first to speak in an English poem of the hartebeest, the springbok, and the quagga. Further on, he does come to 'a region of emptiness, howling and drear', where practically nothing grows, and the fauna are lizards, snakes, and bats. Then at night, sitting apart in the silence, under the bright stars, he loses all feelings of bitterness, anger, or fear in a feeling of immensity and infinity and a sense of the presence of God.

This is not Pringle's only good poem, but it is his best poem, and it conveys the feeling of 'freedom, and joy, and pride', which seems to have brought this courageous cripple, without property or privilege, through a strenuous and exceptionally unselfish life.

[*Book Collecting & Library Monthly*, December 1968]

Admirations
III
Benjamin Britten

Notes on the Libretto
of Gloriana

Lytton Strachey's *Elizabeth and Essex* is not a book which has pleased everybody, but it was the starting-point of this opera. This is not the place to analyse the book's deficiencies, real or alleged, but to assert that it tells skilfully a tense and dramatic story based upon historical persons and happenings. The late Sir Desmond MacCarthy, in his recently published *Memories*, recalls an interesting opinion that *Elizabeth and Essex* is almost a sketch for a play and that Strachey's method was inspired by or borrowed from the Elizabethan stage. Both the composer and the librettist of *Gloriana* were able to see in the book a sketch for an opera, and both are ready to acknowledge their debt to Strachey's dramatic sense. This does not mean that *Gloriana* is wholly based upon *Elizabeth and Essex*, or that it has emerged merely as an operatic version of that book. In the first place the makers of an opera are not under the obligation of even a picturesque biographer like Strachey to stick closely to history or chronology. Secondly, the makers of this particular opera came to be less concerned than Strachey with the amatory motives of the two principal characters and more concerned with the Queen's pre-eminence as a Queen, a woman, and a personality.

It might be said that Queen Elizabeth the First is not only a great figure in European history but in English folklore. Her legendary fame is part of our racial memory, part of every educated or part-educated Englishman's conception of our national character and destiny: therefore to dramatize her life, or any part of it, seems more an act of recollection or evocation than of creation. And what is true of the Queen is to some extent true of the Elizabethan age in general. This does not mean that the composer and librettist simply relied upon Strachey for facts and opinions. They made it their business to extend their understanding of Queen Elizabeth, and of Essex, and of the Elizabethan age, as far as possible, in every relevant direction, beyond its former limits, taking Professor J. E. Neale's authoritative biography as a standard and guide, and going back wherever possible to original sources in art as well as in literature.

Reduced to the barest outline, the theme of the opera may be stated as follows. Queen Elizabeth, a solitary and ageing monarch, undiminished in majesty, power, statesmanship, and understanding, sees in an outstanding young nobleman a hope for both the future of her country and of herself. Essex, young, handsome, bold, of the highest nobility and rank, is perceived by her to be potentially a worthy successor to Leicester and Burleigh, a possible right-hand man or prime minister, who, under her supreme authority and guidance, may in time control and direct the government of England. Essex, for his part, perceives that if he wins the confidence of his ageing sovereign and kinswoman, there may be almost no limit to the power attainable by him. Two human weaknesses make this situation dangerous. They were very well expressed by Sir Robert Naunton in his *Fragmenta Regalia*. The Queen, taken by Essex's nobility, his 'most goodly Person', and his 'kind of urbanity or innate courtesie', conceives a 'violent indulgencie' towards him, which, of its nature, implies the risk of 'non-perpetuity'. Essex, for his part, 'drew in too fast, like a childe sucking on an over-uberous Nurse'; he was 'too bold an ingrosser both of fame and favour'; and what he might have managed by tact, and prudence, and patience, he lost by 'an over-desire and thirstiness after fame'. The Queen, who had been ready to make him, was in the end obliged to break him – a tragedy for both. Loyalty at the court of Elizabeth the First tended to express itself in the language of a lover-like devotion, and in responding to the 'violent indulgencie' of the Queen, in 'playing up' to her, Essex may, in spite of the disparity of their ages, have been half carried away in an illusion of lover-like feelings. An ambiguity in the Queen's feelings towards him may have evoked a response in him. Both were complex characters: the Queen had to subdue her inclinations as a woman to her magnificent conception of her position and her duty as a monarch; Essex, a bold man of action, had an imaginative, moody, melancholy bent.

The liberties that have been taken with chronology and other matters are justified, it is hoped, by the demands of opera and of this particular opera, demands for simplification and concentration. Bacon, Shakespeare, Leicester, the Armada, the Queen's speech at Tilbury, for example, have been set aside, which would have been impossible in any historical conspectus of her reign, or in any chronicle-play or pageant-play. The librettist felt that his business was to afford scope for the musical development of the dramatic central theme.

The libretto is partly in verse and partly in prose. The verse is mostly irregular, with an intermittent use of rhyme. In general the lines have been kept short, often with only two or three stresses, and the language fairly direct and colloquial, in order to sustain a brisk dramatic interchange between the characters. The lines tend to grow longer at moments of soliloquy, prayer, or meditation. Bearing in mind always the paramount requirements of the music, the librettist aimed at giving the words such flexibility, such metrical or rhythmical variations, as seemed fitting to each moment, or situation, or new development. Dramatic unity was the general aim, not metrical uniformity.

From the first the question arose to what extent the language was to be genuine or fake Elizabethan. The best answer seemed that it should be neither. The important things were, first, that it should be operatically suitable – and settable – and, more precisely, settable by Britten; next, that it should have an Elizabethan flavour, so long as this was not procured by any self-conscious 'period' seasonings. It seemed advisable to shun anything that might smack of Wardour Street, Merrie England, Good Queen Bess, or the half-baked half-timbering of debased twentieth-century 'Tudor' stylings.

There seemed no need to be afraid of archaisms; of writing *weareth* or *supersedeth* instead of 'wears' or 'supersedes' (these old endings being pleasing to the ear and useful to the composer) or of using words like *plainings, ensamples, complots,* or *flaskets.* Such words rose up easily from the recesses of the librettist's unconscious memory, and seemed to him, in their settings and his more sanguine moments, to be *mots justes.* No fine combing of the libretto would be necessary to find anachronisms: the use of words of a later than Elizabethan familiarity has been deliberate.

Simple punning or playing upon words was an Elizabethan as well as a later habit. Examples occur in the libretto with the name of Mountjoy in the opening scene, or with Time and Concord in Act 2, Scene 1. To echo now and then the Elizabethan love of antithesis has not been to aim at Euphuism or turgidity. Examples are a phrase like 'the double image of our single bliss' in Act 2, Scene 2, or, in the same scene:

> I with the power of love,
> You with the love of power ...

The recurrent tune associated with the Queen:

> Green leaves are we,
> Red rose our golden Queen,
> O crownèd rose among the leaves so green!

is derived from the following four lines, written by an Elizabethan boy in one of his school-books:

> The rose is red,
> The leaves are green,
> Long live Elizabeth,
> Our Noble Queen.

There is something ancient and persistent and folklorish here: the librettist has lately seen an Early Victorian sampler, worked by a young girl, carrying a plainer intimation of mortality:

> The leaves are green,
> The rose is red,
> This will be seen
> When I am dead.

The occasional ejaculations in Latin put into the mouth of the Queen in the opera were Elizabeth the First's own. She was a superb exponent of plain and memorable English, and a good many of her phrases have been worked into the libretto, some well known, some little known. The prayer at the end of Act 1, Scene 2, is a conflation and adaptation of passages from prayers composed by the Queen in several languages, and her speech to the audience almost at the end of the last scene of all is derived from her so-called Golden Speech to Parliament. The allusions to her intelligence service as her 'eyes and ears', and to her dress figured with representations of those organs, were suggested by the famous portrait at Hatfield, which Lord Salisbury was good enough to show, among other treasures, to the composer and the librettist.

[*Tempo*, Summer 1953]

Let's Crab an Opera

In his book *Benjamin Britten* Eric Walter White recalls that there was no precedent for

> the fact that in May 1952 Her Majesty Queen Elizabeth II gave her approval to the suggestion that Britten should write a Coronation opera on the theme of Elizabeth I and Essex, and that later Her Majesty agreed to accept the dedication of the work and to attend its first performance at a special gala on 8 June 1953 in honour of her Coronation.

The same point had been made by the late Vaughan Williams, in a letter to *The Times* a few days after the gala night. It is worth recalling because peevish complaint is sometimes made of inadequate patronage of the arts by the Royal Family; and because, in spite of this departure from precedent, Royal patronage of the opera is traditional. Mr White recalls that George I and George II regularly subsidized opera in London, Handel wrote an opera about Richard I for George II's Coronation, Queen Victoria 'started her reign by displaying an active interest in opera', and Puccini dedicated *La Fanciulla del West* to Queen Alexandra.

Gloriana was designed as a spectacular *pièce d'occasion* or *pièce d'apparat*, and spectacular it certainly was, diversified with a masque and a Court ball and choral dances, and with such splendid settings and costumes by John Piper that the very sight of them evoked applause. But *Gloriana* was not just a *festa teatrale* or musical pageant: it is an original opera with a serious theme.

It had a curiously mixed reception. No composer or other creative person can expect all his works to arouse instant and general enthusiasm. If they did, there might be something wrong with them; he might be flattering his audiences by giving them what they were used to and saving them from using their brains and imagination. Innovators must expect the possibility of meeting with a dead weight of indifference and must not be surprised by being ignored, patronized, envied, or even hated. But of course disapproval, from persons whose approval is as weightless as a man in space, is no worse than bouquets – from them.

I have lately seen a collection of press cuttings and other material about *Gloriana* which gives some indication of the warmth and coldness, the understanding and the failure of understanding, with which it was received. In looking through this material, I have tried to put on an air of enquiring detachment. If I were to show myself too partial, it might be thought that I have an axe to grind, as I was the opera's librettist. What in fact I do have to grind is a tomahawk for scalping Philistine and puritan art-saboteurs, iconoclasts and ignoramuses, and those who fear and hate anything which does not flatter their prejudices and pander to their appetites. I am old enough to remember the mutilations and daubings and insultings of sculptures by Epstein, and I write in a summer when a figure by Henry Moore has been decapitated – a shameful happening.

'The first-night audience is reported to have been frigid,' wrote Woodrow Wyatt, M.P., in a letter to *The Times* on 20 June 1953. 'If that is correct the reflection is on them and not on *Gloriana*.' The report was correct, the first-night audience *was* frigid. Why? It did not know what to expect, because it was not a regular but an unmusical audience, consisting largely of important persons, some rather far-flung, who were there for official or social reasons or out of loyalty or courtesy to the Queen. A critic of music later reported having overheard in the foyer beforehand the following snatch of conversation:

'Then this is a *new* opera?'
'Yes. It's by this Benjamin Bradford.'
'What's it about?'
'They say it's about Queen Elizabeth and Lord Darnley.'

Were these chatterers interested in anything beyond a plenteous twinkling of tiaras and recognizable wearers of stars and ribbons in the auditorium? Did they perhaps expect some kind of loud and rumbustious amalgam of *Land of Hope and Glory* and *Merrie England*, with catchy tunes and deafening choruses to reproduce the vulgar and blatant patriotism of the Boer War period? If so, they didn't get it. I see the librettist recorded that 'it seemed advisable to shun anything that might smack of Wardour Street, Merrie England, Good Queen Bess, or the half-baked half-timbering of debased twentieth-century "Tudor" stylings' (see page 177 above). And *The Times Educational Supplement* was gratified to find 'no armadas, no cloaks and puddles'. What that bewildered audience got, dramatically, was 'an effective representation of a remarkable queen in her varying aspects of dignity, greatness, generosity, tragedy and human frailty' (Woodrow Wyatt). Joan Cross (according to the *Listener* critic) 'gave the dramatic performance of her career, a wonderful impersonation of the great Queen, domineering, capricious, even spiteful, but a woman with charm and an obvious genius for government'. And Peter Pears, with voice and presence and acting power, most ably sustained the role of Essex.

And what did they get musically? According to Professor Anthony Lewis, who described himself as 'an independent musician', they got 'music of superb richness and invention', which was evidence of 'the continued excellence of the composer's creative powers, responding magnificently to the demands of the occasion' (*The Times*, 16 June). They got 'dazzling' orchestration by a 'great' orchestrator, and 'a variety of musical splendours that astonish the ear' (*Observer*, 14 June). They got, among others, Joan Sutherland, Beriosova and Julian Bream.

It was inevitable that many of the first-night audience, in spite of great distinction in what are generally known as 'other fields', were ill at ease and did not want to be astonished. As I once translated from Voltaire:

> Alas, often the ears of the mighty
> Are mighty long ears.

Upon ignorance, astonishment is apt to have a stupefying effect; upon stupidity, a numbing and chilling one.

They had good cause for alarm. They were faced with 'a work which gleams with intelligence and charm and skill' (*New Statesman*, 20 June), a work of 'striking originality' which was also 'witty and elliptical' (*Manchester Guardian*, 9 June). What! Intelligent, original, witty and elliptical? No wonder a large part of the audience, which in any case might have felt it incorrect to show even a semblance of enthusiasm for something else in the presence of the Sovereign, was petrified. Besides, this was the work of 'one of music's great epigrammatists' (*Observer*). Worse and worse! They could not boo, they dared not walk out.

'It is significant', wrote the *Musical Times* (August 1953), 'that audience reaction at the first public performance of *Gloriana* was wholly different from that at the Gala performance: there was a warm reception, with the customary cheers, and there has been no lack of appreciation at later performances.' The same point had already been made by the *New Statesman*, which noted that the later performances had been 'very warmly received'. Nine months later, after a new production of *Gloriana*, the *Manchester Guardian* (31 March 1954) wrote that although the original reception had been 'stony', it now seemed incomprehensible ever to have missed 'the clear demonstration, clearer even than in Britten's previous operas, of the Verdian quality, in the sense both of kind and of power, of his genius'.

But, first-night 'stoniness' or petrification apart, there was an unmistakable mean streak running through the often generous public and private appraisal. Some critics thought Britten ought to have used the resources of the orchestra more fully, some were troubled by the deliberately quiet conclusion, which was 'moving and poetic' to the *New Statesman* critic. Some resentment was shown at Britten's not having produced a conventionally operatic, popular, lush, rip-roaring, sentimental drama or melodrama, but rather an anthology of linked, vivid, somewhat self-contained scenes and moments.

By a 'mean streak' I do not mean critical doubts, objections, or inadequacies. A pointer is to be found in the *Spectator* (19 June), where Martin Cooper wrote that 'the work has been very generally over-blamed, with an almost sadistic relish or glee that has little to do with musical merit or demerit'. He remarked that envy and resentment had arisen because Britten and his music had been 'news' for about ten years, and it had suddenly seemed to be 'smart' to underrate it. He also mentioned envy of 'special patronage and special conditions of work and performance not accorded to other performers.'

Envy, I remember noticing at the time, was sometimes as plain as buttons left undone, but sometimes tried to conceal itself under a show of tolerant magnanimity or candid friendship or some other disguise. As one gets older, one can quickly see through this most transparent kind of humbug – envy pretending not to be envy.

Evidently in the musical world – as in the literary, which I know better – there are persons who try and compensate for their own infertility and disappointment by deluding themselves and trying to delude others that they know better than productive and forward-looking natures. To analyse cynically and superficially, with 'almost sadistic relish', what is beyond their own powers seems a poor compensation for a lack of self-confidence. And they, and their associate stray dabblers and hangers-on, who try to drug their fear of being alone by idle gossip in clubs, at dinner-tables, or during weekends in the outer suburbia they take with them wherever they go, easily catch from one another, at certain times, a determination to be 'smart' by running down certain creative persons who can exist very well without them – but not without independence, discipline and isolation.

I remember being myself expected at the time to listen to private complaints that Britten throve only on the adulation of a 'small circle'. I replied that I saw nothing wrong with small circles, as I was myself accustomed to moving in them. It is an old grievance of nobodies that somebodies in the arts are dependent upon a 'small circle' of admirers or form part of an exclusive society for mutual admiration. Baudelaire, for example, was publicly abused in his own time for being the centre of a small circle. But surely that was his proper place. How could he make an instant appeal to a wide circle of the indifferent, the frigid, the ignorant, or the impercipient? The smallness of a circle is perhaps made a reproach because it allows no room for squares. The implication is that what is small is negligible; that it may also be choice is an idea too difficult for the unchoosing and unchosen to grasp. And as for mutual admiration, there is such a thing as the recognition of one's peers, and there are such things as kindred spirits.

It must be a lifelong annoyance for persons who have to depend utterly and solely upon their own self-esteem to have to live with the knowledge that their condition is dreadfully ordinary. Their rancour is sadly like that of a plain woman for a pretty one, whom frigid receptions or envious comments do not easily drive to distrust either her features or her make-up, or her ability to make the most of them.

[*London Magazine*, October 1963]

The War Requiem

It is a function of creative men to perceive the relations between thoughts, or things, or forms of expression that may seem utterly different, and to be able to combine them into some new form. Britten's *Nocturne*, for example, which unifies musically a group of poems by different hands, is a notable example of his power to connect the seemingly unconnected. It was a totally unexpected and weightier feat of imagination to see the possibility of combining together the traditional form of the Latin Mass for the Dead – so formidable in its solemn grandeur, so grave in its religious and musical associations – with the utterance of a young English poet killed many years ago in battle.

The popular poet of the First World War was Rupert Brooke, who seemed to many people to embody an ideal image of radiant British youth sacrificing itself for its country. His work was in tune with the conventional patriotic sentiments of the time. But the poetry of Wilfred Owen, who was killed in France just before the Armistice in 1918, after winning the Military Cross, had to wait longer to be known.

Owen was only twenty-five, but his poems were profound, and are profoundly disturbing. They made no appeal to the accepted opinions of his time about poetry or war. They were not about what soldiers gloriously did but what they had unforgivably been made to do to others and to suffer themselves. Owen did not accept what he called 'the old Lie' that it was necessarily glorious or even fitting to die for one's own or any other country, or that a country was necessarily or perhaps ever justified in making the kind of war he knew. As he saw and experienced it, war appeared as a hellish outrage on a huge scale against humanity, and a violation of Christianity. He shared the destiny of millions on both sides, but unlike them he had the sensibility to see what war now really meant, and the power to explain it.

'My subject is War,' he wrote, 'and the pity of War. The Poetry is in the pity.'

Into his poetry went the pity, not of a detached outsider or a sentimentalist, nor simply that of a humane officer for his men, whose lives he cannot save and to whom he cannot hold out hope, but the pity of an imaginative man for fellow-sufferers unable to speak for themselves to later generations. And since right could hardly be on either side in a struggle which, by Christian and humane standards, seemed to him utterly wrong, pity led to the vision of some kind of reconciliation beyond the tortured and shapeless present. This is most explicit in the line from the poem 'Strange Meeting', which comes almost at the end of the baritone solo in the last section of the *War Requiem*, the quietly and simply sung

> I am the enemy you killed, my friend.

It is now clear that Owen was the outstanding English poet of the First World War, and, because the Second World War was a continuation of it, of that too. War has been the central horror of European history in this century; and Owen, mourning young lives tormented and treated as expendable, was to speak as directly to mourners in 1945 as to those of 1918; furthermore, since the fear of war is now universal, his elegies speak to us directly. They are a warning.

To nobody grieving for the deaths of friends in the War which broke out again more than twenty years after his death did Owen speak more directly than to Britten, who has dedicated the *War Requiem* to the memory of four of its victims. Perhaps no composer has shown so remarkable a response to poetry, and no English composer has been more responsive to English poetry. And since there is no motif more predominant and recurrent in Britten's works than that of innocence outraged and ruined, what could be more natural than that Britten, deeply moved by Owen's poetry, should be no less moved by the fate of the man who wrote it, his youth, his promise, his passionate tenderness, his rare talent cut off by the senseless violence of war? Being so moved, Britten's impulse was to set Owen's most memorable poems for singing. It was a sure instinct that prevented him from setting them separately, or as a sequence. Certainly they have a kind of monumental nobility that enables them to stand alone, but he saw, as nobody else could have seen, that they could stand beside the sacred liturgy of the Mass for the Dead, and, musically, be combined with it.

The theme of both is the same: it is death. It is death inseparable from grief and from guilt, death ordained by God for every man, often caused by human stupidity and cruelty, but death associated, in spite of everything, with ideas of mercy, forgiveness, and peace. Owen was the product of a Christian tradition, in which these ideas are inherent. He makes quite clear his disillusionment with the failure of a Christian civilization to practise what it professes, as when he writes of the mutilated wayside Calvary and of those by whom 'the gentle Christ's denied'. This occurs in the poem that is here brought into the brief and beautiful *Agnus Dei*, with the tenor's slow gravity heard so affectingly against the recurrent choral setting of the Latin text imploring the Lamb of God for peace. Then in the *Offertorium* Owen's poem about Abraham and Isaac represents the sacrifice as having actually taken place, in defiance of the divine message from the angel. (It is remarkable how naturally the baritone's opening words 'So Abram rose ...' follow, as if intentionally, the Latin phrase about the seed of Abraham; and how the music recalls Britten's canticle *Abraham and Isaac* (1952) based on one of the medieval Chester miracle plays, and evokes the long scriptural tradition stretching backwards for ages.)

Owen, imbued with ideas of pity and of reconciliation (both of which imply hope), shows himself essentially Christian, and, because of this, the elevation of his poems to a musical synthesis with one of the most solemn of Christian rites, seems strangely in keeping. In achieving this synthesis, Britten has not only written a sublime new Requiem Mass, but has brought out the full force and charity of the utterance of an unforgettable poet. Directly and disturbingly he has given it a new, much wider, and perhaps lasting significance, troubling the deeper levels of our human nature.

There seems to be a general agreement that the *War Requiem*

is the profoundest work Britten has yet produced, and good judges
have called it his masterpiece. At its three first performances – in
Coventry Cathedral, Westminster Abbey, and the Albert Hall – its
reception was not of the usual kind given to a work that impresses
its hearers by musical invention and subtleties, and incidentally
moves them by phases of passion or of gentleness. It was received as
a work of vast scope, in which the composer, by giving it all the
technical resources and emotional power at his command, so
transcends the personal that he seems to comprehend the sufferings,
to transfigure the grief, and to honour the potential goodness of
humankind. It is addressed (and with what poignancy!) to

> Whatever shares
> The eternal reciprocity of tears.

[Preface to leaflet accompanying Decca recording]

The Church Operas

In 1955 Britten was planning a journey to the Far East. Knowing that I had lived in Japan when young, he asked if there was anything he should particularly see or do while there. I strongly recommended the Japanese theatre in its various forms, Kabuki, Bunraku, and Nō – particularly the Nō. I remember describing a Nō play, enlarging upon the emotive effect of its strict stylization, and imitating some of the formal gestures used by the actors.

In the following year I asked Britten about his travels, and enquired whether he had managed while in Japan to see a Nō play. He had, and had been so impressed that he had seen it twice. He then said, in a quiet voice but with what I recognized as a disturbing firmness, that he would like to produce an English version of it, with his own music, and wished me to provide the libretto.

Though honoured to be asked, I thought the project hardly possible. Neither he nor I nor anybody else would want a pastiche of a Nō play, a piece of *japonaiserie*, and as the original depended entirely upon its *mise en scène*, archaic music, all-male cast, and rigidly formal production down to the last detail of masks, costume and movement, it was hardly transferable to the Western operatic stage. What was more, the language and action of the play belonged to an antique Buddhist culture and could only be fully appreciated by highly cultivated Japanese traditionalists. But, like the poets Yeats and Waley (neither of whom ever visited Japan), Britten had been enchanted by the Nō, as I had been enchanted before him, so what was the good of protesting?

There is a repertoire of some 250 Nō plays. It happened that the one seen and heard by Britten was *Sumidagawa* (Sumida River), a drama which, with its theme of outraged innocence, could not fail to move him. I asked him how we could possibly find or create a suitable atmosphere in which to present the intended work: in the Nō theatre there is no applause and the audience sits in a dedicated silence. He instantly saw that the solution was to produce the work in a church. And that is how *Curlew River* and the two successive 'parables for church performance' have come to be known as church operas.

The plot of *Sumidagawa*, in its legendary simplicity and pathos, has a significance not merely Japanese but universal. We decided to transpose this plot from a Buddhist to a Christian idiom, while retaining its medieval temper. In a church in the Fens of East Anglia an abbot, monks, and acolytes would piously enact the story of a demented mother seeking her lost child, her tragic role being sung by a tenor. It was found possible to construct a small, raised, circular stage without proscenium, curtain, or footlights, and to arrange for performers and orchestra to collaborate operatically without the guidance of a conductor. The realization of this scheme owes much to the imaginative, skilful, and devoted labours of Colin Graham.

The plot of the second of these church operas, *The Burning Fiery Furnace*, comes straight from the Book of Daniel. In the character of Nebuchadnezzar, in the cult of Merodak ('the god of gold'), and in the resistance movement of the three young Jewish exiles, Shadrach, Meshach, and Abednego, may be found some relevance to the twentieth century. The success of that extremely difficult experiment, *Curlew River*, and the experience gained from it, had given both librettist and composer freedom to develop this new kind of opera within the limits they had defined. At the same time they had the advantage of interpreting and renewing a story which, being Biblical, belongs to the Judæo–Christian tradition in which the British consciousness has been for centuries deeply rooted.

In choosing *The Prodigal Son* as the theme for the third of these operas, Britten is the latest in a long line of painters, composers, and writers, among them Rembrandt (whose supreme painting of the subject hangs in the Hermitage), Debussy, and Gide. As the best known and loved of all the New Testament parables, it seems to contain the essence of Christianity, with its lavishing of reward and rejoicing upon a forgiven sinner. In accordance with both the two previous church operas and with the Biblical original, the libretto has been made as direct and unornamented in diction as possible. It will be noticed that *The Prodigal Son* has developed in certain ways beyond its predecessors, notably in the fuller functioning of the chorus.

Each of these operas was first presented in the beautiful and ancient church of Orford in Suffolk, as part of the Aldeburgh Festivals in the summers of 1964, 1966, and 1968. The first two have since been performed in cathedrals and churches in many places in England, the Continent, and America. The custom of performing them in a consecrated building was set aside last year, when *The Burning Fiery Furnace* set a successful precedent by being staged, during the season of the Proms at the Albert Hall, before a very large and appreciative audience.

Not everybody has had the opportunity of seeing one of the original Nō plays, to which these church operas owe their inspiration. It may therefore be of interest to add a few words about them. The Nō theatre began to take shape in the fourteenth century, and was developed and refined by Zeami Motokiyo (1363–1443). The rules he laid down were essentially operatic: the action of the play, he said, should develop naturally out of the mood created by the music. The combined effect of action, words, music, and singing was designed not only to have an emotional effect upon the spectator but to make him susceptible to that supreme kind of beauty defined by the Japanese word *yūgen*. This is a word for which it seems impossible to find an equivalent in any European language. It suggests a beauty hinted or half revealed, elusive but significant, and tinged with a wistful sadness.

It would be a mistake to suppose that the refinements of Nō make it a precious or remote or esoteric form of musical drama. 'The purpose of all art', Zeami wrote, 'is to bring sweetness to the hearts of all people and to harmonize high and low.'

[Festival of the City of London
programme, July 1968]

Places

Notes on a Visit
to Ireland

In the dining car of the boat train to Fishguard an English curate, about to visit Ireland for the first time, had just settled himself at a table when he was joined by three Irish girls returning home together. They quickly engaged him in talk, and began to tease him with highly-coloured accounts of what he was to expect. Rather too clean-limbed and solemn, he was not quite sure whether he was being teased or not, and perhaps really believed that if he went to Blarney he would be compelled to hang suspended by the heels from a high tower for several minutes in order that he might kiss the Blarney stone. As they vied with each other to see how much they could get him to swallow, the bright eyes of the three girls grew brighter and their pink Irish complexions pinker.

They had evidently been buying clothes in London, and the one sitting next to him was clearly very pleased with her new grey coat and skirt, which had pink anchors, perhaps of celluloid and as big as teaspoons, sewn on to the collar and cuffs. A little confused and hard pressed by their questions, he told them he was going to Fermoy, and this set them all off at once describing that place to him. The prettiest of the three (she of the anchors) spoke feelingly of the gaiety of Fermoy when it was garrisoned by the English, and then suddenly grew wistful, like one of Chekhov's Three Sisters, and turned her head and stared out into the night, which was framed in a window on her left. Just at that moment a tall and rather severe-looking woman came into the saloon, leading a peaky faced boy by the hand, and looking for a table. Alas, she was wearing a new grey coat and skirt with pink anchors, perhaps of celluloid and as big as teaspoons, sewn on to the collar and cuffs … There was a tense moment when the eyes of the two women met, and each realized instantaneously that it was not an 'exclusive model'

after all that she had bought at that sale in Oxford Street: then with
a bitter grimace the tall woman swept past with such determination
that the eyebrows of her anaemic little boy contracted in bewilderment. One could only hope that the two women were not neighbours, for there are limits to bad luck. In any case, the young woman
next to the curate did not quite recover her former animation.

The next morning, standing in the bows of the boat as it slowly
made its way up the estuary towards Cork, I had the impression of
entering a foreign country. The light, sub-tropical-looking mists
that dangled or drifted over the trees seemed more purely Atlantic
than any on the coast of south-west England, and the trees themselves, and the general disposition of the landscape, and the colour-
washed houses, pale pink, blue or buff, and the stray fishing boats
on the silky water, and the men in them, and even the cynical-
looking cormorants perched on the buoys that mark the navigable
channel, all combined to make me feel as if I were approaching a
remote island, one of the Canaries or Azores, so that I was quite
surprised to catch sight of an English torpedo-boat at anchor under
one of those green hills, and was almost ready to wonder why it was
there. Towards me, stationary at my post of observation, there
flowed a coloured travelogue in slow motion, and presently a large
pink ruin glided by, as if on a pivot. There is a special fascination
about the ruins of modern buildings. This one, I was told, had been
a hotel. But now there were no numbers on the bedroom doors,
for there were no bedroom doors.

It was this ruin which first made me aware of the quietness and
sadness of the Irish atmosphere, and of the part they play in making
that atmosphere seem foreign. There were scarcely any signs of
shipping or industry, and on the long road by the shore only two
or three cars passed: across the water one could hear the swishing
sound of the tyres on the moist asphalt until it grew fainter and
ceased. Throbbing gently, we presently passed a sham medieval
tower at the water's edge. It was inhabited, for there were curtains
in the windows, and a young man was leaning against it and smoking a cigarette. He wore no raincoat in spite of the wetting mist,
and looked at the boat very much as one might look at a passing
cloud. If he had been an Englishman he would have been indoors

or would already have gone off somewhere, instead of standing by himself in that afternoon attitude in the fresh, cool, early morning air, but then he wasn't an Englishman, he was an Irishman, a foreigner.

As the channel narrowed I remembered how at school the history of the country on which I was about to land, this producer of wits, poets, heroes, and beauties, had been either completely ignored or thrown into a false perspective with a strong Orange tinge by means of a few generalizations about over-emphasized episodes. St Patrick got rid of the snakes, and after a considerable delay or perhaps interregnum Cromwell arrived to 'crush the rebels' and 'restore order', and shortly afterwards William III, just to clinch the matter, won the Battle of the Boyne. But the matter had remained unclinched in my mind, for it happened that Easter Week, the Sinn Fein ideal, and the fate of Casement made a strong impression upon my boyish imagination, and in later years, as the fortunate result of a little curiosity, a little reading, a little scepticism, and some experience with Irish individuals, I felt rather better informed. As for Casement, I long ago reached the conclusion that his was the case of a man who allowed his divagation from the usual in his personal relationships to harden into a dangerous political attitude and a wild indiscretion, though certainly without danger changes are not brought about.

For Irish 'rebelliousness' or independence of spirit, in spite of the hopeless ignorance, prejudice, intolerance, injustice, folly and violence that have often gone with it, I cannot help feeling admiration, for when it is clarified by uncommon sense and some knowledge and experience of the world, it shines with a light all its own. It seems a pity that the English do not give in a little more to their sentimental feelings about the Irish and abandon their ever-lurking inclination to 'crush the rebel', for a combination of the best qualities of the two races is irresistible. In this connection I remember an uncle of mine, who used to command an Irish regiment, telling me of the military advantages of combining Irish dash with English moderation. Meanwhile it remains, not merely in a geographical sense, a long way to Tipperary.

Fermoy is dominated by a row of roofless barracks, burnt out in the troubles and left standing – a very suitable monument to the ferocity of the Black and Tans – and near them is a new housing scheme, and near that again the station, which has a somewhat Siberian atmosphere, especially on a windy evening when it is beginning to get dark. Strolling to the end of the platform one sees the empty shells of the barracks again, and beside them the shells, as yet unfilled, of the new houses. So often in Ireland the dwelling and the ruin stand side by side, though as often the ruin stands alone, a reminder of cruelty and disaster in an exquisite landscape. It may be a great roofless mill, full of young trees instead of machinery; or an old tower in a cloud of ivy; or a wayside or upland cottage; or a great burnt mansion of early nineteenth-century Gothic with bunches of twisted water-pipes sticking out here and there like severed arteries; or a mouldering police barracks looking haunted behind overgrown hedges of flowering fuchsia, with the apple-tree beside it in which a sniper was once sniped.

I think especially of Bridgetown Abbey beside the Blackwater, a vast monastic ruin of grey stone which turns a darker grey when rain has wetted it: you approach by a lane all overgrown with brambles weighed down by fat, delicious blackberries that nobody comes to pick, the river glides over its dark rocky bed, trees on a cliff catch the afternoon light, and you scramble impiously over fallen masonry and push aside tall weeds to enter what was once the chapel, inside which, rather oddly, a few nineteenth-century graves keep company with old tombs; from the side of one of these a stone slab has fallen, and inside lies an old thick oaken board which was once the side of the coffin, and the skeleton of a man who died before Queen Elizabeth was born; through the pelvis a nettle has sprung up, and is now in flower.

I think, too, of crossing a couple of meadows to the remains of Kilcolman, where Spenser lived, wrote, empire-built, and rebel-crushed: the bog-water reflects a livid evening sky, and the hay-cocks cast long lilac shadows on the grass; the place is sometimes visited by consumptives from a sanatorium visible a couple of miles off, and one of them has torn up some letters and thrown them carelessly on the ground, so that on an upturned fragment one can read, in very clear writing, '... she said she was hoping ... said that I would never ... last time, darling ... looking forward more than ever ...' That curious headstrong hopefulness of consumptives, how appropriate to be reminded of it in a ruin, and in an Irish ruin!

Not a ruin, but more desolate than a ruin, is the great lead-coloured house at D——, closed up and deserted, with some of its windows shuttered and some not, with black-shadowed ilex thickets and overgrown lawns of a green so vivid under the lowering clouds that it hurts the eyes, with stalactites beginning to form under the heraldic pediment over the door, and a solitary donkey nibbling the grass between the paving stones in the yard outside the coach-house.

I shall claim no novelty for the observation that even today the Irish atmosphere, the Irish character, and certain aspects of Irish life may easily put one in mind of pre-revolutionary Russia. I think I am right in saying that Turgeniev declared that it was the example of Miss Edgeworth which gave him the impetus to write about his own people. Certainly to read a novel like *The Absentee* – so penetrating and amusing – is almost to be reading of Russian landowners who possess serfs and obey alternately the promptings of extravagant self-indulgence and an idealistic social conscience. There is a book of memoirs by Miss Somerville (of Somerville and Ross) which gives a very good idea of the landowners' general attitude of mind in the last century, and indeed there are other books that do the same. It would be amusing to compile a bibliography of life in the Irish country-houses, the breeding-places of that gifted race, the Anglo-Irish: 'The most brilliant and charming people in the world,' a very cultivated Englishman lately remarked to me. 'One day last summer,' he said, 'when I was staying over there at a perfectly delightful house, hip-baths were brought out on to the lawn and filled with cushions, and we sat in them all the afternoon drinking port and eating gooseberries. Such hospitality! Such conversation!'

Such conversation, yes, amongst all the Irish, with their seductive voices and betwitching brogue, but let us admit that their enthusiastic monologues can be terribly boring. Let us admit also that Ireland is a heavenly country to visit, but might be less heavenly to live in. It is so melancholy, so full of the ghosts of feuds and famines, the clouds fly low, the trees sag under the incessant rain, and the very air seems charged and weighed down with a sense of grievance. How could one keep out the climate, how could one keep the Pope and Ulster, Mr de Valera and Mr J. H. Thomas, the land annuities, the censorship and the future at a proper distance, except by taking to drink, going over to Rome or London, or cutting one's throat?

There they are still (or some of them, at least): the extravagantly-built country houses, the walled demesnes and the surviving old eccentrics within. One longs for a Gogol to go round today in a car, on some pretext which would appeal to their vanity, cupidity and curiosity, and observe, collect and record what remains of a class which, as a class, is already an anachronism. Meanwhile there is the Ireland that one hardly supposed could really exist – the long country roads with no one in sight and no traffic but occasional donkey-carts, rare bicycles and very rare cars, roads which serve as a couch for donkeys and pigs or a promenade for turkeys and bare-foot children; the whitewashed cabins, the old women in shawls, the strong cups of tea, the rapid streams and fertile valleys, politeness amounting to flattery, hostility, hospitality, poverty, blessed in-efficiency, and the ramshackle villages and country towns, un-disfigured by advertisements and as free from traffic as England was in wartime. There is the whole bag of tricks, down to the bilingual signposts with their fancy Gaelic inscriptions, and the pleasing green letter-boxes and telegrams. Above all, there is the landscape, which has never suffered from a want of appreciation on the part of those who like that sort of thing.

I choose to remember a very small lake in the hills beyond Killarney, as clear as a dewdrop, with a tumbledown pale blue inn and a few pine trees beside it. Suddenly a spotlight of sunshine travels slowly across the scene, giving it not a theatrical but an almost supernatural beauty. In air and light as pure as this one perceives the connection between the shabby inn and the wits, poets, heroes, and beauties. The hillock of wet grass glows in the sun like an emerald, there is no sound but the appropriate lapping of the lake-water, a tuft of flowering heather at one's feet looks as precious in the sun as something by Fabergé, and as a background to it all the sombre mountains are being slowly suffused with a colour like that of damsons. They seem to grow taller and gloomier and more Ossianic as their impossibly deep purple deepens still further, and the darkening clouds pass over them trailing mile-long scarves of gauzy rain. A faint seethe of sound is audible even from here. It is going to pour again. It has begun.

[*New Writing*, 1936]

A Letter from the
Seaside

You ask for my impressions of this place, so you shall have a few. The day after I arrived they were far from favourable, but variety has crept in since then. In the morning I remember I had some conversation with an Italian ice-cream man. 'We're having a wicked summer,' he remarked as the rain began to patter on his white drill coat, and he turned his back to the sea, which had gone the colour of dirty pewter. In the distance a few old people hobbled into the shelters along the Marina, and a wet blanket of mist and rain was drawn by the wind over the eastern and western heights, over the great blocks of Victorian barracks and the walls of the abbey. In the park the trees were weeping floods of tears, and an empty tram was making a hurried and noisy exit from the High Street.

No wonder the French family, day trippers, felt that England was hopeless. They too retired to a shelter to consume the food and drink they had brought with them (for everybody knows that in England eatable food as a rule is unobtainable, except at exorbitant prices, and drink forbidden, except at odd hours); they wrung the water out of their berets and wondered if it had wetted their cameras, and then, with their mouths full, began to calculate, not without difficulty, since English money is so complicated, how they might avoid spending anything at all.

'Don't tell me it's raining,' said a meek little man with the quietest irony. He was about to step out of the post-office into the deluge. The English are said to take their pleasures sadly, but is it not even more important that they take their misfortunes cheerfully? On days like that one is reminded of Taine's remark that 'le fond du caractère anglais, c'est l'absence de bonheur.'

I retired to lunch at a small commercial hotel, where I found the food surprisingly good, so I have been there a number of times since. As my presence there is unexplained, I am known (I found out by chance) as 'Mr X.' Even more enigmatic is one of my fellow-lunchers, an old woman. Every day she comes into the dining-room at a quarter to one, looking rather furtive under a mop of 'iron-grey' hair, which she wears bobbed in the style of the nineteen-twenties. She wears slippers, and a speckled dress like the plumage of a faded guinea-fowl, and carries a large leather bag stuffed with Heaven knows what possessions: it has a zip-fastener, and is heavy. She then sits down to *breakfast*, which always consists of two boiled eggs. These she eats with much fussiness and daintiness and quick, nervous, bird-like movements. As soon as she has finished she goes out with a specially provided jug of hot water, which I suppose to be used for some digestive purpose. Exactly half an hour later she returns for *lunch*, which always consists of fish. It seems that although in perfect health she has not been out of the house for a year. She spends all the time alone in her room, but does not sew, or read, or write, and has no wireless. *What does she do in there? What is in that bag?* Sometimes she reads *John Bull* over her lunch, and it may be, to judge by her furtive eyes and whisperings, that she sees life and the world as one vast confidence trick. Perhaps she is right; perhaps her bag contains the secret of the universe.

I may say that by way of contrast we are not without a little night life – dancing, drinking, and the mixed pleasures of the flesh. The garrison helps, and as the soldiers get their pay on Fridays, gaiety rather comes with a rush at week-ends. The character of the soldier is a vast subject – something childish, something stupid, something desperate – and as a rule it is only the Scotch or the Irish ones who are interesting to talk to. Speaking of the Irish, a local wild Irish-man, a man of means who wears green suede shoes and has, I am told, morals to match, came into the Hanover Arms the other night with a large paper bag, from which he extracted a succession of sixpenny bracelets. With a low bow he presented one to each in turn of the assembled tarts – one to the fat cheerful tart, one to the fat surly tart, one to the tiny animated tart with bad teeth, one to the tall tart with a mole on her chin. 'Madam,' he said gravely to each in turn, 'allow me to offer you a magnificent specimen of Wool-

worth jewellery.' The gifts were received with shrieks of delight.
'And haven't you any', asked one of the tarts' patrons, a young
butcher, 'in a size just a little smaller – for men?' More shrieks of
delight.

One afternoon I walked over to Kingstrand. There was a strong
wind that dotted the sea with curly white waves, rather stylized.
The sea was streaked with loud blues and greens, and the wind
prevented the fishing-boats, which were turned against it, from
making headway. With their dusky cigar-brown sails they dipped
and fluttered, struggling like moths in glue. Everything was movement, nothing was progress. The waves broke and whitened as
far as the eye could see, the sailing-boats rocked and tilted and got no
further, the grass on the cliff streamed along the ground but stuck
to its roots. At Kingstrand the villas below the cliff were not yet
opened for the summer, and the shuttered beach-huts, their paint
faded by sun and salt, had an air of secrecy, as though a crime had
been committed in one of them. Between the houses and the huts
there is a flat of shingle a hundred yards wide, and here great masses
of pink valerian have run wild. It was all in flower, dancing against
the clean buff shingle and the peacocking sea.

I came back a different way from the way I went, and passed
through that curious region known as the Ness. The first thing you
come to is one of those military follies that occasionally adorn the
English landscape, a city of derelict huts solidly built of concrete but
now overgrown with elder-bushes and nettles, a refuge for tramps,
courting couples, and idle boys on Sunday afternoons: one can still
read a sign which says CANTEEN, and a painted finger points to a sad
edifice with broken roof and windows. A little further on there is a
deep valley with little paths winding among the bushes and hillocks.
Down there one cannot help noticing the wild flowers, and although the place is so near the town I have picked bunches of the
fragrant, the pyramidal, and the spider orchis, and sometimes in
thundery weather a bouquet of mixed flowers with several sorts of
butterflies firmly attached, too drowsy to fly away.

On this particular day I ran into an acquaintance I must tell you
about. His name is Harry. Imagine a disreputable and slightly
formidable young man, unshaven, in shabby clothes, and generally

seeming to be doing nothing. He comes to the Ness because he likes it. He has been coming to it ever since he was a child, and he has not always come alone. Before he married her he used to bring his girl here, but now she stays at home, where there is always so much to do: she has become a woman, but he has remained a boy. Sometimes he brings one of his three children with him, a little brat with a running nose and bandy legs, and lets it tumble about in the grass, eat unripe blackberries, and otherwise amuse itself. But as a rule he is alone, for his brother Ted, who has been here with him a thousand times, has gone to work in the dockyard. Harry likes casual encounters with people he knows or does not know. He likes to watch the ships, knows all about them, has sailed in some of them, has one eye like a hawk's, though the other has a cast in it, and owns a boat of his own, which can be seen on clear days moored in its place far down below and away to the left: now and then it leaves its moorings at night with Harry aboard to engage in activities, I believe, that are not always strictly within the law. Harry likes to see who is about, and to watch the quite public lovemaking that goes on, especially in summer. He likes conversation. He likes a smoke, lying in long grass in the sun. He has a taste for seagulls' eggs, which he collects on the cliffs; he gathers mushrooms, he snares rabbits. He deliberately chose this kind of life in preference to one that would have made him rich, and as people go he is fairly content. When you get to know him you find that he is less rough but not less hardy than he appears. Spare and hard, he is not very tall, has quick eyes, and is almost entirely covered with curly black hair, which flourishes on the top of his head, makes his face swarthy, darkens the backs of his hands, makes his legs look like an animal's, and sprouts out through rents in his shirt and trousers. If he had taken his great chance, there would by now have been no rents in his shirt and trousers: he would have been wearing a coat, a collar, and perhaps a cheque-book as well.

It happened like this. When he was seventeen or eighteen Harry was serving in a smallish boat engaged in coastal trade varied with occasional voyages to Holland and Belgium. In Belgium the captain had a friend, a middle-aged bachelor who owned three shops, a tailor's, a barber's, and a restaurant. This individual was an anglophile and wished to adopt a young Englishman to help him in the conduct of the three businesses and be a companion to him, saying that if the young man turned out well he would make him his heir: could the captain recommend anybody? The captain recommended Harry, and Harry was installed. But the boy could not manage to learn Flemish; he was looked askance at because he was a foreigner; in spite of the kindness of his patron he found that after three months he could bear his exile no longer; so one night he crept out of the house, joined a boat, and returned to England – and the Ness.

When the weather allows it I like to sunbathe or swim. For a swimmer the sea here tends to have three chief disadvantages – roughness, coldness, and at times swarms of jelly-fish. They do not sting, but are disagreeable to touch, like cold sago. The swimmer has the pleasure of being able to take his exercise lying down, and since, being a swimmer, he is solidly built, he does not greatly mind the low temperature of the water, and can often stay in it for an hour or so at a time. If he has an eye, he can enjoy seeing the land from the water, and when he is not swimming, the water from the land. This morning, for instance, the sky hung low, darkened and discoloured like a bruise in sunburnt flesh, and the sea, ominously calm, was streaked with a milky green that belongs to northern seas alone and never, even to them, for long. Smoke, blackish or sulphurous yellow, coiling from a thin and distant funnel here and there, seemed to enter the windless air and spread like some dark substance injected into a vein. Far away to the left a fog signal made a noise like a cow deprived of her calf, far away to the right a dredger was clanking and creaking in the outer harbour. In the garden not a leaf moved, the curtains hung motionless at the windows, and the girl who was sitting in a basket chair on the balcony put down her sewing and looked out to sea, but it was impossible to tell where the sea ended and the sky began.

A little later the sun came out, and all the bathing children became children of light. Three very fair and slender little girls in pale blue, pale yellow, and white bathing-suits hovered at the water's edge, and people sat on the shingle and idled in boats, like figures in a painting by Seurat. A boy with red bathing-drawers waded into the sea and stood, with the water up to his waist, gazing

at the horizon. His biscuit-coloured torso, apparently severed from
the rest of him, rested on the calm surface as if on a sheet of glass.

But after this picturesque description I must add that my attention was attracted by a splashing figure in shallow water, and I
immediately recognized it as Elsie. I must tell you about Elsie: I got
to know her a couple of weeks ago, when I was sunbathing one
morning on a lonely part of the beach. I was approached by a young
girl who asked me if I would guard her clothes while she bathed,
but I could not imagine anybody wanting to steal them. She
rapidly undressed beside me, which seemed a little forward, talking
and giggling as she did so, and then sat for a time with nothing on
above the waist, displaying her unripe breasts. There was some
reason for thinking her a half-wit, and some for thinking her less
of one than she seemed. Her bathing consisted of a floundering
exhibitionism in the shallow water a few yards from my feet, and
her movements were punctuated with loud cries of delight and
invitation. When she came out she talked incessantly, and presently
came to the point.

'Where do you live?' she asked.
'Over there,' I replied.
'Is your wife there?'
'No.'
'Why not?'
'Because I haven't got a wife.'
'Do you live with your Mum?'
'No.'
'Who looks after you?'
'Oh, various people.'
'Wouldn't you like me to look after you?'
'Thanks, but I'm very well looked after.'
'Who do you sleep with?'
'It depends.'
'Do you sleep alone?'
'Sometimes.'
'Don't you get lonely when you sleep alone?'
'Not a bit.'
'Wouldn't you like to sleep with me?'

'You'd never stop talking.'

'What would you do if I walked into the bathroom when you were having a bath, and you were standing up and facing the door?'

'I always sit down in my bath, but it's quite likely I might tell you to buzz off and not be so nosey.'

'Wouldn't you like to marry me?'

'Not today, thank you.'

'What's your name?'

'Mickey Mouse.'

'Oh ... You fibber! Oh, what a fib! God is listening to you. How can you tell such fibs when God can hear us?'

'I'm sure God has a great many more interesting things to listen to.'

'Oh ...'

'By the way, why don't you go and drown yourself?'

'Would you rescue me?'

'Certainly not.'

'But don't you like me?'

'You talk such a lot.'

'Would you like me if I didn't talk so much?'

'I can't answer any more questions today.'

The sun was nice and warm, and I lay back and closed my eyes. She began to balance stones along my outstretched arm, arranged them in patterns on my chest, and then, giggling delightedly, began to build a little cairn on a really rather personal foundation.

'Now, now,' I said ...

As a nice contrast to Elsie I will give you an account of my visit to Lady Chalkham, with whom I have been to tea. We may as well begin with Lady Chalkham taking a photograph down from her mantelpiece and handing it to me.

'A tremendous beauty, isn't she? It's Princess Eudoxia. She used to stay with us before the War.'

'To dear Ada,' ran the inscription, 'Cordially, Eudoxia Victoria of Blundenburg-Stettin.' And what a handwriting! What energy! What confidence! What pre-War brio! Lady Chalkham herself must have looked rather like that: a back like a ramrod, a bang of

hair, a skirt shaped like a cornucopia. Looking at her across the tea-
table with curiosity and admiration, one could not help seeing her
in terms of her past. She is a work of art, a product of all kinds of
lucky chances and patient cultivations, a perfect specimen of a kind
of woman that will never be produced again. By her gestures and
contours, her voice and manner, one imagines an early environment not without stateliness, in which convention allowed a
charming playfulness. This well-preserved ancient monument was
once a little girl in bustle and ringlets, bowling a hoop or learning
a collect, or crossing demure little feet in black kid boots buttoned
up at the side; an ingénue, flushed at dances, whirling in the polka
or fondled in conservatories; a young woman reclining in a punt,
with a Japanese fan in her hands, wearing balloon sleeves of broderie
anglaise and a hard straw hat tilted over eyes fixed on a young man
in a tall collar and white flannels. One may guess at the flutterings,
the palpitations, caused by the first visit to the theatre, the first
pointed compliment from a man of experience, the first disillusionment, the first glass of champagne, the first lingering kiss;
one may try and gauge the innocence in which, like many women
of her class and generation, she had married, and the way in which
experience delighted and ripened and completed her.

Somewhere there must be an early photograph in which she
appears to be yearning towards the camera, her head turned over a
bare shoulder thrust up from a fuzz of tulle like an egg emerging
from the fluffy recesses of a hen, and gazing at it one might call up
one by one little scenes from her past, each with its convention of
clothes and behaviour, its setting and witnesses, like the successive
movements in a ballet, in that long training which is as necessary
to produce a personality as any other kind of expert or artist. I see
her sitting at a dressing-table, with its silver-backed brushes and
little book of *papier poudré*, lifting her soft arms so that the loose
sleeves fall back from the elbow, and slowly going through that
beautiful lost movement, slowly withdrawing the long, jewel-
headed pins from a huge hat heaped up with white roses; gathering
up her skirts in one hand as she crosses the road; pausing to consult
a watch suspended over her left breast from a diamond brooch in
the form of a bow; writing to the dentist in the third person;

peppering the backs of post cards (views of Venice, Cairo, or St Petersburg) with exclamation marks; seeing poverty in the distance and Naples from a porthole, and watching the slow-motioned withdrawal of Alps, vast, useless, and dazzling, from the steamy windows of a railway carriage; settling a feather boa round a collar supported with stiffeners; feeling relief at taking off her stays from her sixteen-inch waist; stepping, with card-case and parasol, into a carriage to pay calls, and driving off between banks of ferns in a smell of horses; bathing in water-logged black serge with white pipings; going motoring in an ulster, thickly veiled, perched high above the ground, and moving off with a jerk in a cloud of blue vapour amongst respectful but sceptical yokels, who step back in alarm as the machine snorts by; attending weddings, funerals, garden parties, musical evenings; appearing on lawns, the decks of yachts, racecourses; playing diabolo, bezique, puss in the corner; arriving at a tango tea, wearing a small hat adorned with two ospreys as lavish as horses' tails, carrying a flat leopard-skin muff as square as the top of a table, and hardly able to put one foot before the other because of the tightness of the skirt round the ankles, a skirt split upward from the hem for four inches, attention being called to this provocative opening by two red buttons as big as half-crowns. A little later she follows the fashions of the early war years, going out in a plumed shako, a frogged coat, a tent-shaped skirt, and high laced boots; at one moment she passes, to the music of Suppé, under a striped awning in the direction of a fountain, at the next she is bending graciously over wounded soldiers in beds, a little troubled by the mingled smell of men, flannel, and iodoform ...

'Why are you looking at me so quizzically?' she asked.

'I was thinking', I said (and I was still holding the photograph of Princess Eudoxia), 'that it's odd to have known that world and this world.'

'Ah, those were the days,' she said, as one would expect her to say.

I looked at her and then I looked out into the sodden garden, where the fuchsia-bushes were covered with coral earrings and those earrings were covered with sliding raindrops. I was thinking of other aspects of life in pre-War days, for I had been looking through an old local almanack of the mid-nineties. Two things especially struck me. One was the large part that religion then played in the life of the town: missionary societies, bands of hope, synods, Lord's Day Observance societies, and so on were continually holding meetings; 'sacred concerts' took place on the pier; and much was made of 'a three-days conference on the Second Coming.' The other thing that struck me was the frequency of suicides among the working class. An engine-driver cut his throat; a baker threw himself from the western heights 'during a state of temporary insanity'; a maidservant 'was killed by falling over the cliff', two bottles of a drug being found where she fell; a bootmaker was found dead on the downs 'with a half-full bottle of poison beside him'; an artilleryman 'shot himself and died immediately'; and a messenger-boy 'died from taking carbolic acid' among the bramble thickets at the Ness. In the meantime, the English love of minding other people's business was being indulged, for several meetings were being held 'in support of the persecuted Armenians'. Most curious of all, two seamen were committed to prison for refusing to serve on a steamer that took the Prince of Wales to France. Why did they refuse? I offer you this (since I have just seen a review in which you are called 'a writer with a social conscience'), as a theme for a story.

[*New Writing*, 1937]

Views of Brighton

Until 1914, by all accounts, Brighton had still an air of festivity. Since then it seems to have increased in size, in civic pride, in ordinariness, and in respectability. Formerly proud of itself as a setting for free and easy behaviour, it was a siren among watering places, something between a mermaid and a barmaid. Nowadays it is proud of its 'improvements', its up-to-date paddling pools and public conveniences, its satellite suburbs, its efficient police, and so on. The object of those who control its destinies seems to be to make it as like other places as possible instead of keeping it what the nineteenth century made it, an original playground: so in recent years people who would formerly not have dreamt of going anywhere but Brighton for their holidays have gone increasingly across the Channel, to Ostend for instance, to enjoy themselves, to get a drink when they want one, and to let themselves go. Brighton is now a reformed libertine with false teeth: it has lost its bite. A week-end at Brighton, formerly a synonym for a spree, now means little more than a week-end at Tunbridge Wells. Certainly Brighton pullulates on Bank Holidays, but less vigorously than Southend, Margate, or Blackpool. Like most of England now, it is an example of local government by the lower middle class of the lower middle class for the lower middle class. This is the class which has already almost established in our country a classless society: it has squeezed out the upper and lower classes, who had much in common, for neither had anything to lose by the freedom of their behaviour, the one being protected by money and position, the other by lack of these things. So Brighton has lost its aristocrats and eccentrics, of whom fine examples survived until lately, and it has lost its swash-buckling cockneys, those peasants of the pavement. The standards of Hove have prevailed. From Southwick to Peacehaven, and further in both directions, pukka mediocrity has come to stay, everything is in its place, everybody conforms, and the suicides at Black Rock now fall plop on to a concrete promenade instead of into the untidy sea. So clean, so quick an ending.

Brighton still has two assets, one inalienable and the other still largely intact – its atmosphere and its older buildings. Much has been written about the Brighton air; doctors know about it, for it is a doctor itself; but even more remarkable is the Brighton *light* – the dazzle, the sparkle, the aquamarine afterglow – and in this the buildings play a part, for they reflect it. Why on earth have our painters so neglected this town? A canvas here and there, a Conder or two. But did anybody before Sickert *feel* Brighton and record it on canvas as tellingly as he has done? How pleasant it is to find that an artist of a younger generation has, so to speak, been seized with Brighton. It takes liveliness to respond to the light and the buildings; together they promote liveliness; and a lively talent is needed to record their co-operation. Mr Piper has that talent and has found a medium that suits him. Let anybody look at his drawing of Sussex Square, entitled 'Kemp Town', with those grandiose façades baking in brilliant sunshine against a dark sky, or his 'Regency Square' with its crowded and curving balconies, and see if they cannot regain at a glance something of what Lord Alfred Douglas calls 'that first fine careless rapture of the middle eighties and the early nineties'.

If Mr Piper gives us views of what is familiar he does it in such a way as to convey surprise. The Pavilion never grows stale, it is astonishing even if one sees it every day; and Decimus Burton's Brunswick Terrace has something of fantasy in its ordered solidity and on an autumn afternoon looks almost like a quayside palace in St Petersburg. Nobody will accuse Mr Piper of confining himself to the obvious: that dancing line of his has its source in a roving eye. He has for instance caught, and caught most successfully, the very odd view that meets the gaze of anyone who looks east on emerging from Brighton Station – a herringbone pattern of oyster-coloured roof-tops, arabesques above a white church by Barry – and he has done an impressive west front of that neglected landmark, St Bartholomew's, built in the eighties and dominating one of the less showy parts of the town. In doing a job that gives pleasure to the beholder he has cleverly adapted an old medium to modern needs, and will add to the name he has already made as an original and curious interpreter of our vastly varied architecture.

[Review of *Brighton Aquatints* by John Piper, *Spectator*, 29 December 1939]

Kilvert's Country

August 1939. A Londoner in the morning, I found myself in the evening helping with the hay on a remote Welsh hillside. To get there I had to go through a small market town which became notorious a few years ago for the discovery that one of its respected citizens, a professional man who used to read the lessons in church, was a murderer. Through the sham-Gothic machicolations of the Jubilee Clock Tower crouching detectives watched him as he crossed from his office to the chemist's to buy arsenic 'for dandelions'. His first 'dandelion' was his wife, neatly done away with in the neat villa with its hanging wire baskets of geraniums and its ornamental ironwork painted dead white. The second 'dandelion' was a professional rival. 'Excuse fingers!' said the murderer, pressing his guest to a doctored scone. Everybody remembers him, and if a statue had been put up to him his memory could not be more alive. For me the scene of his activities is also familiar as the scene of more innocent events that occurred before he was born; for me the town enshrines two legends, that of a murderer and that of a diner-out and player of croquet.

Arrived at my hillside, where the dense foliage of a sycamore seems almost an architectural adjunct of the grey stone farmhouse, I felt at home although among strangers, for they were hospitable and cheerful, with delightful manners. I hope they were as pleased to know me as I was to know them. There was a special reason for this: I happened to have a detailed knowledge, derived from the diary of that diner-out and player of croquet, of persons and events in the parish seventy years ago. I wanted to know the place as it is now, to see it in detail, and to meet and listen to its inhabitants. My hosts were pleased, I think, by my curiosity. The stuff of that diary, with which they were already partly familiar, for they too have curiosity and the Welsh love of reading, was largely the stuff of their own knowledge of persons and places, but seen from a different angle and through a temperament – that of an impressionable youngish clergyman who flourished in the eighteen-seventies. His name was Kilvert: two volumes of his diary have been published and have much extended his fame; indeed, he has been compared by reviewers to Dorothy Wordsworth, to Proust, to Pepys, to Amiel, to Gerard Manley Hopkins, and to D. H. Lawrence!

Staying in the region where he wrote his diary, I found myself trying to see people and things from various points of view. I wanted to see them as freshly as possible from my own point of view, though this was partly determined by memories of an earlier visit to the same neighbourhood; I could not help seeing them to some extent from Kilvert's point of view; I wanted to know what the local people, some of whom can remember him, thought about Kilvert and what they think of him now that they know him, much more intimately, through his diary; and I wanted to know their points of view in regard to their surroundings and any other subject on which they might care to express an opinion. All this suggests a purposeful programme and perhaps a ponderous intellectual nosiness, but in fact I was simply out to enjoy myself. I did enjoy myself (a change of environment, good weather, an exciting landscape, human contacts) and I found myself involved in a sort of experiment with time. I hasten to disclaim any visionary powers: what I mean is that being so much concerned with points of view I gained a new impression of part of the pattern of life, of *intersecting planes of experience,* and a strong impression that the people and the place were significant while 'the passage of time', as it is so oddly called, was not. I found I could not at all think of time as a thing that 'passes' or indeed as a 'thing' at all. Everything conspired, so to speak, to show that life, in any particular aspect, can be viewed, like individual character, as a combination or crystallization of certain elementary tendencies.

One blazing midday, after a bathe in the ice-cold pool under the ferny waterfall, I made my way over some rough ground to a house called Whitehall. In Kilvert's day it was in ruin, and he has left a charming, nostalgic, and rather Hardyesque account of it: a house with a past, it had been the scene of wild merrymakings after hard work. Since his day it has been rebuilt and lived in and has again fallen into ruin: the ivy and the owls were once more busy, under a vertical sun, with their spellbinding. Kilvert, it occurred to me as I stood among the ruins, had made allusions to the Franco–Prussian war. My own attachment to this neighbour-hood is inextricably mixed up with memories of the German war of 1914–1918, when I was last here; and now there was about to be another German war. I am not trying to establish the slightest direct connection between the tendency of this remote house to fall into ruin and the tendency of the Germans to invade France. I only say that the cliché about 'time standing still' suddenly acquired a meaning for me: time became no more than an atmo-sphere in which every human word or deed gave out a sound, so to speak, which was only an echo or a repetition, and which went on vibrating but was only audible, like sounds on the wireless, when one happened to be attuned to it.

Nothing that happened to me during this stay in the Welsh countryside is more real to me than something that happened there three winters ago to somebody I never knew. A young married woman with several children, the wife of a farmer away up in the hills, went on horseback on Christmas Eve to the nearest market town (that same town where the murderer lived) to do some Christmas shopping. There was snow on the ground and in the afternoon a wild snowstorm set in. Friends tried to dissuade her from returning home, but off she went: she wanted the children to find their stockings full in the morning. In the darkness and the blizzard she lost her way. She was found by a search party on Christmas morning, frozen to death, face down in a snowdrift, with the presents for the children clutched in her hand. A sophisti-cated person might say 'Serve her right!' or find the story somehow sentimental, but locally it has become a kind of legend, and the dead woman, her maternal instinct thwarted by circumstances over which she had no control, a kind of saint or martyr. I had heard two or three versions of the story when I went one Sunday to an 'anniversary' at a local chapel. (These anniversaries, half sacred and half secular, are simply eisteddfods on a small scale.) A dear old man got up and recited, with feeling, a ballad of his own composing about the young mother lost in the snow. It was listened to with rapt attention and deeply admired. A real folk-poem, it was in its way a work of art, and therefore timeless; in one's mind it set up the figure of the homegoing woman like an equestrian statue, perpetuated a Christmas Eve and prevented its snow from ever melting.

When I praised the beauty of the countryside, whether under snow or lavish with summer, to an old labourer in a lane he said I mightn't think it so beautiful if I had to get a living out of it. This I readily admitted, but when he began to talk he talked like a poet, by which I mean that he gave utterance to sensuous impressions, emotions, memories and opinions in clear and memorable phrases that could only have been evolved by a person with a heart and a head and a special matured-in-the-wood wisdom of his own. I don't want to generalize about the Welsh character, but many people in this parish did seem to me to have what may be loosely called poetic feeling. The toilworn farmer pointing out the features of the landscape or recalling the past; the woman singing 'God be with you till we meet again' over the washtub; the girl fetching a bottle of perry across the hayfields; the roadmenders stopping work to look up at that rare sight, an aeroplane; the two miners holidaying in a minute tent pitched in the bracken; the naked boy cleaning out the bathing pool; the voluble blacksmith; the eccentric recluse with his books and curiosities and half-ruined house (I must write of him another time) – all these people seemed to have the faculty of turning fact into legend, of living a legend: they seemed almost to be conscious of being characters in an endless epic – in which Kilvert and the murderer and the frozen woman also have their places. You can't live on a heath and be vulgar, said Hardy. It seems that to live on this heath makes people see things in their true colours and gives them a power of speech. They help one to understand why Wales has a literature of its own, a living language, tendencies that make up a character, a rhythm, a pattern, a vibration, variable but persistent and timeless.

The unpopulous landscape, which emigrants spurred by enterprise and economic pressure have long been deserting for distant countries and other servitudes, retains its richness and wildness. Here I sit, sweating from a long walk, on a bank of heather in the afternoon sun, listening to the tiny artillery of the seed-pods of the gorse bursting open in the heat, bursting with life. Between me and the climbing flowery hills lies the Rhos Goch, a sinister bog where many have been drowned; over there is Llanshiver with its dark past, and Cefn-y-Blaen, where giants once lived; and there is the road to Newchurch-on-Arrow, up which Kilvert, bearded and repressed and dressed in black, used to stride to see his sweet but *maladive* Emmeline. The more you know, the more it all fits together. All is of a piece. It is all a play in which we are all acting. The unities are observed. There are only thirty-six possible situations, though they are capable of being infinitely varied. Time is no object, for nobody knows when the play began or when it will end. Whitehall is in ruins again; and in another Whitehall they are preparing for another war against the Germans.

[*Horizon*, March 1940]

Marginalia

[William Plomer kept no diary, but occasionally
he wrote out in the margins of a scrapbook
the notes that follow.]

Leonard Woolf

1951

Leonard Woolf, speaking to me of Virginia's unpublished diaries,
said she was 'censorious', but that her censoriousness was not 'the
real Virginia'. Quite true.

10 June 1961

Staying with Leonard Woolf at Monk's House, Rodmell, he being
eighty. Behind the house, in an untidy corner, as we were going
to look at a new-born puppy, I noticed on the ground a Victorian
bust, apparently in stone, of a serious-looking man. I asked who
it was. 'It's James Stephen, the one who was Colonial Under-
Secretary.' A pause, then rather scornfully: 'He looks it, doesn't
he?' Another pause. 'I invariably use it to pumpship on.'
Note: Belated instance of the now old-fashioned and extreme anti-
Victorianism of 'Bloomsbury'.

25 June 1962

Leonard on a visit to Rustington. I told him that Bob Gathorne-
Hardy was engaged in editing the memoirs of Lady Ottoline
Morrell. 'She gave them to Virginia and me to read,' he said. 'They
were no good. She kept buttering people up.'

He once reviewed a book by Bosie Douglas in the *Nation*, and received a letter threatening him with an action if he didn't apologize. He consulted Maynard Keynes, who advised him to do nothing. Later, he put his name to a document asking for a Civil List pension for Bosie. This brought him a letter of thanks from Bosie, expressing surprise that Leonard, of all men, should have supported his claim.

28 January 1965: Rodmell

Leonard said that when Tom Eliot was living in Emperor's Gate ('surrounded by curates') he sent the Woolves a typescript of one of his longer poems (I think one of the *Four Quartets*) and sent copies to Mary Hutchinson and McKnight Kauffer. He invited them all to read it critically and then assemble and make their opinions known to him. Whatever Mary Hutchinson and Kauffer said he dismissed as of no interest, but when it was Virginia's turn she said she thought too many lines ended with a present participle. 'That's a *good* criticism, Virginia,' he said. Leonard remarked sardonically that, all the same, 'Tom only made one or two alterations.'

Leonard said he thought *A Passage to India* much the best of Morgan Forster's books, but all the business in the caves was absurd and unbelievable. He said there was some absurdity in all M.'s novels, but supposed they were 'quite good as the Jane Austen sort of novels'. I remarked how on re-reading some of them I had been struck anew by the oppressively feminine influences under which M. had evidently grown up. I said I supposed that if one grew up with a lot of old women it must do a good deal to one's outlook. 'But Morgan *is* an old woman,' he said. 'He always has been.'

21 March 1967

After spending the night at Rodmell, I said: 'Leonard, I hope you slept well.' 'I always do, you know,' he said pleasantly. 'I have only had one bad night in my life. It was in Ceylon. There was a blind child that had been brought from India, and they stuck pins into it all night with the idea of curing its blindness.' He later asked the parents if they would like a European doctor to see the child. They said they would, and he arranged it. The doctor said there was nothing to be done: the child was hopelessly blind.

E. M. Forster

1951

Morgan Forster told me that once having formed an adverse judgment of somebody he has always tended to make it final, and not to 'make allowances'. He admitted that this was wrong. His mother used to tell him that he was 'revengeful, like your father's family'.

Leonard Woolf told me that Morgan was 'the touchiest man in the world'. That fits in. I know of instances where Morgan, offended or annoyed by somebody, has 'written them off' ruthlessly.

3–4 January 1969

At Cambridge for Morgan Forster's ninetieth birthday. John Morris and I stayed at the University Arms Hotel, and Bob Buckingham brought Morgan to dine with us. He ate heartily, ordering himself melon, trout with vegetables, and some sort of peach melba. He chose to share our claret, which he much enjoyed. He wore no spectacles, but had no difficulty in dissecting his fish. Later, when we were sitting in the lounge, some sort of head waiter or chasseur came up with an autograph book and invited Morgan to write his name in it. Morgan hesitated a moment and then said he would. 'Perhaps,' said the man, rather as if granting a favour, 'you would like to put your name on the same page as Mr Maugham's.' 'No, I shouldn't,' said Morgan instantly, 'I'll put it on another page.' Slightly taken aback, the man then agreed and found another page, and Morgan signed his name. The man then boasted that there were some famous names in the book, especially that of some cricketer or other, of whom Morgan had never heard.

I noticed that the hair at the back of Morgan's head was still dark. He was alert, and said how much he liked a couple of stories I told him, notably one about Gandhi. He said, 'I like to hear interesting things, but I don't say anything interesting,' and twinkled.

Bob reckoned that our combined ages (Morgan 90; John 73; Bob and I 65) came to nearly 300.

Not much to say about the luncheon at King's, except that it was very nicely done, and gave a feeling of being a private party, which in fact it was. Morgan showed every sign of enjoyment and was standing, or sitting, and talking or listening from 12.30 to 3.0, when Bob led him away. I picked up Morgan's hand and kissed it as I said good-bye, and he snatched up mine and kissed it heartily.

Benjamin Britten at Aldeburgh

25 June 1960

Driving back from Orford with Benjamin Britten's sister Barbara, she told me something of the family origins. The Brittens were yeoman farmers, I understand, in the region of Tenbury – Herefordshire and Worcestershire borders. One John Britten, I understood her to say, was the original of *John Halifax, Gentleman* (which I have never read) and a friend of Mrs Craik. Something went wrong – one son married his housekeeper and left everything to her; another took to drink. The property or inheritance was dispersed. Ben's grandfather had to go and make his living in Birkenhead, which he disliked. He died, leaving a widow with, I think, ten children, of whom Ben's father was perhaps the eighth. Some friend invited the widow to Maidenhead, where she ran a dairy. This was regarded as a disgrace in the family. Barbara can remember being told to look the other way when a milk-cart approached bearing the words 'Britten's Dairy'. Ben's father would have liked to be a farmer but became a dentist and settled in Suffolk. His wife was a London woman. Barbara was born in Ipswich; Ben, I think, at Lowestoft, where he spent his childhood – so his strong attachment to Suffolk is not hereditary, but his attunement to 'the country' no doubt is.

21 May 1965

Marshy walk with Ben along the waterside at Orford. I led him on to talk about his family, having first asked him about his Aunt Queenie, whose portrait of him as a child he gave me some years ago.[1]

His mother was the eldest of her family; Queenie was her next sister. Ben's father, attracted by Queenie, became engaged to her. But when he saw her elder sister, he switched his attention to her, and turned against Queenie. Queenie never married, got religious mania, and ended in an asylum.

An enigmatic illegitimacy in the background – I think it was Ben's grandmother whose paternity was unofficial; her father's name was said or supposed to have been Montmorency.

Strange stories of various characters, including the dipsomaniac uncle, who gave him early musical encouragement before being shut up in a 'home' for good. Then Aunt Somebody married a clergyman who later became a canon of Worcester. She was reputed to be fond of children, but they were childless. After many years of married life – he was a missionary in India – she was left a widow. When one of her relations said to her, 'Well, Judith[2] (if that was her name), considering how fond you are of children, I wonder you and Harry never had any (if it was Harry),' she got very red in the face and said, 'Well, Harry never mentioned it.'

9 June 1966

Ben: 'I may not be the best living composer, but I'm certainly the busiest.'

June 1968

Barbara Britten told me that in a local paper at Lowestoft when she was young there appeared an obituary notice which much amused the family, especially her father, and was often quoted by them:

[1] Now in the National Portrait Gallery [R.H-D.].
[2] Perhaps it was Julia.

His picture hangs upon the wall
For all who pass to see,
He was a kind and father dear
Though many thought him not so.

Arthur Waley

6 January 1960

On a television programme with Arthur Waley at Teddington,
by way of marking his seventieth birthday. He was unwilling for
me to put the question why he had never been to China or Japan.
He said whatever answer he gave might appear slighting: the
fact was he didn't really like travelling. He hoped no allusion would
be made to Ezra Pound, towards whom he showed a strong
antipathy.

28 June 1966

Arthur Waley died last night. Only two or three days ago his wife
Alison wrote to say he hoped I would come and see him. I hoped
to be able to go to Highgate soon. Too late now. I knew he was
dying, from what Celia Goodman told me. (It was, she said,
cancer of the spine.) I think of Osbert Sitwell's feelings, losing two
friends within a few days – Malcolm Bullock and Arthur.

Arthur was a great man. Taste, learning, independence, unique-
ness. Quite inadequately recognized as a poet. All his Orientalist
learning was, in a sense, the obsession which made him a poet, and
conditioned his poetry.

He was always so kind to me. I remember how he told me,
about 1930, that I had been influenced by modern Japanese writers.
I remember him crouching silently on the floor at a party in
Mayfair in the 1930s. Why was he so sad-faced and sharp-witted?
Was it defensive? To think he was a Rugbeian!

I remember giving a joint poetry-reading with him at the Royal
College of Art, I think in the 1950s. And later doing a talk with
him on television. I don't think he had ever been in a television
studio before. 'William,' he said, looking sadly round, 'you and I

don't belong here. We belong to the Middle Ages.' And I remember how he kept his eyes tightly shut before the cameras, while talking, because he felt the bright lights oppressive. Poor old Beryl de Zoete was looking at us on a screen in some other room. I could no longer understand a word she said. She seemed toothless and senile. And I remember Arthur at a party in his house last autumn, his affability, and how he looked tired. No wonder: he was born in 1889.

Laurie Lee

Sunday 16 October 1960: Stroud

Staying here for the annual Religious Drama Festival. Two poetry readings yesterday afternoon, with Laurie Lee and others. Today misty and still. Free at mid-morning, I decided to go for a walk until lunch-time. I saw a signpost marked 'Slad' (L.L.'s village) '2 miles' and felt strongly inclined to see the setting of *Cider with Rosie*. There is a gradual climb along one side of a steep and partly wooded valley, decreasingly populous after the first mile.

All at once I saw two unmistakable figures strolling Sladward ahead of me – L.L. and his wife (Mary Campbell's niece). I hesitated whether to turn back or to overtake them and intrude upon their privacy. I decided to intrude and called out 'You're being followed!' If I was unwelcome they quite concealed it, and L. asked me if I would walk on with them to Slad: I said I would, but must return to Stroud for lunch. He at once began pointing out features of the landscape and when we met a couple of locals – an oldish man accompanied by a boy and carrying a basket of earthy carrots newly dug up – there was an exchange of Christian names.

At the top of a steep bank on the left of the road was a bungalow called, I think, Hazeings. L. described to me a 'duchessy-looking' woman who used to live there. He said he used to work in her garden for twopence an hour, later raised to threepence. She had no water laid on, and at the same rate of pay he carried water up to her from the brook (the Slade) at the bottom of the steep bank on the right. He used to save the money to buy chocolate. Once on an outing with other boys he ate some chocolate from a sixpenny bar:

'It tasted sour in my mouth; I couldn't help thinking it had cost me a whole Saturday morning.'

The sun now came faintly through the mist, lighting up the calm October beechwoods and the few houses below in the valley. Where a mill had stood was a great tangle of bushes and travellers' joy. Across the valley, high on the slope, a fine old Elizabethan farmhouse was pointed out to me by L.L., who said it was on or near the site of an abbey. It stands on the original road from Stroud to Slad. I remarked that the view could have changed little for centuries. (The road we were on was comparatively new.)

We came in sight of the village or hamlet of Slad, perched high on a sort of shelf, beechwoods above, farmlands below. Before we got there we passed a house against and a little below the road, on our right, with a wonderful old stone-tiled roof, and, on the north side, some small Gothic windows said to be from the old abbey. A great feeling of peace and ancientness. Just beyond this house there was a vertical pipe among some bushes, giving out rapid, heart-like throbs (? hydraulic ram). It had been working ever since L. could remember. He said, 'When I hear that, I know I'm home.' We then passed one of several seats once put up by a farmer as a memorial and for the benefit of wayfarers. There are no wayfarers now and the seats are falling to pieces: on the back of one are the initials L.L. carved by their bearer as a boy: they won't be there long.

We now arrived in Slad. He showed me the pretty little stone village school (c. 1840) and the wall against which he used to bounce a ball. Then we went into the pub (small) where he and his wife were staying for lunch. Several cars parked outside and several locals within. Greetings, chaff, introductions. After a drink I had to leave them and chose to walk back to Stroud, having refused a lift offered by the village schoolmistress.

Extraordinary nowadays to see a man so conscious of his roots and as much in love with his native place as, say, John Clare. One might call L.L. the last of the peasant poets: although quite used to 'the world' (he and his wife were just back from New York) he retains his naturalness and doesn't exploit it (? except perhaps a little to attract women).

It was either discreet or delicate of him, or both, not to mention the W. H. Smith prize, which he is due to receive in nine days' time at the Savoy (I, with Harold Nicolson and C. V. Wedgwood, being one of the judges).[1]

Royalty
Spring 1951

Queen Mary, walking in the garden at Trent Park with Hannah Gubbay, heard the cuckoo, and said immediately, with some urgency and even alarm, 'Where's my money? Where's my money?' Hannah was worried and thought the Queen had lost her bag or purse, but it appeared that it was H.M.'s custom, on first hearing the cuckoo, to turn her money. Steps were taken to have the Queen's bag fetched from the house, and when she had it she said, as she looked towards the trees, 'And now I suppose that wretched bird won't oblige again.'

27 July 1952: Houghton

Conversation with the Queen Mother about Elizabeth I. She said she greatly wished she had had a classical education. I asked her if she had had any classics at all. Only a little Latin, she said. She rather wistfully wondered how there could be a 'new Elizabethan Age' when people were too easily satisfied with second-hand things, cinema, television, newspapers, etc.

Talking of the opera, I said I had looked at the libretto of *Merrie England*, out of curiosity, and that it was so silly that it had to be seen to be believed. She had enjoyed the music, she said. She hoped there would be some 'rousing tunes' in the opera.[2]

She was with Princess Margaret, and sometimes they exchanged glances of beautiful understanding, love, and sympathy. Princess Margaret talked a good deal to me about the radio programme 'The Critics', which she listened to, she said, regularly.

[1] It appeared later that he didn't know I was one of the judges.
[2] i.e., *Gloriana,* on which I was then working.

Miscellaneous

August 1959

The bodily ailments of the young often heal quickly; the wounds inflicted upon their self-esteem may never heal. The bodily ailments of the old are slow to heal, or get worse; but wounds to their self-esteem are seldom grave – it has become too indurated.

Overheard:
'She's not my wife, she's not my girl-friend, she's not my daughter, she can do what she likes.'

19 November 1959: Street, Somerset

After A. E. Housman's death his papers came to his brother Laurence here. Among them were two essays, one on Burns and one on Swinburne, both of which Laurence destroyed. Before getting rid of the essays, he read to my local informant, a friend of his, the opening of the one on Burns, which was to the following effect:

> If you can imagine a Scotch commercial traveller in a Scotch commercial hotel leaning on the bar and calling the barmaid 'Dearie', then you will know the keynote of Robert Burns's verse.

I am inclined to ask how much Housman knew about Scotch commercial hotels and their staffs and clients.

28 September 1965: Brighton

Admiral Godfrey told me that once, after he came back from India in the 1940s, he was dining alone at the Travellers. Harold Nicolson was at the next table and was not forthcoming. After some desultory conversation, John Godfrey remarked that he had been re-reading a lot of Kipling and mildly suggested that 'We could do with another Kipling today.' Harold made no answer, rose from the table, and went away. The next time John saw him in the club, Harold cut him dead.

Osbert Sitwell told me that once at Renishaw when Arthur Waley and Louis Kentner (a pianist) were staying with him, all three were out 'motoring' and passed a golf course. Kentner, by way of making conversation, said, 'And have you ever played golf, Mr Waley?' 'Once,' said Arthur. 'And did you enjoy it?' 'If I had enjoyed it,' said Arthur, 'I should have played it again.' 'And did you find it difficult?' 'About as difficult as playing the flute.'

12 December 1968

Cassell's gave a luncheon at the Savoy for Robert Graves, who had this week received the Poetry Medal from the Queen. I sat next to him. When I told him I had lately met Wilfred Owen's brother and spoke of the latter's autobiography, Graves said: 'Homosexual! The trouble is, he hides it. He never says Owen was homosexual. All that about "the poetry is in the pity", it's as if you or I were looking at a battlefield covered with the bodies of beautiful girls.'

Speaking of his meeting with the Queen, Graves said he told her that as she is descended from Mahomet, she ought to make it known, and that would make the Pakistanis in this country so pleased. 'I never thought of that,' said the Queen.

17 May 1969

At the Poetry Dinner at the Rembrandt Hotel, over which I presided, a Nottinghamshire member told me that there is an elderly chemist still living in Nottingham whose grandfather, or great-grandfather, carried on the same occupation there, being spoken of in those days as an apothecary. He relates that Byron's mother once came over from Newstead, and said that if Lord Byron were to come in and ask the apothecary to make up a poisonous draught, she wished him to dilute it with distilled water. Shortly afterwards Byron came in and said, 'If Lady Byron comes in and requires you to mix a poisonous draught, you will oblige me by diluting it with saline.' The apothecary supposed that these visits were the result of a great row between the mother and son.

16 September 1970

Patrick Mahoney as a very young man acted as secretary or bear-leader to Maeterlinck in America. He told me today that when Maeterlinck, breakfasting with his second wife, opened a newspaper and saw in it that his first had died, he said, '*La vipère est morte.*'

In the nineteen-twenties Sir George Sitwell, talking to Constance Sitwell, said: 'Such a mistake that Edith didn't take up lawn tennis.' This is a perfect example of period (i.e. Victorian) idiom. I can remember old people saying 'Such a mistake ...' It was a euphemistic way of condemning other people's behaviour. To 'take up' a game seems deliciously condescending. And who ever speaks of 'lawn tennis' now? The thought of Edith as a tennis player is far-fetched.

Short Stories

Miss Bourbon-Hapsburg

'It's apt to be a bit smutty,' she said, 'but I think we'll have coffee
out on the balcony. Such a beautiful day, it seems wicked to be
indoors.'

So to put an end to such wickedness she and her nephew went
out on to the balcony. It's a nice balcony with nice plants and
tolerably comfortable chairs, and it was certainly a beautiful day.
Before the nephew sat down he went to the balustrade and looked
up and down the street, which is one of the quietest in Kensington.
The houses are large mid-Victorian villas, detached from one another and surrounded by shrubby gardens. Having always been
occupied by people with money they have not been suffered to
decay, and look as if they might stand for ever, basking in the sun or
looming in winter fog. They have that air of secrecy suitable to
homes that are castles. Through a lighted window a passer-by may
catch sight of a table laid for dinner; a silent car with a silent
chauffeur waits outside this gate or that; the milkman and the postman, the month and the year come and go; crocuses push up, leaves
flutter down, church bells in an adjacent square are heard on Sunday
mornings, and what goes on behind these heavy façades one might
almost never know and never guess.

But life, like murder, will out. A woman and her nephew, for
instance, were taking coffee publicly on the balcony. And they were
not the only people tempted out by this early summer's day, for
they noticed somebody coming out on to the balcony of the house
opposite them. A rather remarkable somebody, in fact. A woman,
not very tall, dressed in mauve, and rather uncertain in her movements, as if no longer young, she was wearing a wide-brimmed hat
of floppy straw, untrimmed, but tied on to her head with a broad
black ribbon in such a way that it looked like the sort of hat a

woman might have gone motoring in when motoring was still a novelty. The ribbon ended in a big bow under her chin. And she was smoking a big cigar.

'Ah,' said the aunt, 'she's come out. I did want you to see her. Our most distinguished neighbour. She always wears that hat in fine weather.'

'Who is she?'

'Well, if you want to know, she's a Miss Bourbon-Hapsburg.'

'Ha, ha,' said the nephew. 'Very funny.'

'I knew you wouldn't believe me, but it's her name nevertheless.'

'Oh, I see,' he said. 'Eccentric Elderly Recluse Found Dead. Little is known of Miss Smith, formerly of Bournemouth. Said to be the daughter of a prominent Army officer, she was believed to be wealthy, and, claiming royal descent, changed her name some years ago by deed-poll to Bourbon-Hapsburg. The postman, failing to get any reply, informed the police——'

'Oh, very clever,' said the aunt. 'But you're quite on the wrong track. You see, she's the real thing.'

'Impossible!'

'But why? If you found a Romanov keeping a beauty-parlour in New York you'd be no more surprised than I was the other day when I heard of a Hohenzollern who keeps bees in Nicaragua. So why should you boggle at a Bourbon-Hapsburg in Kensington?'

'It's the combination of the two names——'

'What could be more natural, considering how mixed the two families are? And she's not morganatic or wrong-side-of-the-blanket or anything. She may not be out of the top drawer as far as precedence goes, but she's pukka – the daughter of a minor Hapsburg who married an obscure Bourbon collateral. Did you know that there are some quiet Bourbons in Italy who branched off about three centuries ago?'

'I certainly did not,' said the nephew, gazing across the road with heightened curiosity.

Miss Bourbon-Hapsburg, like themselves, was taking coffee. The sun beat down on her hat, her hat cast a deep shadow over her face, and she was apparently offering a lump of sugar to a white dog on her lap.

'And is she now busy', he asked, 'learning nothing and forgetting nothing?'

'I don't know what she remembers,' said his aunt, 'but I know one thing she has learnt. However, I'll come to that presently. First of all I'll go and get the glasses. But you'll have to go indoors of course to look at her. I should hate her to think she was being spied on. It would be so un-English.'

While she was getting the glasses her nephew watched Miss Bourbon-Hapsburg sipping her coffee and puffing at her cigar. When she came back he went indoors and took up his position at a window, taking care that he could not be seen. He carefully focussed the glasses, and his line of vision travelled over some baroque architectural detail until it caught the straw hat, which seemed as near as if he could touch it. The dress seemed more uncompromisingly mauve. Unconsciously, but most obligingly, the lady suddenly tilted her head back to take a puff at her cigar. He saw her big nose and her grenadier moustache, caught the scintillation of a diamond ring on a long, narrow hand, saw her pull at the cigar, take it out of her mouth again, and then, making a sort of spout of her pendulous lower lip, blow out a slow jet of dove-coloured smoke. She had the benign air of one who enjoys an excellent cigar and is at peace with the world. He put the glasses down, and went out to rejoin his aunt on the balcony.

'What an apparition,' he remarked. 'She looks perfectly contented.'

'I believe she is,' said his aunt, 'and I'll tell you why. She's had her share of Hapsburg luck, and you know what that means. Her grandfather bled to death as the result of a mosquito-bite. One of her great-aunts was assassinated. A maternal uncle had trouble with his glands and grew to a height of eight feet. Her sister eloped with a footman and was drowned on her honeymoon, but they brought her round by artificial respiration, unfortunately too late, for the footman, who was temperamental, had already cut his throat, believing her to be dead. Her mother went mad. And her father – oh, I forget what happened to her father, but I know it was something perfectly frightful. What with all that, and then the War, and going through two revolutions, and the boom, and the slump, this good creature felt she had had enough. So what did she do? She had always been an Anglophile, so she settled in England, and quickly turned into something like an Anglomaniac. Could she possibly have chosen a more English street to live in than this? And she has a little place in the country, where she takes, I'm told, the keenest interest in her garden. She likes weeding very much. Kneeling on a little mat in all weathers, wearing an old raincoat and filthy gardening gloves, she won't let a single weed escape her. She also breeds Sealyhams: that's one of them sitting on her knee. She's joined the Church of England and the Times Book Club, and has taken up archery, bridge, needlework and croquet. She's got extremely bad taste in furniture, pictures, music, and all that sort of thing, and has a very few, very stupid and very well-bred friends. Except in one or two ways, like her cigar-smoking, she's now much more English than the English, but her idea of us is what we mostly were thirty years ago, when she first knew us. She likes to quote Kipling – it sounds rather funny with her foreign accent – and she subscribes to the Navy League, the Primrose League, the Anti-Socialist Union, and things like that.

'Oh, you may laugh, I know all you young men call yourselves Communists nowadays, but that's not what *she* believes in. What *she* believes in is a nation of shop-keepers, keeping a straight bat, the old school tie, and the sacredness of the family. She believes in going to church, weeding the garden, taking the dogs for a walk, and doing good without ostentation. When she was a girl and was called on to a balcony to bow to the crowd she never knew that somebody mightn't chuck a bomb at her. But now nobody calls her on to the balcony, she stays off it or goes on to it as she pleases, and there's nobody to bow to – unless it be the milkman, who'd never throw anything at her but a cheerful good-morning. So don't you dare to laugh at her! Has it occurred to you that perhaps she appreciates this country better than we do ourselves? One can't say that she's "learnt nothing and forgotten nothing", for she's learnt how to enjoy a quiet life, and even if *her* England only exists in her own imagination – even if she can bear the climate and turn a blind eye to the squalor and put up with all the cant and boredom and stupidity and the things that make us angry or disheartened – well, don't you think that, considering her origins, she has at any rate been wise?'

'I don't know,' said the nephew, watching the person in question finishing her coffee. 'Unless it's wise to exchange one world of fantasy for another.'

As he spoke he saw Miss Bourbon-Hapsburg open her bag, take out her handkerchief, wipe her Bourbon nose and Hapsburg lip, and with what, given the facts, seemed rather a regal gesture, throw the stump of her cigar into the garden.

[*Spectator*, 29 January 1937]

A Friend of her Father's

When I came to England in the thirties I was the most extraordinary *ingénue* you can think of. An only daughter, in fact an only child, and my mother a widow, and with all sorts of fixed ideas, bless her heart.

My father was a schoolmaster. After leaving Cambridge he was offered a post in a school in Natal supposed to be modelled on an English public school. He married my mother and took her out there with him. That was some time before the 1914 War. Neither of them ever left South Africa after that. They were happy, made their home there, and when I arrived on the scene, towards the end of the 1914 War, they decided to bring me up as a South African.

I dare say that sounds quite simple to you. Well, it wasn't. First of all, Natal is, or was, always supposed to be the most English part of the Union. It was all very well for my parents to call themselves South African, but they were, and remained, extremely English. My father's job kept him in one place, and although we sometimes travelled about in South Africa during the holidays, we were almost as much outside things as if we were tourists. My parents came little into contact with the Dutch and neither of them ever learnt a word of Afrikaans – except perhaps the word one says to stray dogs to make them go away. It would never have occurred to them to learn it. I see now, though I didn't realize it at the time, that both of them thought of themselves, I suppose almost unconsciously, as belonging to a superior race which had won the right to a predominant position in South Africa. I don't suppose it ever occurred to them that the Anglo–Boer War ought never to have been fought. I know they believed that England had behaved in a very magnanimous way after that war, and that the Dutch ought to be eternally grateful to them accordingly. If they ever heard of Dutch people who were resentful because the country had been invaded, their farms burnt, their menfolk killed and their women and children put in concentration camps, they wrote them off as Nationalist hotheads. The Nationalism of the Dutch was something they simply didn't try, I'm afraid, to understand. From hearsay, or from what they read in the papers, they thought of the back-veld Dutch as being uniformly narrow, ignorant and unimaginative.

I don't at all want to give you the impression that my parents were just jingo imperialists, automatically despising other races than their own. Not at all. Both had an Evangelical background, they were kindly souls, with views in some ways liberal, but they were terribly conventional. They had never really questioned the ideas they had been brought up to take for granted. After the 1914 War they didn't understand how things had changed. It was possible for people like them to live in what seems to me now an amazingly unrealistic kind of isolation. I don't mean that we didn't see other people, but the people we saw were nearly all people with much the same sort of ideas they had themselves. Why, I can even remember old ladies in Pietermaritzburg, widows of English colonels and archdeacons, whose ideas and mannners had become rigid in the nineties at least. They were held up to me as models of what a lady should be. And very good models too – but in the sense that an early Rolls-Royce is a good model, if you see what I mean.

So you see, I was supposed to be brought up as a South African, but I was really brought up to be a sort of English girl that had ceased to exist, and an expatriate at that. As you can imagine, my ideas of England were decidedly quaint.

When I was quite young my father died, and my mother was left with only just enough to live on and keep up the sort of appearances she thought necessary. I rather wish now that she had married again, some rather breezy sort of man perhaps, who would have shaken her up a bit. I know she did have an offer, but turned it down, I think because she was devoted to the memory of my father.

My mother had a prejudice against large schools for girls and was dead against boarding schools, so my education was a bit sketchy. I did go to school as a day-girl for a time, and went through agonies of shyness – a thing you mightn't expect to find in a so-called 'new' country. Looking back, I should say my mother intended me to be what she would have called presentable, without a South African accent, and eligible for marriage to what she would think a presentable young man. She wanted me to enjoy myself at tennis parties and dances, and I did enjoy them, but I felt terribly innocent and unworldly compared with the girls of my own age that I met.

As I began to grow up, the question arose how I was to qualify myself to earn a living, and as what. Certainly not as any kind of secretary or typist. My mother believed that to be a typist was just to be an irresistible temptation in the way of one's employers. It was obvious that I wasn't musical, and that was rather a relief to her, because she thought too many South African girls went to England hoping to be pianists and singers and wasted a lot of their own time and their parents' money failing to rise above mediocrity. I didn't want to teach, or to be an actress or a mannequin. My only talent was for modelling in clay, so I said I would like to be an animal sculptress.

'A *what*?' said my mother. 'But, Valerie, how could you ever earn your living by that? And it sounds so Bohemian.'

The odd thing is that I stuck to my intention, I got her to let me go to an art school, I held a small exhibition in Durban which did well, I got a few commissions for dogs and horses, and then I was unexpectedly awarded a bursary for a year's study and travel in Europe. That drove my mother into a flat spin. She was awfully proud of my success, and madly apprehensive about what might happen to her ewe lamb. Who would look after me if I fell ill? And what about the dangers of the White Slave Traffic? She was worried because we had hardly any relations or friends left in England. When my mother began counting on her fingers the people she thought she could ask to be protective towards me she very soon found she had far more fingers than she needed.

'Fancy,' she said, 'I was just going to count Aunt Evelyn. I quite forgot she was dead, one had always thought of her as something permanent. Then it's no good my writing to the Greenvilles, her last letter was so very strange, she has never been the same since her husband left her. Betty Blossham would be just the person, I've known her since I was *that* high, but as she seems to have settled in British Columbia for good, it's no good applying to *her*. Cousin Felix, when last heard of, was a confirmed black sheep. As you will be in London, Muriel Pepperday can hardly help you, bogged down in Northumberland with arthritis. Your father never quite approved of George Softly, whose children are now just about your age, and although I used to be devoted to Millicent, I don't know whether I should be now, she seems to have led such a rackety life – two divorces, and a witness in that dreadful case last year. I don't think she would do at all. We're so dreadfully out of touch after all this time.'

I wasn't much interested. Why *should* one be interested in other people's ageing pen-friends – or pen-relations either?

'Of course,' said my mother, 'there are, I suppose, the Foats. Ever since your father died I've gone on sending them a card at Christmas. It seems a waste really, as they never do the same for me, and I only met her once and didn't greatly care for her, she seemed so patronizing.'

'The who?' I said.

'The Foats, dear. I don't believe you're listening.'

'I am,' I said. 'Tell me more.'

She then explained that my father and this man Foat had been at Cambridge together. His first name was Tisbury, and my father always spoke of him as Tizzy. When my father became a schoolmaster, Foat became a political journalist. They had been close friends when young. Prigs of a feather, I expect. But whereas my father always remained a kind of liberal, this Foat had become, so I understood, a rather jaunty kind of Left-winger. My father had kept up with Foat, more and more disliking his political views and the paper he wrote for, and they exchanged letters about once a year. I imagine my father wrote and said that his wife had been ill but was now better, that I was growing up and therefore made him feel older, that Smuts was that rare thing a practical idealist and South Africa's greatest hope for the future, and that our garden had been sadly afflicted by either a drought or a hailstorm. In return I suppose Foat said nothing about the weather, made some sarcastic remark about Smuts or the Conservatives in England, and some

complimentary one about one of the international organizations
he supported; then, as he was determinedly 'modern', gave some
unnecessary clinical detail about his wife's last confinement, and
probably ended up with a sly dig at God, in whom he knew my
father believed. But I had much vaguer ideas then: all that's what
I think *now*.

'He's what they call a political commentator, dear,' my mother
explained, 'on some influential paper, and they live near the sea,
a jolly family I expect, perhaps a little free and easy but thoroughly
nice, I'm sure, or your father wouldn't have liked him. Anyway
there's no harm in my writing and putting out a feeler or two.'

Having grown up in the time when people still left cards on one
another, and all that sort of thing, my mother still thought of
English ways as being formal, so I rather liked this suggestion of
freeness and easiness. There might be less fear for me, in such a
family, of doing or saying the wrong thing. It was only by experience that I was to learn to what extent things had loosened up
in England since my mother's girlhood. My chief comfort was that
I had the work of my hands to look forward to.

Some friends offered to give me letters of introduction to people
in England, and one couldn't very well refuse. My mother cautioned
me against using these letters:

'You wouldn't want people to feel you were just a duty foisted
on them, some unknown Colonial girl they're asked to take notice
of, when there's no earthly reason why they should, and people we
don't even know. With the Foats it's different, he having been
such an old friend of your father's.'

I was beginning to imagine myself already submerged in the
complicated cross-currents of English life, all alone, and stretching
out a claw-like hand to one thin life-line that might not bear my
weight – the ghost of my father's long-ago friendship with this
Foat. In fact my initiation into English life turned out to be far less
hazardous than I expected.

Some South African friends, the Okeleys, were going to take
care of me on the voyage, a still youngish married couple, childless,
and just about old enough to have had a daughter of my age. They
were going to England for six months, had often been there before,

and had been lent a small house in Chelsea where they offered to let me live with them until it was time for them to go back to South Africa. Nothing could have suited me better.

2

I liked the Okeleys awfully, enjoyed every minute of the voyage, and arrived in England feeling a bit less like some Victorian maiden awakened from a spell than I had felt when we started. We arrived at Southampton in November, and instead of thick wet fog there was a cloudless sunny day, almost warm. I knew vaguely that England was an overpopulated industrial country, but it gave me such a jar to find that one was never out of sight of houses and people and traffic that I almost failed to have the conventional reactions about little green fields, quiet nooks, immemorial elms, wonderful policemen and all that.

London was madly exciting. I was so simple that I thought to be living in Chelsea was like almost all one's dreams come true. The Whistlerish views of the river, the short dark days and pouring rain, going out to dinner through a real London fog, the warm, bright rooms with people laughing and drinking, and the beautiful clothes and furniture; then the theatres and the galleries and exhibitions, and my first contacts with people successfully doing the kind of work I was doing myself – oh, it was all so heavenly! Without the Okeleys I should have felt absolutely lost and bewildered, but they made everything so easy for me. Being South African, too, they knew exactly the sort of things to explain to me.

As Christmas came nearer I loved the streets jammed with traffic and the brightly lighted shops crammed with people and lovely things, and the tingling frosty air. I wished I was going to spend Christmas with the Okeleys, but they were going to Switzerland for ten days, and it had already been arranged that I was to go to the Foats, and then, as soon as I got back to London, settle down to work in earnest. Jerzy Tralaeff had agreed to take me as a pupil for three months and you can just imagine how keyed up I was about that. But I was a bit shy about the Foats. When I had told some

friend of the Okeleys that I was going to stay with the Foats, all
she had said was 'Lumme!' and I hadn't quite liked to ask her why.
The Okeleys themselves knew of Tisbury Foat as a more or less
public figure in the world of political journalism, but they had
never met him. They said they supposed I should find everything
'very prog', including the conversation.

'Very *what*?' I said.

'Prog,' they said. 'Short for progressive. If you look at the back
of some intellectual weekly, in the personal column, you'll see
things like "Broad-minded prog couple offer jolly accommodation
near Potter's Bar. Discussion circle. Vegetarians preferred. No
restrictions." '

'You don't really think the Foats will be like that?' I said. 'I
should be terrified.'

They said they were only teasing me and they had no doubt
that the Foats lived very comfortably and would give me a very
pleasant time. But they thought it a bit odd, and so did I, that Mrs
Foat hadn't taken the trouble to write to me. All I had had was a
typed postcard from Tisbury Foat's secretary telling me I was
expected on such and such a day and that such and such a train was a
good one to take. Not a word as to whether I was to be met or not.
Never a word of welcome. And a P.S. saying 'We don't change in
the evenings.'

'I suppose that's prog,' said Mrs Okeley. 'Most people would
have said "We don't bother to *dress* in the evenings." "We don't
change" probably means "We sit down to dinner in the same
sweaty sweaters and downtrodden sandals we've been wearing all
day." They probably call dinner "supper" anyway. We can't *wait*
to hear your account of it all, and we wish you, dear, a prog
Christmas as well as a merry one.'

As it was my first Christmas in England you can imagine how I
was looking forward to all the trimmings and incidentals. I had
already seen enough in London of the preparations for Christmas
to understand that the glittering cosiness of an English Christmas,
shut in from the outer darkness, must be of dream-like magic, with
all the holly and mistletoe, and the coloured festoons, and the
Christmas tree and the crackers, and the wonderful food and drink,

and the presents, and the sound of church bells, and the carol-
singers outside, and with a bit of luck the sight of deep, crunchy
snow everywhere. 'Just off to spend Christmas with the Foats,'
I wrote to my mother. 'Will describe it all later.' In fact I didn't
describe it all later: somehow when one is a long way off from one's
own people and in a strange environment it's awfully difficult to
explain things to them – at least it is for me – I'm an awfully bad
letter-writer.

As I think I told you, the Foats didn't live in London, they lived
on the South Coast, at a place called Atheling-on-Sea. So in due
course I set out by train, taking with me what seemed likely to be
suitable clothes and what seemed suitable presents for my host and
hostess – an ash-tray and a tea-cosy. I couldn't very well take
presents for the children, because I didn't even know how many
there were, let alone how old they were or what they were like.

The day I went down, just before Christmas, was overcast, grey,
inclined to drizzle, and almost warm. I suppose I knew that a white
Christmas in the South of England is rare, but somehow I was still
half-hoping for snow. Do you realize that I had never even *seen*
snow then? I certainly didn't see it when I got out at Atheling
station. I felt a bit nervous. I didn't know if anybody had come to
meet me. Evidently nobody had. The few, rather over-dressed
people who had got out of the train seemed much more self-
confident than I was. I heard a cry of 'Darling!' in rather an affected
voice and saw a couple of middle-aged women embracing, pressing
their faces together but kissing the air and not each other, a chauffeur
touched his cap, and in no time everybody had vanished, and I was
left with a rather heavy suitcase and a feeling of not being des-
perately wanted, like an emigrant who has missed the boat.
Uncertain what to do, I wandered out of the station to see if there
was a taxi or bus or anything. There was a taxi and I took it, but
when I looked out and saw through the grey drizzle first a lot of
ugly little brick bungalows huddled together, some of them still
building, and then a series of new-looking villas, rather pretentious,
too close together and with macrocarpa hedges and a lot of white-
wash, and wrought-iron gates, and pergolas and things, I could
just have howled.

I suppose it was half-baked and romantic of me, but I had some-how thought of Atheling as having lovely stone or flint cottages, old and simple, and a little High Street with Georgian shop-fronts, and an ancient church with mossy tombstones and huge trees round it. When we passed a filling-station I just shut my eyes. But I had to open them almost at once, as we turned into a short drive and drove up to a house. I gave the man a tip, probably too big, and rang the bell. If ever I felt like a fish out of water, it was then.

The door was opened by an untidy girl of about fourteen who said, 'Oh, it's you. Come and dump your case.'

She led the way upstairs and showed me into a bedroom.

'You're in here,' she said. 'Tizzy's working and Molly's out, but she'll be back to tea. Come down when you like.'

The room was clean and tidy – and cold. There was an electric fire, but it hadn't been turned on. The only pictures were two caricatures, one of Bernard Shaw and the other of some politician of those days, perhaps Ramsay MacDonald or somebody. And there was also a large framed poster, Russian I think, of a brawny woman holding a sheaf of corn. There were some books on the bed-table, but not a single one that appealed to me – titles like *An Approach to Biology, The Economics of Socialism,* a couple of Left Book Club choices, something about the Spanish Civil War, a donnish whodunit, and a really ghastly compendium called *Weekend Fun,* with sea-shanties, conundrums, suggestions for round games and cold drinks, and fancy recipes. My heart sank, and I went downstairs.

If I were to describe it all in detail I should never be done. You see, I was so impressionable. By, for instance, my mother's standards the Foats' way of living was what she would have quaintly called Bohemian, though it could easily be given a harder name, and their manners were pretty casual. But they were really very hospit-able, although I must have seemed like a Martian or something to them. As it happened, staying with the Foats was important for me. Incidentally it taught me that nobody is so conventional as the unconventional. Yes, it certainly taught me that.

The family consisted of Mr and Mrs Foat, three children and a nephew, who was about my own age and sort of adopted. Tisbury

Foat was generally called Tizzy, but his children called him Cadsir. Apparently some old buffer of a neighbour had once had a row with him about cutting a tree down or something, and had ended by saying, 'You're behaving like a cad, sir!' They had all thought this exquisitely funny. Tizzy was a stocky, active man with a quiff, bright darting eyes and horn-rimmed spectacles. He had a very active brain, he was garrulous and a bit cocky, thought he knew everything, and never doubted that his own opinions were right – and yet one couldn't help admiring him and even liking him, there was something vital and warm about him.

Molly was quieter, and a bit schoolmarmish, with biggish feet. It seemed funny at first to hear her children calling her Molly, but I got used to it. There was something calculated and solemn about her slovenliness and her (to me then) awful freedom of speech. It was as if her whole personality was fixed in a sort of permanent fancy dress. I believe she was quite a simple person underneath it all. She had once taught biology, and I always seemed to see a sort of ghostly blackboard behind her.

The eldest son, Wells, was called after a writer, H. G. Wells, whose books I have never read. I always imagine that they're prog in a very old-fashioned way. I didn't see Wells then. He was at some smart-aleck technological school in Sweden. Next came Phyllida. It was she who had shown me in when I arrived. She didn't talk much. She was mad about music. I think it was a way of escape from her family. She was always playing the gramophone or blowing a recorder. She liked to play simple, folksy tunes and to hear the most gnarled and harsh modern music. The youngest girl was called Monday because she had been born on one. Then there was Andrew.

I remember how he came into the room, and how Tizzy said, 'And this is Andrew. He's really Molly's nephew, but to embarrass him we often pretend he's our son. We're not at all what he has been used to, but he's wonderfully tolerant.'

'Tolerant's just the word,' said Andrew. 'This is the first real home I've ever had.'

He smiled, and his eyes almost disappeared, not because his face was fat, but because he just had that sort of eyes. And he had such a

deep voice. I felt much more at ease with him than with the others.
I thought he was awfully attractive.

Tea was brought in by a dark-haired woman I hadn't seen before.
I heard that she was a Basque refugee. When Molly told me about
her, Tizzy began to explain about the Spanish Civil War. I must
say he was terribly boring about it. I didn't want to know about it
at all, and he wanted to show that he knew *all* about it. He really
seemed to know all the answers to that, and to everything else.
Perhaps if one is a journalist one has to give oneself the air of knowing everything. I suppose I ought to have felt flattered at being told
all about the Spanish Civil War by a well-known political commentator, but I found it a terrible strain to look as if I was listening
intelligently, and even more to think of questions to ask now and
then. My face became rigid, I could feel it, with an expression of
false alertness. Oh, how he did love explaining!

In the middle of it my gaze wandered round the room, and the
thought did cross my mind that it looked rather bleak. There were
no sprigs of holly over the pictures, no Christmas cards on the
mantelpiece, nothing. Tizzy was watching me.

'The solemn thought has just occurred to me', he said, 'that
Valerie may have expected to find here the usual English bourgeois
Christmas, with holly and all that.'

'Well – ' I hesitated.

'Oh, *gosh*, Cadsir!' cried Phyllida, her voice rising to a shriek
at her father's absurdity. 'Not *holly*! She *couldn't* have!'

'I don't see why not,' said Andrew.

'Well,' said Phyllida, 'I *mean* –'

Evidently the matter was beyond discussion.

'Soon after Tizzy and I were married,' Molly remarked, 'we
made up our minds to ignore Christmas altogether.'

This was a cue for Tizzy to put the rest of the world in its
ridiculous place.

'We saw', he explained (as who can't?), 'that it was just a
primitive survival——'

'Tied up,' said Molly, 'with a really fantastic superstition——'

'And now simply a pretext for commercial exploitation.'

'Oh, poor Christmas!' I said. Then, anxious to be conciliatory,

I said I did suppose that Christmas *was* now terribly exploited, perhaps more in England than in South Africa. Nobody pursued the comparison.

'It was quite simple,' said Molly. 'We decided never to allow a sprig of holly or mistletoe into the house, and never to eat turkey and Christmas pudding either at Christmas or any other time, or mince-pies. We don't happen to like them. We also decided never to give Christmas presents or send Christmas cards to anybody.'

'Oh, but how awkward,' I couldn't help saying. 'What do you do when people send *you* presents or cards?'

'If they send *us* presents,' said Molly, 'we just write and thank them, and explain that we ourselves don't celebrate Christmas.'

I thought that pretty cool.

'If they send us cards,' she said, 'we ignore them, and they generally dry up.'

I remembered how my mother had said she always sent them a card and never got one from them.

'Oh, by the way, Tizzy, you would hardly believe that Mrs Thringle at East Weston has sent us a card with robins, church bells *and* a coach in the snow. If it were from anybody else in *this* neighbourhood, one would suspect a practical joke.'

'She's obtuse,' said Tizzy. 'Let's see it.'

'Naturally I tore it up at once.'

'Oh, Molly,' said Monday, who was about seven, 'why couldn't *I* have it?'

'It was awful,' said Phyllida. 'I saw it. You wouldn't have liked it.'

'I would, I would!' Monday began to cry.

'That child has a low I.Q.,' said Tizzy. 'She has the mental age of an infant half her size. If you want pictures of robins, Monday, the ferocious little brutes are very well illustrated in J. F. Huxwin's *Birds for Beginners*, which is on the shelf in the W.C.'

'Oh, Cadsir,' said Phyllida, 'don't *nag*!'

'Shut up, Phyllida. I don't know, Valerie, how your father's ideas on education developed, but I remember that before our son Wells was born Molly said to me that we had a chance to give an entirely new meaning to the term, a liberal education.'

'Yes, I did,' said Molly. 'We decided to treat him as an equal. Absolute sex-equality. Early sex-education, and *thorough*. Straight answers to all questions. Freedom of speech.'

'*And* of action, Molly.'

'*And* of action, of course. Rational diet, rational clothing – and as little of that as possible. We decided that Pogsdon was the only school for him, and to Pogsdon he went. So does Phyllida.'

'Another thing,' said Tizzy, 'none of our children were to be brought up on fairy tales. That meant particularly the brothers Grimm, Hans Andersen, and that pernicious, Freudian *Alice in Wonderland*, with its obscene imagery and nasty class-consciousness.'

'*And*,' said Molly, 'we were resolved to protect all our young from militarism and from even recognizing the *existence* of the Royal Family – or of Christmas, which is such flagrant propaganda for both, what with the broadcast from Sandringham, the firing-off of crackers and the red coat of that sinister father-figure, Santa Claus.'

I wondered whether I was not the victim of some elaborate leg-pull. Were they trying to shock me, or what? I asked Andrew when he took me out for a walk the next day.

'Oh no, they were perfectly serious,' he said. 'They meant every word of it. But if I were you, I wouldn't press them for reasons. There's nothing they like better than being pressed for reasons, and they're so awfully generous with them. You see, they call themselves rationalists.'

'And what about you? Are you one too?'

'Oh, I'm not anything really. I wasn't brought up to any ideas in particular. Of course to me rationalists seem a bit superstitious. One would think it was just as *unlucky* to bring holly into the house as to bring in peacocks' feathers or flowering may, as some people believe. And of course when Tizzy and Molly tell other people who give them presents that they themselves don't believe in Christmas, other people think them mean, and don't ever give them anything again.'

'But what about the children? Aren't they allowed to enjoy Christmas like other children?'

'Oh, goodness, no! They've none of them been christened, so

they've got no godparents, and they can't hang up stockings, which they're not allowed to wear anyway, so they haven't got any. I was never christened either, but that was just an oversight, not on principle or anything. As they told you, Tizzy and Molly, when they were first married, decided to cut Christmas whenever they met it. And now they humiliate it a bit more by making quite a fuss of its humble rival, New Year's Day. They even sent out cards last New Year.'

'No!'

'Yes. With an abstract design, quite non-committal, and underneath there was an inscription saying, "A New Year greeting from Tisbury and Molly Foat, from Wells, Phyllida, and Monday, and from Andrew Downing." '

It was the first time I had heard his surname. I liked it.

'Obviously,' he said, 'you did come here expecting a proper Christmassy Christmas. I must say I should like it myself.'

'Would you? Oh goody!' I could have hugged him.

'Though I'd never let on, to them.'

'In South Africa', I said, 'we do rather dream about a real English Christmas. But it doesn't matter, of course,' I added politely, 'because I'm very glad to be here.'

'Well, this is Atheling,' he said, pointing to a white house with a hard tennis-court. 'What do you think of it?'

'I don't want to keep on seeming disappointed, but it's rather like a South African residential suburb, everything looks so new and smart.'

'You do judge everything by South African standards, don't you?'

'If I do, I can't help it. I've been there all my life. And one can't help expecting an English village to be old and mossy.'

'It's just the newness', he said, 'that made Tizzy and Molly come and live here, and the sea, of course, and the easy distance from London. Some of these houses belong to stockbrokers and company directors who commute comfortably every day, some to retired people, and some, like that showy one with the thatched roof and the sun-loggia, to theatrical or racing people who come down for week-ends with fast cars and flash women. What Tizzy likes, he says, is that there's absolutely no sense of community. He says it's all so beautifully impersonal. You can live here for years and never get to know anybody at all. There are no bores like local bores, he says.'

'But I suppose there's a church,' I said, 'and a good deal of social activity centred on that – oh, but I forgot, he wouldn't care for that.'

'There's no church, anyway,' he said. 'Only a few years ago this was all fields going right down to the sea.'

As we walked along by the sea I asked Andrew about his earlier life. He said he had never known his mother, and he had been abroad a lot with his father, who had been killed in an accident. Then he had been more or less adopted by the Foats, when he was fourteen. He said Tizzy let him have his way in most things, and was more like an elder brother than an adoptive father. I think he couldn't help feeling a bit outside the family, and as I was an outsider too, this rather brought us together. But we didn't really need bringing together. We just naturally took to one another. When Tizzy and Molly noticed this, which they very soon did, they just took it for granted, and I am glad to say there was none of that heavy facetiousness one would have had to put up with in some families.

On Christmas Eve the sun shone quite brightly. I was careful not to say that by South African standards it could hardly be called sunshine at all. I sent a cable to my mother to wish her a happy Christmas. I knew she would be feeling a bit lonely without me. I had never been away at Christmas before. At home she and I generally went to the midnight mass. As there was no church actually in Atheling-on-Sea I thought I would go to the early communion at the nearest church on Christmas morning instead. I had never missed communion on Christmas morning since I had been confirmed. I don't want to suggest that we were terribly pious at home. Not at all, we were just naturally Church of England. I always loved the Church, and belonging to it. But I hadn't quite realized what effect my saying that I intended going to church would have on the Foats.

It was at lunch-time, and Tizzy had been explaining how there couldn't possibly be another World War, I think it was for economic reasons. Nobody contradicted him. When he paused to pop some food into his mouth I said, trying to make my voice quite casual:

'By the way, are there any churches near here?'

'There are several,' said Molly. 'Are you interested in architecture?'

'Yes, a little. But of course I'm more interested in sculpture, and I know there are some wonderful things in English country churches. But I asked because I want to go to the early service tomorrow morning.'

I shall never forget the look on Tizzy's face, and Molly's, and Phyllida's too. I suppose that what I had said was the most – what shall I say? – the most *scandalous* thing ever uttered in that house. It was exactly as if one had stood up in church and declared oneself an atheist. There was a silence in which you could have heard a *New Statesman* drop.

'You *can't* be serious, Valerie,' said Molly.

'Of course she isn't,' said Tizzy. 'She's pulling our legs.'

'But I'm perfectly serious,' I said.

'Can I go too, Cadsir?' asked Monday.

'Idiot, of course not,' said Molly.

'But surely,' I said, 'I'm not the only person in the house who will be going to church tomorrow? I'm sure your maid is a Roman Catholic, and will be going to mass.'

'My dear Valerie,' said Tizzy gravely, 'you don't understand. Our good Concepción is a militant atheist and violently anticlerical. Why, in Spain she was secretary of her local branch of B.T.M.'

'?'

'The Basque Anarchists' Rally.'

'Oh.'

'But, Valerie, seriously, why do you want to go to church? Are you helping with Mass Observation or something?'

I had never heard then of Mass Observation, so I quite misunderstood him.

'Oh, it's not just *observation*,' I said. 'When I go to mass I always go as a communicant.'

Molly laughed abruptly. An expression of something like in-credulous distaste spread over Tizzy's face, as if some dreadful tropical insect had come into the house.

'But it's just a pantomime!' he burst out. 'It's a sort of mockery of cannibalism! Eating the god! Primitive beyond words! You can't really mean that you *believe* in it!'

'Of course I do!' I was jarred by his crudity, and felt myself getting rather red in the face. 'And I simply can't imagine *not* going to church at Christmas. I *always have!*'

'There's no doubt', said Molly, 'that Dombrovski is right when he says that habit is the greatest unconscious force there is.'

'Who?' said Phyllida, but nobody answered her.

'I'm *not* an idiot, am I?' Monday appealed to me.

'Of course not,' I said.

'But where on earth', said Tizzy, his voice becoming almost shrill, 'did she *get* the habit? That's the question. Certainly not from her father.'

'My father was a churchwarden for as long as I can remember,' I said quietly.

I think that is the only moment I know of when Tizzy was reduced to silence. It was as if I had said my father had contracted leprosy or something.

'The nearest church', said Andrew, who had not yet spoken and evidently felt it was time to come to the rescue, 'is at East Weston. It's only about a mile and a half. I'll take you there if you like.'

I could have kissed him. As a matter of fact, on Boxing Day I did.

We were horribly teased by the Foats about our churchgoing. Except that I thought them frightfully blasphemous I didn't really mind, they were so nice, and much more like Christians than they suspected – like Christians standing on their heads and walking backwards, if you see what I mean – like the kind of Christians who ask 'Are you saved?'

Whether it was because Andrew was interested in me that he got interested in the Church, I don't know, but before I left Atheling he had made up his mind to be received. He asked me to be his godmother at his christening. I said I would. Soon after that he asked me to be his wife. As you know, I said I would.

I forgot to say that I didn't give the Foats the Christmas presents I had taken for them. I gave the ash-tray surreptitiously to Andrew, and kept the tea-cosy for myself. I also forgot to say that Monday Foat has just married a clergyman. I hear it nearly killed Tizzy and Molly. But Monday always did seem to be the rebellious one. What is the opposite of 'prog'? 'Retrog', I suppose. And I suppose that is what she is, and what Andrew and I are too.

[*Winter's Tales: 2*, 1956]

Poems

Martin Luther King

(Phrases in quotes are King's own words from a discussion with Gerald Priestland broadcast by the BBC, 4 April 1968, the day King was shot)

You saw the moon set, you saw the sun rise,
   They shot your body down.
Not by moonlight, in white-hot daylight
   They shot your body down.
You lie in the grave and stretch out your arms
   Where they laid your body down.
                  pp   Yes, yes!

You went to judgment in the evening of the day
   When they laid your body down.
We knew moon-rise, we saw star-rise
   When they laid your body down.
And your words came out to meet us that day
   When you laid your body down.
                  ff   Yes, yes!

SOLO: 'I must go on and do my work'
CHORUS: He said, and meant it;
SOLO: 'And do what conscience tells me is the right,'
CHORUS: Nothing could prevent it.

SOLO: 'I live each day under a threat of death,'
CHORUS: They laid the trap, and set it.
            He said, not being given to pretend,
SOLO: 'I know that I can meet a violent end,'

CHORUS: Foresaw the end, and met it.
SOLO: 'I have a dream,' he said, and told his
                                        fellow men,
            'Truth crushed to earth will rise again.'

TUTTI: Only one way to change the heart –
                        To change the heart!
            Only one proper way to die –
                        To live no lie!

CHORUS: Martin!
SOLO ECHO: Martyr!
CHORUS: Luther!
SOLO ECHO: Renewer!
CHORUS: King!
SOLO ECHO: Awakening!

TUTTI: Let this be our defence –
            No lies, no violence.

                                    [Written 1968]

Machine-Tool Man

Metrical to him the steely whizz,
the soothing sibilant seething
of well-oiled functioning tools
in a fully equipped machine-tool shop,
stainless, Swinburnian, smooth.

Arc, spot, and butt welding-machines,
drilling, morticing, grinding machines
obsessively busy themselves,
screw presses, fly presses, kick presses, toggle presses
oilily pressing, compressing, unpressing,
folding and tube-bending machines
speedily bending, easily folding,
polishing spindles spinning and polishing,
bending rollers rolling and bending,
cylindrical surface and centreless grinders,
guillotines slicing what might have been butter.

For servicing joints, bearings,
stroke shapers, the lot,
trust him with a grease-gun
or for needed degrees of de-greasing
toting a handy hot gas-heated de-greaser.

Who said stroke shapers?
Why not shape strokers?
Machine tools at rest
to him are shapely as odalisques resting,
machine tools at work

he sees as a bevy, a brilliant
ballet kept to perfection
by implied, predetermined imperatives –
Drill, grind, and press!
Kick, fold, and bend!
Spin! Roll! Butt!
Screw!

[*London Magazine,* August 1971]

Adopted Son

For the first time a room to himself.
He stands by the bed in a loud silence,
Feeling watched, feeling judged;
Only four feet high
Stares at himself in a long mirror
As an actor stares, miscast.

Unrehearsed, this child
Feels a kind of stage fright,
Was only told 'You're a lucky boy!'
Uncoached, must take on
For two strangers the part of a son.

For comfort of a kind he touches again
Those two towels, clean and soft.
'Why are there two?' was what he asked
His new mother, so-called.
'A face towel, and one for your bath.'
'Gosh, I've never had two before.'
'Well, they'll make you nice and dry.
I hope you like these blue pyjamas.
Often at night we hear an owl,
You won't mind that. *Who? Who?*
This room gets the morning sun.
Whenever you like, Jason,
Come down. You know your way.
We'll have tea. There's a chocolate cake
Specially made today for you.'

In the room not one sound;
From the window nothing, nothing but trees.
No traffic! What a place!
Carpets everywhere. If somebody
Sneaked up outside the door
No more noise than a cat.
This high bed's as soft as dough.
'Whenever you like, Jason,' she said,
'Come down.' Okay, I will.

Downstairs, resolutions
(Long-term) are being rehearsed.
'To let him feel we belong to him
We must take his side, make sure
The least promise is faithfully kept,
Never say *Don't* or *You must*.
I love him already. Some day
When his young blood drives him out,
No reproaches! Let him go
In new clothes, without guilt.'

[Written 1972. Published in
People Within, Thornhill Press, 1973]

Former Migrants

Outdoors, in metal canisters on wheels,
Indoors, all gaping at a box of tricks,
How might we seem to former migrants here?
Addicts of felony and trash smeared thin,
Drugged by the instant, with collapsed
Imaginations, passive, levelled down.

By Blake, along this now unlikely coast,
'Celestial voices' were 'distinctly heard';
Hudson, lone exile from the Purple Land,
'Wrote as the grass grows'; Jefferies, true
Life-loving countryman, was downed by pain;
And Wilde, in this unconscious town, displayed
The importance of being frivolous and rash:
Beyond the aerials, these perpetual stars.[1]

[Written November 1972. Published in
Eight Sussex Poets, 1973]

[1] William Blake occupied a cottage at Felpham, W. H. Hudson wrote *Nature in Downland*, Richard Jefferies died at Goring, and at Worthing Oscar Wilde worked on *The Importance of Being Earnest*.

Cupboard Love

In the front garden snowdrifts of snowdrops,
Predictable daffodils, floribund litterbug roses;
In the back garden leathery greens, then treasure-trove
New potatoes, wigwams of huge runner-beans.

Behind the front door Victor, no drop-out,
Rather a drop-in or opt-out, a marginal man,
An old man, with Beulah, the much older wife
Strangers supposed him, till put right, the son of.

It began back in 1914. Newly widowed,
Beulah married and mothered him. Victor,
A taciturn peasant, with nothing to lose but his life,
Demurred at the war. 'Take no notice,' she said.

'All will be over by Christmas. Till then
You can hide in that roomy great cupboard upstairs.'
Enwombed for four years; when he came out he remained
A homebody; went daily to garden at Atheling Grange,

Kept himself to himself, never seen in a pub or a club.
Someone did say: 'Victor, what happened to you in the war?'
'Never got through me medical, so was exempt.'
For fifty years more was exempt from the world.

When he followed its monstrous reflection in print,
On radio, then, caught in the act, televised,
He found it too wild to be false. 'I'm content
To be out of it all', he said, and very soon was.

Beulah survived him; somehow she knew that she would.
The earth is his hidey-hole now. The snowdrifts
Of snowdrops increase, and somebody else
Puts up the annual wigwams, and gathers the belt-like beans.

[*Listener,* 30 November 1972, and
New Poems 1973-74, 1974]

Painted on Darkness

A sunlit branch of four reflected roses
Bright on the darkened window of that room,
That locked and shuttered, memory-haunted room,
Startles by tint and stillness, perfectly composed.

Each rose transmuted, sweeter than itself,
In pure vermilion stands out strange and new
Against the haunted glass intensified,
Painted on darkness, as a poem is.

[Written 1971–73. Sent to Sybil Cholmondeley 15 March 1973 with a letter
saying:
'With this I send you a short poem which, slight as it is, took ages to shape itself.
It began with the reflection in a murky pond of a branch of sunlit, young,
brilliantly green horse-chestnut leaves, and seems to be partly about the suggestion
of a parallel with art in the idea of a transmuted image, and partly about the
association of an image with memories of the dead.']

Having Wonderful Time

Having repulsive time,
Glad you aren't here.
Rushing from place to place,
Now in a sterile room
In another airport hotel
(Or is it the one before last?),
Unable to read tonight,
Unwilling to listen to news
Of cruelty and lies,
Glad you aren't here.

As the days come fluttering down
From deciduous calendars,
And clicking watches and clocks
Keep an exact account,
Like a growing overdraft –
Advanced, for experiment,
Without security –
Seeing it rise like a flood
At a menacing speed,
Glad you aren't here:

But able to think of you
As a continuance
Among the still alive,
And hoping not to be here
Tomorrow, cheerfully
Biting the pith of *now*,
I write an ugly card

With just a touch of truth,
'Having wonderful time
In this kitsch caravanserai.'

[Written 1972–73]

A Radio Interview

In memory of Cecil Day-Lewis

'When young,' he was told,
'I seem to think, and wouldn't you say,
You turned your back on the old,
Then got swinging into your stride
In your own way?'

When the dying poet replied
His voice went faltering firmly back
With difficult steps, difficult steps,
Over his former training-track
To recall the pace he could never regain.

'And what,' he was asked,
'Of those menacing years, that terrible phase,
With the Hitler thing, and the war in Spain?
Did you still feel hope?' One single phrase
In his answer rang with emphasis:
He clenched the words 'I was full of hope!'

Incredulous at hearing this,
'How could he?' a listening friend cried out
(Not an especial misanthrope
But his youthful veins had been drugged with doubt
And frustratedness, as if injected.)

'How little I knew him! I supposed dismay
Universal then, and the very air
We breathed infected
With anxiety, apathy, despair.

'Unravelling all day
My ignorance, I understood
Hope of a sort myself had lacked,
Gathered perhaps with the stored and stacked
Harvest of early fatherhood.

'Myself had been several ways displaced,
Putting out premature flowers in haste
As shallow transplants do;
Slow the renewal of a broken root,
Slow, slow before I grew
Soundly, and set some fruit.

'Hope in me was long asleep
Though awake in dreams. I couldn't accept
Utopian reckonings. Even now I keep
To a private path, as then I kept –
But when mine crossed his, a pleasure!'

Children of a horse-drawn day
In a high-speed world, at our leisure
We felt, as coevals may,
Compatible in a brotherly way.

[*London Magazine*, December 1973]

Index